Gerd Spittler,
Michael Bourdillon (eds.)

African Children at Work

D1610051

Beiträge zur Afrikaforschung

ISSN 0938–7285

Herausgegeben vom Institut für Afrikastudien der Universität Bayreuth

Band

52

LIT

African Children at Work

Working and Learning in Growing Up for Life

edited by

Gerd Spittler and Michael Bourdillon

LIT

Gedruckt mit freundlicher Unterstützung des
IGK Arbeit und Lebenslauf in globalgeschichtlicher Perspektive

Gedruckt auf alterungsbeständigem Werkdruckpapier entsprechend
ANSI Z3948 DIN ISO 9706

Bibliographic information published by the Deutsche Nationalbibliothek
The Deutsche Nationalbibliothek lists this publication in the Deutsche
Nationalbibliografie; detailed bibliographic data are available in the Internet at
http://dnb.d-nb.de.

ISBN 978-3-643-90205-4

A catalogue record for this book is available from the British Library

©LIT VERLAG GmbH & Co. KG Wien,   LIT VERLAG Dr. W. Hopf
Zweigniederlassung Zürich 2012   Berlin 2012
Klosbachstr. 107   Fresnostr. 2
CH-8032 Zürich   D-48159 Münster
Tel. +41 (0) 44-251 75 05   Tel. +49 (0) 2 51-620 320
Fax +41 (0) 44-251 75 06   Fax +49 (0) 2 51-23 19 72
e-Mail: zuerich@lit-verlag.ch   e-Mail: lit@lit-verlag.de
http://www.lit-verlag.ch   http://www.lit-verlag.de

Distribution:
In Germany: LIT Verlag Fresnostr. 2, D-48159 Münster
Tel. +49 (0) 2 51-620 32 22, Fax +49 (0) 2 51-922 60 99, e-mail: vertrieb@lit-verlag.de
In Austria: Medienlogistik Pichler-ÖBZ, e-mail: mlo@medien-logistik.at
In Switzerland: B + M Buch- und Medienvertrieb, e-mail: order@buch-medien.ch

In the UK: Global Book Marketing, e-mail: mo@centralbooks.com

Contents

Introduction

Michael Bourdillon and Gerd Spittler

This book is about relationships between work and learning as activities in children's lives in Africa. Work is a fundamental human activity, in which children take part. Learning is just as fundamental to life and particularly important for the young, who have to develop technical and social skills to play a constructive role in their communities. In the contemporary world, learning is strongly associated with schooling, widely seen to be essential in being able to compete in the world and to the development of young people and their communities. But learning—education in its broadest sense—is not confined to formal schooling: the United Nations Convention on the Rights of the Child (1989, article 29) states that education should be directed at the development of children to their fullest potential in a variety of spheres. The studies presented in this volume pay attention to the fact that much learning takes place outside the school context, and particularly in social activities of work. The authors consider how children learn through work, and in some cases how work can help or hinder learning through school.

What is childhood?

In many Western contexts, children are defined primarily by their age. In Germany, persons below the age of 14 years are children in the eyes of the law, while persons between 14 and 18 are adolescents. The Convention on the Rights of the Child does not make this distinction and defines all persons under the age of 18 as children: this somewhat arbitrary definition serves for certain legal purposes, but tells us little about how young people grow and develop into adults. In Africa before the introduction of civil registers and schools, such clear age distinctions were unknown; and are still uncommon today in many areas. Hardly any distinction is made between children and adolescents. A distinction is made between children and adults, but in different ways. In many societies rites mark the transition from childhood to adulthood, but these rites only take place every few years and, although they provide clear cognitive distinctions, they do not define the actual growth of young people (Dougnon, this volume). In some societies, one is called a child until one marries and has children of one's own (Martin, this volume), in other societies the change in status comes even later (Spittler 1990). In practice, the process of growing, learning, and becoming a full member of society is a gradual process with no clear divisions. In this volume, we have not used any fixed definition, but most of the authors are interested in the work of persons who are less than 15 years old, in other words those who correspond to the Western defi- nition of children.

To complicate matters further, the process of growing up differs in different cultures and socio-economic situations. Although people take for granted ideas of childhood that prevail in their own particu- lar settings, comparative studies show the ideas and practices sur- rounding childhood to be social constructions (James and James 2004). In the past, psychologists, the most renowned of whom was Jean Piaget, have examined the way in which children develop, and systematised the process into clear stages that characterise altering competencies and behaviour. Such systemisation, however, resulted from research conducted in North American and European settings. More recent studies reveal that such stages do not apply across cul- tures (Rogoff 2003). Children develop competencies and patterns of behaviour depending on what is expected of them and what guidance they receive. Essays in this volume show some of the ways in which such development can take place.

For most Western people, a basic difference between adults and children is that children do not work. In Africa, on the other hand, most children work from an early age, well illustrated in the chapter by David Lancy, who shows taking on various tasks to be part of the education of children. Nevertheless, the ideal of childhood as free from work—or indeed care generally—remains strong, not only in Western societies but also among elites everywhere. The first question about this ideal is whether it is realistic. A carefree childhood is possible only if children can depend on adults who have adequate resources to provide for them. There are structural reasons why the kind of support that is available to children in high-income countries is often not possible elsewhere. In high-income countries, children under 14 comprise 17 per cent of the population; in sub-Saharan Africa, children under 14 comprise 42 per cent of the population (Frost 2010) and incomes of adults supporting them are much lower. Many African families rely on children to help produce a livelihood: without such help, more children would be malnourished, impeding both physical and cognitive development. Besides, many children have to support themselves and younger siblings in communities ravaged by war or disease or extreme poverty. The chapter by Stanford Mahati provides an extreme example: young migrants escape the collapsed economy of Zimbabwe, to support themselves—and sometimes their families—by working in South Africa. There is sometimes a tension between what these enterprising youth see as their responsibilities and interests and how aid workers perceive their deviance from internationally accepted norms of childhood.

Even where a work-free childhood is possible, the question remains as to whether it is ideal. In this volume, Barbara Polak shows how children eagerly participate in work activities of the family, at first playfully but with growing competence. Far from feeling exploited by their parents, young children are demonstrably eager to participate, which imposes a responsibility on parents and older siblings to ensure that they work only within their sphere of competence and that crops are not ruined. Here, work is participation in family activities—participation that is not possible where work is separated from family life, and from children in particular, as is so often the case in wealthy urban societies. Other articles in this volume show that children perform small tasks even at the age of three (Lancy, Köhler, Spittler). In the course of time, these tasks grow in size and complexity; and we discuss below how children can learn through work. The idea that children should work, within the limits of their strength and their knowledge, has now come into conflict with the spread of schooling. However, this conflict does not mean that all children have stopped working. Their work can lead to their spending less time at school (Spittler, Katz, this volume); alternatively, the parents may decide that some children should go to school, while others should work (Alber, this volume); or children can combine school and work (Martin, this volume). Children's work can also help to pay for their schooling.

As children acquire competence in family activities, they gradually take on their share of responsibility for family welfare, starting with simple tasks like fetching drinking water for older workers. In many societies, young children aged eight years or even less, especially girls, are expected to take responsible care of infants and younger children while adults are working or otherwise engaged. In pastoral societies, as among the Tuareg of Niger described by Gerd Spittler, young children and girls learn early on to take care of domestic animals, and boys grow up taking responsibility for the family wealth in their herds—in this case of camels, but elsewhere of cattle.

A key feature of several of the chapters is that the welfare of children is seen in the context of the welfare of the family in which they live. Spittler, Polak, Erdmute Alber, and Jeannett Martin show children treated differently to ensure that the various needs of their families are met. Children's life trajectories are affected by decisions concerning family livelihood in situations where resources are scarce. While attention is paid to the needs and capabilities of individual children, more important in these cultures is the welfare of the group to which they belong and on which they depend.

The chapters by Alber and Martin point to another social construction: that of the family. It illustrates how this concept need not be confined to the nuclear family of parents and their children. Child care and rearing is taken on by a wider group of relatives and friends, and children's responsibilities and services extend to this wider group. Although relatives do not always treat foster-children with the same concern as that extended to biological children, Alber shows social pressures to support fairness to fostered children. In risk-prone poor rural areas a system of fostering provides some security for children, which usually more than compensates for the risk of inadequate support when children move from their natal homes.

Martin describes children negotiating their workloads to fit in with requirements of schoolwork. Polak shows young children free to participate in work activities at their own will, subject to controls to prevent them from damaging crops. This is a common pattern. Older children are expected to participate but do so willingly and often with enthusiasm. Cindi Katz describes Howa children exercising initiative in acquiring competencies that will help their standing in their communities. From an early age, children actively direct their learning and developmental trajectories.

Manfred Liebel's account of the African Movement of Working Children and Youth presents young workers not simply as passive victims, but in various ways taking initiatives to gain some control over their lives. And they speak positively about the work that enables them to do this. Isaie Dougnon, Yaw Ofosu-Kusi and Phil Mizen, and Mahati describe children exercising agency in deciding to migrate, sometimes to very difficult situations that require enterprise and ingenuity.

The family or domestic economy in Africa

In today's Western world, work is conducted mostly in firms or institutions while family life belongs to the private sphere. Only domestic work is carried out by the family, yet for this reason it is often not counted as work. Now, more than at any other time in history, family and work are regarded as opposites. The former is dominated by love, feelings, care for others, while the latter is dominated by efficiency, calculation, and financial interests. It seems difficult to find equilibrium between career and family. Balancing work and life pre-occupies ordinary people as much as it does sociologists.

People tend to impose their own views on foreign cultures, so that, for example, children's work—often called 'child labour'—is assumed to be deserving of condemnation and abolition, in much the same manner as slavery. People in the Western world also find it difficult to see the family economy, within a system where capital-ism dominates, as anything other than an anachronism. However, the division between work and family is not obvious everywhere: in most societies, the domestic or family economy unites the two worlds of work and family. Men and women, children and the elder-ly, work together, not only for domestic purposes, but also in pro-duction. In history, this type of domestic or family economy pre-dominated from the beginning of the neolithic period until capitalist industrialisation. Even today, the close connection between the do-mestic sphere and business management is apparent in the term 'economy' (which originally meant 'household management'). In Western industrialised nations, the domestic economy has lost its meaning. The global spread of capitalism, however, has not under-mined the home-based economy everywhere. In many parts of the world, especially in Africa, the domestic economy is still the most widespread form of economic organisation. This holds true not only in rural areas, but also in cities. Much of what is called the informal sector is based on domestic economy (Verlet 2005).

What exactly is meant by a domestic economy? It is character-ised by the close relationship between production and consumption. A family, often consisting of two or three generations, forms the core, so that domestic economy and family economy are sometimes equated. But frequently the two are not identical, because a domestic economy can include people who are not related to the family. The chapters in this volume offer many examples of economies that devi-ate from the familiar patriarchal type of domestic economy: matri-local ones (Spittler), polygamous ones (Dougnon, Katz, Köhler,

Polak), and even domestic economies where foster children play an important role (Alber, Martin).

A domestic economy is not the same as a *household*. A domestic economy is an institution that independently organises the work of its members and operates autonomously. A household also makes economic decisions, but often its members work for employers outside the household, and the income is used fully or in part as a contribution to the common household budget. So very often we find a mixture: the basic model is a family economy, but individual members temporarily or permanently work outside it. This may also apply to children who work in towns that are a long distance from their homes (Mahati, this volume), although in some cases children who travel break with their homes (Ofosu-Kusi and Mizen, this volume).

In family economies that operate in a capitalist context, the members of the family frequently divide their energies between the family enterprise and waged work. In Africa, young men seek employment far from their families for varying periods of time; while they are gone, their work at home has to be performed by other family members, especially children (Reynolds 1991; Dougnon, Spittler, this volume).

Is children's work in the family economy good or bad?

A family economy always implies children's work. Instead of seeing this from a Western point of view as burden or exploitation, it is useful first to focus on the children's achievements, on the way they acquire knowledge and skills or assume responsibility for their family. The children are generally proud that they have learned how to do a particular job and are able to make their own contribution to the family economy. Often early work is mixed with play (Lancy, Katz, Polak, Spittler, this volume). But even when working has priority over playing, this is not automatically damaging to child development. Suzanne Gaskins (2009) has shown that Maya children's working activities help them to develop social skills and problem-solving capacities.

There is no doubt, however, that, under certain conditions, children's work in the family economy may also have adverse effects. How much a particular child has to work depends on how many siblings he or she has, and their position in the order of birth (Spittler, this volume, Kramer 2005). It depends even more on the degree to which the larger economy is embedded in the capitalist system. Children may be involved in the work process to a greater or lesser extent, or involved in different ways. When family economies compete with capitalist enterprises, there is pressure on prices and work. Families often make up for this by working harder, which frequently means that children are expected to work more, either by starting at an earlier age or by doing extra work. When family economies depend on trading its produce with outsiders, this means stronger pressure on the members of the family, including the children (Nieuwenhuys 1994; Dougnon, this volume). In Africa this has been observed particularly in systems of irrigated agriculture that produce for markets (Dougnon 2007: Katz, this volume). Labour migration can help a family economy because money flows back into the domestic economy. But more than anything else, it means that the family members who are left behind, including the children, have to work harder. Today's global conditions have often transformed family economies to survival economies, excluded from lucrative markets (Verlet 2005). Here, too, the children are often heavily burdened.

In all these cases, it is not helpful to lead or support campaigns to prohibit children's work while the structural causes remain unchanged. Legislating against child labour can worsen the situation for poor families, instead of improving it. In practice, it seems more important to take working children seriously, and to understand the reasons they themselves give as to why they work. Liebel (this volume) takes seriously what an organisation for working children says about their work.

Child work or child labour?

The terms 'work' and 'labour' are sometimes used synonymously; more usually, however, the term 'child labour' is value-laden with strong negative connotations, in contrast to any work by children that may be beneficial. It is often defined as work that is in some way harmful to children and their development; in practice, harmful work is usually merged with employment of young people below a specified age, arbitrarily adopted as an international minimum-age standard. Often the term 'child labour' is associated with paid productive work (not usually for the paid work of children from rich families in such sectors as entertainment and advertising).

Western watchdog organisations and media, supported by some academics, have produced reports based on a sense of outrage at forms of work that contradict their own romanticised image of childhood, and which are geared towards abolishing 'child labour'. This dominant focus on the negative appears in a new handbook: *The World of Child Labor. A Historical and Regional Survey* (Hindman 2009). The first section, 'Understanding Child Labor', includes an informative and balanced chapter, 'Social Science Views on Working Children' by Ben White. This is followed by 'Toward an Integrative Theory of Child Labor' by G.K.Lieten, which in fact has less to do with theory than with the eradication of child labour, starting from a 'concept of child labor… restricted to the production of goods and services, including work in the household, that interferes with the normative development of children as defined in the UN CRC and that transgresses the ILO conventions on this issue' (p.30—thus merging harmful work with work below the arbitrarily established minimum age of employment). Section 3 on 'Less Developed Regions of the World' contains eleven chapters, seven of which begin with the title 'Worst Forms of Child Labor'. The fourth section deals with 'Action Against Child Labor'. This volume typifies the many studies on child labour that concentrate on 'worst forms of child labour' and discuss measures to 'stop child labour'.

There are certainly exploitative forms of child labour that should be abolished. No activity can be properly understood, however, by focussing solely on negative aspects. The fact that in many cases and cultures children benefit from their work means that benefits and harm need to be considered together and weighed against each other.

Related to their exclusively negative perspective, studies on 'child labour' commonly have a further theoretical weakness. Few of the researchers describe and analyse actual children who take part in the work process. They concentrate on labour relations and exploitation but fail to describe what the children do in practice, what skills and knowledge they possess, and how the children themselves perceive their work. Indeed, such studies often reveal more about the values and opinions of the researchers, and of the organisations campaigning against child labour and financing research on the topic, than of the people most intensively involved in the work of children such as the children, their parents, and their employers.

A further theoretical weakness common in studies of 'child labour' is their assumption of the universal and unquestioned validity of their Western concepts of 'childhood' and 'work', failing to consider that these are social constructions and that alternative equally valid constructions are possible. Further, they are rarely interested in the diversity of family frameworks. In cultures where children's work is part of the social fabric, it is mostly embedded in a family or domestic economy. In order to understand it, therefore, we need to know the structure of this domestic economy and how it functions within and outside capitalism.

These theoretical weaknesses have practical consequences. Claims by parties concerned about children's rights and working 'in the best interest of the child' are empty without careful study of the contexts in which children actually work, and their own perspectives on, and agency in, the work they do.

There is no lack of publications that condemn child labour in Africa. But there are still too few studies that examine carefully the realisation and context of children's work, and those that exist have often been conducted hastily and superficially. There is a serious lack of authoritative ethnographic studies by authors who have spent time observing children at work, and talking to the children, their parents, and their employers. This volume is a step towards filling this gap.

Paths to learning

In contrast to outrage at child labour, the widespread view in African cultures is that work is essential to rearing children and preparing them for constructive adult life. According to this view, work provides necessary discipline and experience of responsibility. Work is also a way of learning many skills: those required for running a household, for example, and those required for economic activities such as agriculture and various crafts. Also, through work children learn how to relate to family and communities. In this volume, such benefits are well illustrated in Lancy's chapter on the 'chore curriculum'. Children willingly undertake various kinds of work as a way of interacting with those around them, and acquiring growing status in their families. Many Africans believe that concerns about 'child labour' are imposed by people who do not understand African cultures and the situations of African children.

The perspective that work is essential to rearing children fits psychological research on fundamental human learning processes. In her book, *The Apprenticeship of Learning*, Barbara Rogoff (1990) argued that the most fundamental way in which children learn is through participation in social activities. Similar to the way an apprentice learns a trade by observing, imitating, participating under guidance, before fully competent, Rogoff argues that children learn by watching others, then playfully imitating them, practising, and finally participating fully and competently in the activities. A common social activity for this kind of learning is work: through it children learn not only the skills of the work, but also the culture in which they have to live and the ways in which people within it relate to each other.

Such learning is as important for many facets of life as learning in the classroom is for others. It is the way in which girls learn skills of maintaining a home and caring for children, and much of the world's agriculture and many other productive activities depend on skills learned in this way. In Western societies, children are often encouraged to invest time and effort in developing skills in sport or the arts from an early age, but practice in productive skills are often discouraged.

In learning through practice with others, children and young people cannot be passive recipients of knowledge, but have to take part actively. This is well illustrated in Iris Köhler's chapter on learning pottery in a village in Côte d'Ivoire: children take the initiative in imitating and learning from an established potter. Indeed, much learning in any field depends on students exercising agency according to their interests.

One particular competency that is important for children living in communities with scarce resources is how deal with risk and adversity. Successful coping with adversity has been widely recognised to give children the confidence necessary to deal with problems in future. Particularly important in this respect can be a child's contributions through work in helping to overcome family crises: work thus provides a path to protective competence (see Boyden 2009). In this volume Dougnon, Ofosu-Kusi and Mizen, and Mahati show children learning to cope with risk and adversity through migration, with varying degrees of success; Dougnon presents migration as a rite of passage through which a boy acquires maturity.

The changing world demands new kinds of learning, illustrated by Katz's and Spittler's chapters. Spittler shows a growing appreciation of literacy and language skills even in traditional occupations like long-distance trading. Apart from learning important skills through participation in community activities, children now have to learn to deal with state officials and foreign countries in the wider world. This needs knowledge of things outside the community, sometimes new languages and knowledge of new technologies. Schools provide a means whereby a large number of children can acquire standardised skills under the guidance of relatively few specialised teachers.

Work and school

There is a widespread belief that work impedes schooling, thereby entrenching a cycle of poverty by preventing children of the poor from improving their situation. Sometimes work and school compete for children's time (Alber, Katz, Spittler, this volume). It is important therefore to consider what research tells us about the incompatibility between work and school generally.

Numerous studies show correlations between work on the one hand and poor school performance on the other. There are, however, two major difficulties in interpreting these correlations. First, there are numerous exogenous variables: to take some obvious examples, poverty generally correlates both with more child work and with poorer results at school; lack of education of parents also correlates with both; in poorer communities, where children are more likely to be working, access to schools is often more difficult and the quality of schools is often poorer. Consequently, careful multivariate analysis is required to establish a direct link between work and schooling.

Second, even when a direct link is established between work and schooling, the direction is not always clear. Is it the failure of the school system that drives children to work, or the attractions of work that keep children from school? The answer can occasionally be determined by using longitudinal studies, which are slow and expensive and still require strict multivariate analysis; or by applying instrumental variables on the rare occasions that appropriate ones can be found (validation of instruments used in econometric studies is frequently inadequate). While incompatibility of school and work can be established in certain specific situations, the general pattern is not so clear. Economist Eric Edmonds, in his extensive review for the *Handbook of Development Economics*, shows that long hours of work correlate strongly with poor school attendance, but that the pattern is less clear when the hours are shorter; the inverse relationship between hours of work and school attendance rises sharply at something over 30 hours a week (Edmonds 2008: 3641–3944). Most children work far less than this: in an earlier study of 36 developing countries, Edmonds and Pavcnik showed that 80 per cent of working children worked for fewer than 20 hours a week, including unpaid non-productive work within the household (2005: 203, Table 1). Research, therefore, does not support an assumption that part-time work is generally incompatible with schooling. Indeed, limited work sometimes improves nutrition and helps to pay for school expenses: some specific case studies show part-time child workers to have better attendance than non-working children (Bourdillon et al. 2010: 119).

There is a further question about the value of investment in schooling where school quality is poor. Apart from problems of accessing schools from poor communities, there are problems with how relevant school learning is for children in African communities, where the prospects of utilising minimal education to find employment are low. School systems in Africa were initiated by missionaries and colonial powers, usually in an attempt to bring African societies into line with Western ideas of 'civilisation' (Serpell 2011): sometimes parents fear that schooling results in children losing respect for their own culture and losing the values that go with that respect. Schooling can also restrict opportunities to learn skills that are important for local livelihoods (Spittler, this volume). In many schools, learning of any kind is extremely limited and failure rates are high (Glewwe and Kremer 2006; Hallack and Poisson 2007). Ofosu-Kusi and Mizen (this volume) depict children who have decided that work, even in harsh circumstances away from home, affords a better chance for the future than staying at home and at school. Sometimes, bullying and abuse make schools hazardous to children, especially to girls (Leach et al. 2003). When children and their families resist schooling, therefore, it cannot be assumed that their resistance is based on ignorance and prejudice: it should be taken seriously.

On the other hand, we have pointed out that children can learn in a variety of ways through appropriate work. Consequently, far from impeding human capital formation, work can be integral to it. In his introductory essay in the *World of Child Labor*, economist Patrick Emerson (2009: 8) points out, 'Though almost every theoretical study [by economists] of child labor posits a fairly rigid relationship between child work and diminished human capital, there is very little empirical evidence to support or refute this assumption.'

So it remains questionable whether children's work entrenches cycles of poverty. In many situations, children and their families use children's work as a way of dealing with crises and sometimes of opening up opportunities for future improvements. These possibilities are lost in studies that focus only on detrimental aspects of work.

Rights and values

Concerns about work and schooling are related to larger concerns about child protection, and roles of academic researchers in this area. We have criticised the value-laden nature of the 'child labour' discourse: there is a tradition in sociology and anthropology of researchers putting their own values aside and trying simply to describe and analyse the values of the people studied on their own terms. However, most academics interested in childhood studies are concerned about the welfare of children. In this volume, for example, Martin and Alber show concern about a child being deprived of schooling, and Ofosu-Kusi and Mizen show concern about how children are treated on the streets. Liebel is personally committed to supporting organisations of working children. When tension arises between the researcher's values and those of the people studied, what is the best way to decide what lies in the best interests of the children?

One response is to rely on international conventions, such as the UN Convention on the Rights of the Child and the African Charter on the Rights and Welfare of the Child, about which there is widespread agreement. There is a style that gives to such documents a moral standing, binding on all (for a full discussion, see Archard 2004). We suggest that a minimum ethical demand is that any particular application must be assessed in terms of outcomes for the intended beneficiaries. There is a more fundamental danger that an uncritical and decontextualised insistence on rights fails to recognise different social constructions of childhood (a weakness we pointed out with reference to discourse on 'child labour'): rights documents and interpretations of them often reflect the constructions of economically and politically powerful people. Such instruments are agreed by politicians rather than by the communities in which the children live.

Several chapters in this volume point to problems in applying universal standards to children in widely differing circumstances. Liebel points out that the African Movement of Working Children and Youth demands the right to appropriate and light work, whereas many activists in child rights believe that children's right to protection requires preventing them from working until they reach a certain age. Dougnon discusses conflicts between the interests of UN conventions, governments, and local people concerning child trafficking and youth migration, and Mahati shows similar tensions. Statements of rights based on an idealised childhood bear little relationship to the realities of children living in difficult circumstances such as street children (Ennew 2000): does the right to shelter mean that they have to be rounded up and deprived of their freedom? Moreover, it has been pointed out that such international instruments and agreements often reflect Western emphasis on the individual, while in many African societies the emphasis is on the good of family and community: Alber and Martin provide examples of decisions about individual children being based on what is needed by the family. And we have commented on the need to respect resistance to schooling.

These tensions raise the question of the purpose of child protection. It is often seen as safeguarding children from particular hazards. A more comprehensive view of protection is concerned with safeguarding opportunities for young people to develop meaningful lives in the circumstances in which they live. Fundamental to such protection are the social relations surrounding the child: to safeguard the child from particular physical hazards in a way that damages the relations of children with their families and communities is questionable protection. Finding appropriate forms of protection requires a thorough knowledge of the situation of the children and the specific culture in which they live.

Does this mean that we have simply to accept the values of the societies we are considering, and accept uncritically the places of children within them? Questions can be asked of learning through participation in family work. One problem is that children learn social practices and values that can be hurtful to certain members of the society. Participation in household chores often results in boys and girls taking for granted the heavy responsibilities of household work expected of women in a society. Such work may also instil social inequalities: certain children are expected to do certain kinds of work on the grounds of the status of their families. It is possible for adults to take for granted extensive work of children, a particular problem when it interferes with school. The traditional herding by boys in pastoral societies can occupy much of the day far from the homestead, impeding effective schooling. Demands on family labour in peak agricultural seasons can interfere with school timetables. Demands, particularly on girls, for hours of cooking and cleaning in the home can leave inadequate time for both study and leisure. Such conflicts are sometimes a matter of necessity and poverty; sometimes they are simply due to adults taking for granted cultural demands made of children and failing to realise that changing educational needs are not always compatible with these demands. When schooling competes for time and attention with traditional learning through participation, respect for resistance to schooling conflicts with children's need to acquire classroom skills in the modern world. While questioning such practices in terms of well-being and development of children, one has to be aware of potential unintended consequences of any intervention, particularly in relations between the children and their communities. Is there any way of resolving such conflict?

Academic research cannot resolve these questions definitively, but it can contribute to answers by collecting sound empirical data and providing a careful analysis of children's activities, and how these fit into their lives, both in the present and in future. We have criticised the selective collection of data and the lack of theoretical awareness in many 'child labour' studies. If academic research is to help in understanding, evaluating, and providing for the genuine needs of children, it must be conducted according to high academic standards (see Bourdillon, this volume).

Problems with applying rules rigidly in a variety of cultural situations occur also in relation to ethical research, which must be reflective and take into account relations between researchers and participants. Research institutions now widely demand ethical procedures to ensure that subjects who provide information suffer no harm from the research and, ideally, benefit from it. Ethical rules are useful in that they offer a guide for such reflection, but they do not guarantee ethical relations between researcher and researched: indeed, in the kind of ethnographic research presented in this volume, rules applied literally (such as demands for written consent from children or illiterate adults) can work against a respectful and ethical relationship between researcher and those providing information (see Chenhall *et al.* 2011). While individual chapters have not discussed ethical procedures in their research, we as editors believe that all the chapters arise from research conducted according to high ethical standards, based on concern and respect for those participating in the research.

So, in this book, we present some empirical studies, which look at both positive and negative outcomes of work in relation to learning and to developing young lives, and which take into account perspectives of children and of the adults in their communities.

Acknowledgements

Most of the chapters in this book arose from papers presented at a workshop organised early in 2011 by the International Research Centre *Work and Human Life Cycle in Global History*, based at Humboldt University in Berlin. This Centre, founded in 2009 and directed by Andreas Eckert, pursues fundamental research on the subject of work, focusing on the connections between work and life cycle. Initially, a life course was associated with careers and the problems of ageing populations in Western countries. But soon it was realised that in many parts of the world, especially in Africa, children constitute an important part of the workforce and their work merits serious study.

To discuss these questions, Gerd Spittler, a former fellow of the Centre, organised a workshop and invited a group of scholars from different disciplines to take part. Most had studied children's work in domestic economies; some had focused on child labour in capitalist companies. Although they disagreed in their theoretical and political positions, they had one thing in common: they had all carried out carefully conducted ethnographic or historical research in Africa. Ten of the twelve presenters of papers at the workshop are represented in this volume. Three additional papers are by African scholars (Dougnon, Mahati, and Ofosu-Kusi).

Apart from the presenters of papers, the participants at the workshop included fellows of the research centre and several discussants who contributed significantly to the debates: Andreas Eckert, the director of the research centre; Julia Seibert, a member of the Centre's scientific team, who had studied the labour question in colonial Congo; and the Bayreuth-based anthropologist Kurt Beck, who had studied the work of nomads, peasants, and craftsmen in the

Sudan. Hans Bertram, of Humboldt University, unlike all the other participants at the workshop, has done no fieldwork in Africa; however, he is a well-known sociologist specialised in the study of modern family relations, and much interested in the question of what work means for children and adolescents in Western societies.

We wish to express our thanks to Andreas Eckert and the International Research Centre who accepted the idea of the workshop and financed it. The Centre also financed the editing of this book. This included not only a printing grant, but also an English correction service. If the book is written in readable English, this is not least due to this valuable correction service.

The book is part of the series 'Beiträge zur Afrika Forschung' edited by the Institute of African Studies and the International Graduate School (BIGSAS) in Bayreuth. We are grateful to the editors for agreeing to include this book in the series. We are also grateful to Veit Hopf and the Lit-Verlag for publishing this book.

References

Archard, David (2004): *Children: Rights and Childhood* (2nd edition). London & New York: Routledge.

Bass, Loretta E. (2004): *Child Labour in Sub-Saharan Africa*. Boulder & London: Lynne Reiner.

Bourdillon, Michael, Deborah Levison, William Myers and Ben White (2010): *Rights and Wrongs of Children's Work*. New Brunswick, etc.: Rutgers University Press.

Boyden, Jo (2009): Risk and Capability in the Context of Adversity. Children's Contributions to Household Livelihoods in Ethiopia. In: *Children, Youth and Environments* 19, 111–137.

Chenhall, Richard, Kate Senior, and Suzanne Belton (2011): Negotiating Human Research Ethics. Case Notes from Anthropologists in the Field. In: *Anthropology Today* 27 (5), 13–17.

Dougnon, Isaie (2007): *Travail de Blanc, travail de Noir. La migration des paysans dogon vers l'office de Niger et au Ghana (1910–1980)*. Paris: Karthala.

Edmonds, Eric V. (2008): Child Labor. In: T.P. Schultz and J. Strauss (eds.): *Handbook of Development Economics*. Amsterdam: Elsevier Science 4, 3607–3709.

Edmonds, Eric V. and Nina Pavcnik (2005): Child Labor in the Global Economy. In: *Journal of Economic Perspectives* 18 (1), 199–220.

Emerson, Patrick M. (2009): The Economic View of Child Labor. In: H.D. Hindman (ed.): *The World of Child Labor. A Reference Encyclopedia*. New York: M.E. Sharpe, 3–9.

Ennew, Judith (2000): Why the Convention is not about Street Children. In: D. Fottrell (ed.): *Revisiting Children's Rights. 10 Years of the UN Convention on the Rights of the Child*. The Hague, etc.: Kluwer Law International, 169–182.

Frost, Ashley (2010): Youth Dependence. In: *Population Bulletin* 65 (2), 4–5.

Gaskins, Suzanne (2009): Work before Play for Yucatec Maya Children. Chicago. In: R. Shweder (ed.): *The Child. An Encyclopedic Companion*. Chicago: University of Chicago Press, 1040.

Glewwe, Paul and Michael Kremer (2006): Schools, Teachers, and Education Outcomes in Developing Countries. In: A. Hanushek and F. Welch (eds): *Handbook of the Economics of Education* volume 2, . New York: Elsevier, 945–1017.

Hallack, Jacques and Muriel Poisson (2007): *Corrupt Schools, Corrupt Universities. What Can Be Done?* Paris: International Institute for Educational Planning.

Hindman, Hugh D. (ed.) (2009): *The World of Child Labor. A Reference Encyclopedia*. New York: M.E. Sharpe.

James, Allison and Adrian James (2004): *Constructing Childhood. Theory, Policy and Social Practice*. Basingstoke: Palgrave Macmillan.

Kramer, Karen L. (2005): *Maya Children. Helpers at the Farm*. Cambridge: Harvard Univ. Press.

Leach, Fiona, Vivian Fiscian, Esme Kadzamira, Eve Lemani and Pamela Machakanja (2003): *An Investigative Study of the Abuse of Girls in African Schools*. Sevenoaks: Department for International Development.

Nieuwenhuys, Olga (1994): *Children's Lifeworlds. Gender, Welfare and Labour in the Developing World*. London: Routledge.

Reynolds, Pamela (1991): *Dance Civet Cat. Child Labour in the Zambezi Valley*. Harare: Baobab Books.

Rogoff, Barbara (1990): *Apprenticeship in Thinking. Cognitive Development in Social Context*. New York: Oxford University Press.

Rogoff, Barbara (2003): *The Cultural Nature of Human Development*. New York: Oxford University Press.

Serpell, Robert (2011): Social Responsibility as a Dimension of Intelligence, and as an Educational Goal. Insights from Programmatic Research in an African Society. In: *Child Development Perspectives* 5 (2), 126–133.

Spittler, Gerd (1990): Lebensalter und Lebenslauf bei den Tuareg. In: G. Elwert, M. Kohli, and H. Müller (eds.): *Im Lauf der Zeit. Ethnographische Studien zur gesellschaftlichen Konstruktion von Lebensaltern*. Saarbrücken: Breitenbach, 107–123.

Verlet, Martin (2005) : *Grandir à Nima (Ghana). Les figures du travail dans un faubourg populaire d'Accra*. Paris: Karthala

The Chore Curriculum

David F. Lancy

Introduction

While claims that anthropology has ignored children (Hirschfeld 2002) have been successfully countered (Lancy 2008, 2011a), children's work has undoubtedly been slighted. The anthropological study of children's play has yielded an enormous amount of scholarship—an annual conference, newsletters, journals and an entire shelf of scholarly volumes. The anthropological study of children's work has been limited, by comparison. This imbalance does not reflect any grounded reality: children in most societies spend as much time doing useful work as they do playing (Harkness and Super 1986). Rather, it reflects an inherent bias on the part of anthropologists whose culture provides no legitimate role for children as workers. And in the vast annals of developmental and child psychology, 'work' as a category of children's experience—worthy of study and analysis—is virtually absent. Hence, this volume, growing out of the Berlin conference organized by Professor Spittler, should be seen as a contribution towards redressing this unfortunate omission.

In my first attempt to review and synthesize the material on children's work, distinctive patterns emerged that crystallized into the expression 'chore curriculum' (Lancy 1966: 149). In the second survey, further analysis refined and enhanced the value of the concept (Lancy 2008: 235–242). I hope to take it one step further. The term 'chore' is somewhat self-evident, except that in contemporary society, we use it to characterize relatively minor tasks, completely peripheral to the 'important' work that is done exclusively by adults. However, in the archives of ethnographers and historians we find that children are expected to assist in a variety of critical areas of domestic and corporate production including the care of infants, gardening, herding and foraging. There is a widely acknowledged distinction between the work that all children are expected to do (contingent upon age and gender) and realms of endeavour that are optional or, contingent upon the child's interest and aptitude. A chore is any task that all boys or all girls should master by a roughly agreed upon age and carry out willingly and efficiently. Among the Kpelle, these include running errands, fetching water and firewood, tending younger siblings, weeding in the fields, caring for livestock, daubing mud on the walls of houses under construction, sweeping out the compound and so on (Lancy 1996). The chore inventory is mandatory and corresponds, in the parlance of contemporary (US) discussions of children's education, to the 'core' that all pupils are expected to master. In my study of Kpelle children, I found that they may also elect to pursue non-mandatory skills such as weaving, basketry (see also Köhler, this volume) and becoming a blacksmith. These are not part of the chore inventory and the pattern of skill acquisition and mastery is somewhat different (Lancy and Grove 2010).

The term 'curriculum' in chore curriculum conveys the idea that there is a discernible regularity to the process whereby children attach themselves to, learn, master and carry out their chores. While the academic or core curriculum found in schools is formal and imposed on students in a top-down process, the chore curriculum is informal and emerges in the interaction of children's need to fit in and emulate those older, their developing cognitive and sensorimotor capacity, the division of labour within the family and the nature of the tasks (chores) themselves. In the remainder of this chapter, my goal is to delineate and illustrate the common elements of the chore curriculum.

A note on methodology

The methodology used in this chapter involves canvassing the ethnographic record, assembling illustrative cases and teasing out broad, 'culturally invariant' patterns. It is referred to as *ethnology*. In a

recent exemplar, MacDonald describes her review of the ethnographic record on boys learning to hunt as a 'cross-cultural synthesis'
leading to an analysis that is of necessity, 'qualitative, as the relevant
evidence from the ethnographic literature is either anecdotal or generalized and includes limited quantitative data' (2007: 390). The
current survey of children's work grew out of a comprehensive
review of the ethnographic record pertaining to childhood (Lancy
2008). In that review, approximately 1350 published and unpublished reports were used, and since publication, an additional 250
sources have been found and added to the corpus. The material is
comprehensive with respect to geography and subsistence patterns.
This corpus is canvassed for all descriptions of children's work,
however brief, and then this smaller but still extensive corpus of
cases is systematically searched and organized around common
themes, such as the child's acquisition of 'sense' (see below).

The pre-school or play stage of the chore curriculum

In *Becoming a blacksmith in Gbarngasukwelle* I described children's
amazingly detailed and faithful replication of the blacksmith's forge
in an episode of make-believe. The blacksmith's compound was a
happening place in the village, consistently attracting a crowd of
enthralled spectators and gossips, young and old (also true in a Kuba
village, cf, Binkley 2006: 106). Children could watch the action of
the smiths and eavesdrop as village affairs were retailed. They thus
built up a stock of script material that could be woven into their
make-believe play. The boy playing the smith, in particular, had
obviously absorbed a great deal of the processes, both technical—he
constructed reasonable replicas of bellows, anvil, tongs—and
social—assigning the roles of novice, wives and helpers to his playmates. The terminology for tools, actions and relationships used in

the 'script' was also a faithful rendition (Lancy 1980a).[1] The town chief's court proved a similar magnet with similar engagement by children as spectators and later, dramatists (Lancy 1980b; see also Read 1960: 84).

Ethnographic descriptions of work activity enacted in make-believe and play with objects are rich and varied and even include archaeologists' reconstructions of childhood based on the discovery of miniature or crudely made artefacts assumed to be toys (Park 2006: 56–7). In the domestic sphere, we see children playing at food preparation, cooking and feeding the family. In these vignettes we occasionally get a glimpse of development over time in children's make-believe:

> When [very young Kaoka] pretend to keep house they make no sexual distinction in the allocation of the tasks. Boys and girls together erect the shelters, plait the mats, cook the food, and fetch the water. But within a year or so, although they continue to play in company, the members of each group restrict themselves to the work appropriate to their sex. The boys leave the cooking and water carrying to the girls, who, in turn, refuse to help with the building. (Hogbin 1969: 38)

Similarly, Goody (1992) describes a continuum from make-believe to 'for real' food preparation in which older children model for younger ones, real but scaled down pots. These may substitute for toy pots and if the mother is willing, edible ingredients go into the pot rather than grass. In a second illustration of this development from play to work, I was able to observe the 'canoe curriculum'. Ifaty village in southwest Madagascar depends primarily on marine resources and a modest-sized outrigger sailing canoe is the primary means of accessing such resources as well as marketing them. Virtu-

---

[1] In using this vivid example, I must acknowledge that blacksmithing is not a chore. In fact, becoming a blacksmith requires an apprenticeship. But, as I indicate elsewhere, the play stage is found across the task inventory, from chores to relatively simple crafts to full-fledged, complex crafts requiring an apprenticeship (Lancy 2011b).

ally all adult males use such canoes almost daily. On the beach and in the shallows, I observed (almost simultaneously): a) a 2-year-old splashing alone in a tide-pool, learning about water; b) three boys around 5 years old clambering over a beached canoe, learning an agile dance from thwart to gunwale; c) two boys about 7 years old independently preparing and then sailing model canoes, making appropriate adjustments to sail angle and rudder; d) two boys of 8 years playing with an abandoned outrigger in the shallows. They climbed on, paddled it, capsized it, took turns as captain and mate; e) when two young men began to rig and prepare to launch a full-size outrigger, the boys paddled over to watch this unfold and; f) shortly after they sailed away, a boy of about 10 came paddling in to shore in a half-sized canoe. Based on previous and more thorough studies of the canoe curriculum, I am confident that these experiences prepare boys to become mariners with little need for any formal instruction (Wilbert 1976: 318).

When children re-enact activities they have witnessed these are not just generic scenes but quite precise and thoughtful replications of complex systems. Katz's (1986: 47–8) descriptions of Sudanese boys' make-believe enactment of two contrasting agricultural systems provide a case in point. Aside from farming, children learn critical skills through play in varied environments. Among pastoralist societies, we find 'Dhebar boys... using camel and sheep droppings to practice herding sheep and lambs' (Dyer and Choksi, 2006: 170). Tuareg boys, who will eventually care for substantial camel herds, begin their lives as herders tending a kid they treat as a playmate (Spittler 1998: 343). Franz Boas describes Baffin Inuit boys 'play-hunting' seal using miniature harpoons fashioned by their parents (Boas 1901: 111).

Of course, children's play 'pre-school' is not limited to chores but may prefigure virtually any customary adult activity, including for example the processes involved in carrying out trance-induced shamanism (Katz 1981). In order for children to take the initiative and get a head start on learning their culture, chores included, the 'culture' must be an open book. The public nature of most adult activity facilitates children's engagement at a safe distance where they are not interfering. Anthropologists often note adult awareness and sympathy towards children's mimicry. 'When adults are asked about children's mimetic play they reply: "That is how they learn"' (Fortes 1938/1970: 23). Another example is drawn from the Sisala. 'When a boy first goes to the farm with his father, he is told to sit in the shade of a tree and observe what his elders are doing. When he asks to help, someone gives him a hoe with which to play' (Grindal 1972: 29).

John Bock has been the scholar most noted for empirical tests of the hypothesis that play equals preparation for work. In field studies among peoples in the Okavango with varied subsistence patterns, he has demonstrated that the likelihood of children mimicking specific adult activities in play closely tracks the relative importance of those activities in the local subsistence system. Furthermore, he has carefully demonstrated the process whereby girls build up skill in grain processing through 'play-pounding' (driving a pestle into a mortar to hull grain but without actual grain) which can then rapidly develop into the real thing, functioning from the outset at a high level of skill (Bock 2004: 274). We have evidence then, from a multiplicity of sources, of children playing at the tasks and production systems that they will later assay in earnest. We also have more limited evidence that this play activity is 'educational' but several disclaimers are in order.

Children's motivation to engage in make-believe and object play cannot be attributed solely or even primarily to the desire to learn their culture. The essence of play is its purposelessness. Still, there is little play that does not echo adult activity. Play with toys that are uniquely toys (as opposed to miniature or discarded tools) is associated almost entirely with high civilization and social class. In upper class households in Egypt circa 2300 BCE, one finds an array of professionally made toys that would not look out of place in a contemporary toy store, such as a wooden crocodile with articulated

tail and jaws (Wileman 2005: 31). This implies an attitude of indul-
gence: that parents expect children to play just for fun.

In contrast, village children draw primarily on the scenes from
their direct experience (Power 2000: 272) because unlike bourgeois
children they do not have access to manufactured toys, storybooks,
videos and other sources to launch them into more inventive fanta-
sies (Gaskins, in press). And, in contrast to contemporary bourgeois
society where parents engage with and encourage their child's
fantasy play, villagers do not engage directly in children's play
(Lancy 2007). '[Sisala] parents regard an interest in children's play
as beneath their dignity' (Grindal 1972: 25). Lastly, not all chores are
foreshadowed in play. Little girls may care for an infant sibling in
lieu of playing with a doll, for example (Broch 1990: 110) or assist
their mother in a market stall in lieu of pretending to market
(Paradise and Rogoff 2009: 113).

Running errands

Margaret Mead, reporting on her first field study in Samoa, provides
one of the earliest characterizations of the centrality of work in
childhood.

> The tiniest little staggerer has tasks to perform—to carry water, to
> borrow fire brands, to fetch leaves to stuff the pig… learning to
> run errands tactfully is one of the first lessons of childhood…
> these slighter tasks are laid aside for harder ones as soon as the
> child becomes strong enough or skilled enough. (Mead 1928: 633)

Running errands nicely illustrates key characteristics of the chore
curriculum.

Fetching and carrying is inherently staged or laddered. 'Very
young children (age 3) may start with one or two sticks of wood, or
yams in a carry net, but by age 8 they are carrying firewood, water,
produce and messages' (Zeller 1987: 544).

A barely mobile toddler may be asked to carry a cup from its
mother across an evening family circle to its father. The same toddler
will tag along as an older sibling makes a longer delivery excursion,

in effect serving as an understudy. Errands can vary by length and territory, between close kin and strangers, can involve loads of varying size and fragility, and can include an exchange of some kind including a market transaction. Adults match their assignments to the child's level of skill and size and each new assignment ratifies (and motivates) the child's growing competence.

The stalwart little helper publicly advertises the quality of its upbringing and its worthiness as a potential foster child, enhancing the family's reputation. On the other hand, children are favoured as errand runners 'because adolescents or adults seen in close proximity to neighbors' houses might be suspected of adultery, theft or witch-craft. And boys are favored because their virtue isn't as fragile as girls'' (Lancy 2008: 238). Learning to become an errand runner rarely entails teaching by an adult. Children observe and replicate the process with only minor guidance from an older, sib role model.

Anthropologists often note with some degree of awe how early the child embarks on the chore curriculum and how significant is their contribution to the domestic economy. Ottenberg notes that, among the Afikpo, babies are routinely cared for by their 4- or 5-year-old siblings (1968: 80). Among the Hadza, groups of children forage in the vicinity of camp while their parents are gone on longer expeditions. From 4 years of age, they successfully gather baobab fruits, tubers and small birds and mammals, providing up to 25 per cent of their daily diet. Marlowe notes: 'foraging simply emerges gradually from playing' (Marlowe 2010: 156; see also Tucker and Young 2005: 169).

Even with change in the village economy, such as the introduc-tion of cash crops, children's work remains crucial. For example, in the coffee industry children make varied and valued contributions. The youngest plant seeds in small plastic bags to germinate new plants, they also collect coffee cherries that have fallen to the ground at harvest. Somewhat older children are responsible for weeding and spreading chalk. 12- to 15-year-old boys are responsible for spraying urea as a fertilizer and assisting with trimming, which may involve climbing trees to lop off branches with a machete. All help with the harvest and with sorting the cherries. Agile boys are only too happy to climb into the branches to collect the fruit that adults cannot reach (Ruiz, 2011: 169–171).

Work and identity

It is not enough to acknowledge that children are kept busy doing chores or that being helpful makes them 'fit in'. The very identity of the child may be largely defined in terms of the work that he or she does. Throughout human history children have been seen as an investment. Parents have them and raise them so that their labour can support the household, and eventually provide an old-age pension or social security (Clark 1994; Reynolds 1991). Among the severely impoverished Papel in Guinea-Bissau, infant mortality is extremely high: roughly one-third of all children born alive will die before they reach the age of five. In spite of these dire statistics, and the fact that women work extremely hard to eke out a bare survival, Jonina Einarsdottir found that mothers were not interested in reducing their fertility; on the contrary, they wanted as many children as possible. They operated on the assumption that the more you have, the more likely there will be a few who survive and 'help with work, contribute to their emotional well-being, take care of them in old age, secure them a respectable funeral, and ease their entrance into the afterlife' (Einarsdottir 2004: 86). A Kpelle mother asserts: 'What makes a child good? If you ask her to bring water, she brings water. If you ask her to cook she cooks, if you tell her to mind the baby, she does it. When you ask her to plant rice she doesn't complain' (Lancy 1996: 76). Given these widely shared views, it should not be surprising that for the Nuer (and many others), it is only when:

> the boy tethers the cattle and herds the goats… cleans the byres and spreads the dung to dry and collects it and carries it to the fires [that] *he is considered a person.* (Evans-Pritchard 1956: 146, emphasis added)

In some societies the association between chores and identity is made even more explicit. Among the Giriama, a two- to three-year-old is labelled, in effect, 'water carrier'. An eight-year-old girl is called a 'maize pounder', a boy of the same age is *muhohomurisa* or, 'herd boy' (Wenger 1989: 98). In pre-modern Russia 'our ploughboy', 'our herd boy', and 'our nanny girl' were habitual terms parents used to address their children (Gorshkov 2009: 15). And among the *Tchokwe'*, 'children are identified through the roles they assume [for example] *kambumbu*are children... who help parents in the field or with fishing and hunting' (Honawana, 2006: 41–42). On the other hand, an adult seen carrying out chores normally assigned to children would be an object of scorn and pity and Russian children:

> who could not learn how to do work appropriate to their age were subjected to mockery... a girl who could not learn how to spin by a certain age was called a 'no spinner' (*nepriakha*); if a girl could not weave cloth by age fifteen, she was called a 'no weaver' (*netkakha*). Boys who had not learned how to make bast shoes were called 'shoeless'. (Gorshkov 2009: 23)

Aside from nomenclature that marks the child's developmental progression as a worker, we find numerous examples of adults turning these transitions into minor rites of passage. These include: a Kaoka boy's first pig (Hogbin 1969: 39); a Vlach 6-year-old being given his first shepherd's crook (Campbell 1964: 156); a Kutenai boy's first bow and arrows (Grinnel 1923: 115); a Netsilik girl's first caught salmon, her brother's first goose (Balikci 1970: 45); and 'When [an Mbuti] boy kills his first "real animal," he is immediately acclaimed as a hunter...[and honoured by cicatrization]...an operation performed... by one of the "great hunters"' (Turnbull 1965: 257). On the other hand, certain areas of work are considered inappropriate for children (just as certain tasks are reserved for males, others females). The Kwoma prevent children from prematurely assuming more difficult chores because tasks are associated with rank, and moving to a more challenging assignment is tantamount to a promotion (Whiting 1941: 70). Koori boys are not permitted to touch 'real' hunting weapons (toy or scaled-down are OK) as that would demean the adult hunters who have earned the privilege (Basedow 1925: 86).

Chores also play a major role in the differentiation of gender—especially before the appearance of secondary sex characteristics.[2] Among the Kel Ewey Tuareg, goats are tended by boys and girls, but only boys tend camels (Spittler 1998). In West Africa, weaving is the province of women among Akwete Igbo, and 3-year-old girls pretend to weave, eventually picking up the skill through watching and helping their mothers. For the Baulè, males weave and boys acquire the skill through a lengthy, formal apprenticeship (Aronson 1989). Stereotypically, among Hadza foragers girls forage and boys hunt (Marlowe 2010). Almost universally girls are preferred as caretakers for younger siblings and sons are conscripted for this chore only when a daughter is unavailable (Ember 1973: 425–6).[3] Indeed, it is common to see two clusters of children in open areas of the village or farm. Girls gather together in a corner with their young charges playing in a subdued fashion. Boys, on the other hand, roam more widely, engage in a panoply of games, some quite noisy and boisterous, and seem generally carefree (Read 1960: 82).

The Kerkenneh Islands are typical in transitioning girls into responsible roles well before boys. 'By the age of four most little girls have some real responsibility in the household. Little boys are babied longer and are discouraged from imitating their mothers because that is women's work' (Platt 1988: 282). Indeed, boys in many societies are defined as much by their freedom from work—relative to girls—as by the specific work they do (Pope-Edwards

---

[2] Iris Köhler has written (personal communication 25/7/11): 'Within the society I explored, I can validate the connection between chore curriculum and identity building: Very small children are allowed to play and 'work' tasks of both sexes. People say that they 'don't know yet who they are' and how to act their age.'

[3] A significant exception to this generalization occurs in a few, highly egalitarian, foraging societies, the Central African foragers known as pygmies in particular (Henry, Morelli, and Tronick 2005: 200).

2005: 87). In many cases, a boy or man doing 'women's work' would be the object of ridicule.

The onset of middle childhood marks an important transition in the child's identity. As Edel describes, Chiga children have been busy play/working and learning to do a variety of useful things. But by around seven or eight (earlier in some societies) the child falls into a routine of predictable, competent, essential work. Earlier, 'any assumption of adult ways and attempts at adult skills or responsibilities is praised and applauded' (Edel 1957/1996: 178). Now they can be relied upon to do their chores without guidance, instruction, scolding or praise. Girls, in particular, can largely replicate and substitute for their mothers.

The child has reached a point in its development where they he or she starts to 'get noticed' (Lancy and Grove 2011) due to their evident intelligence or common sense, referred to among the Kipsigis as *ng'omnotet* (Harkness and Super 1985: 223); *wijima* among the Sisala (Grindal 1972: 28). 'Intelligence in the village is associated with qualities like self-sufficiency, obedience, respect towards elders, attention to detail, willingness to work and effective management of younger siblings and livestock' (Lancy 2008: 168, see also, Wober 1972). Most, if not all, of these signs of maturity, relate to the child as worker.

The transition from child to adult is often marked by a rite of passage or initiation, seen as a precursor to marriage and adult standing. However, work may play a critical role in this transition. 'Fully adult Hadza men are referred to as *epeme* men. When a male is in his early 20s and kills a big-game animal, he becomes an *epeme* or fully adult male' (Marlowe 2010: 57). Among the Warao, a prospective bridegroom is judged on his ability to garden, hunt, fish and above all, make a canoe: any deficit is a bar to marriage and adult status (Wilbert 1976: 327). Contemporary anthropological accounts describe many cases of a breakdown in the chore curriculum resulting in a failure to marry and establish an adult persona. Among the Bumbita, a breakdown in traditional socialization practices due to missionary interference and temporary out-migration of youths has denied them knowledge of how to cultivate yams. A young man, who cannot grow yams, cannot support a family (Leavitt 1998: 178). For many, the obligation to attend school pulls them out of the chore curriculum. Youth from foraging societies may be particularly vulnerable as they miss out on hunting and gathering expeditions and fail to learn the local ecology. For Cree children:

> By the time they finished their schooling, they had become foreigners to Cree tradition, not only by failing to acquire skills and knowledge of the land but also by lacking an appropriate attitude for life on the land. Thus, formal schooling led to the weakening of the existing social system. (Ohmagari and Berkes 1997: 207)

The linkage between social structure and chores is also founded on the idea that 'work builds character'. In a Nahua village, the elders see children working less and showing, as a result, diminished vigour and toughness (Sánchez 2007: 94); while Russian peasants believed that if children are not put to work early, they will never develop into responsible adults (Gorshkov 2009: 14). Zelizer describes the battle that unfolded during the first quarter of the 20th century between those who felt that labour was harmful to children and interfered with their schooling, and those who thought that work built the child's character and that early employment staved off idleness and deviance (1985: 57, 72).

Role models

If I were discussing contemporary bourgeois society this section might be labelled 'Teachers'. But as analysis reveals (Lancy 2010a), active, child-centred *instruction* is quite rare outside the contemporary elite. Rather, children assume responsibility for learning their culture, chores in particular, while relying on those more expert to serve largely in the capacity of models. Again, contrary to contemporary views on what is 'natural' (Lancy 2010b), the model, especially for boys, is as likely to be an older sibling or peer as a parent. As examples, I cite Amhara boys who are said to trail after young males 'like retainers follow a feudal lord' (Messing 1985: 213). Hadza boys 'almost never go hunting with their fathers, at... 8 or 9 years old, they go hunting for small animals, usually in twos' (Marlowe 2010: 157). By imitating their sib-caretakers Marquesan 'toddlers learn to run, feed and dress themselves, go outside to urinate and defecate, and help with household chores' (Martini and Kirkpatrick 1992: 124).

There are several reasons for the choice of peers as role models. From an early age, children are placed under the care of older siblings who introduce them into the neighbourhood playgroup, e.g., 'Mayan toddlers learn primarily by observing and interacting with their sibling caretakers...' (Maynard 2002: 978). At the threshold of the chore curriculum, children are far more likely to be in the company of peers than parents. Weisner notes that Abaluyia 'children care for other children (under a mother's or other adults' management) within *indirect chains of support*' (1996: 308, emphasis added). That is, toddlers are managed by slightly older siblings who are in turn guided by adolescents, while adults serve as rather distant 'foremen' for the activity, concentrating primarily on their own more productive or profitable activity. This phenomenon is well illustrated in Polak's study of Bamana families engaged in bean cultivation (Polak 2003, 2011).

There is considerable evidence that siblings are more patient and sympathetic mentors than adults (Maynard 2002). A contrasting pair of anecdotes is very revealing. Raum observed a Chaga mother and her little daughter cutting grass to take home to feed the cattle. Tying the stalks into a bundle is difficult but the 'mother refuses requests for help by saying: "Haven't you got hands like me?"'(1940: 199). Now consider a vignette of Pushtun children gathering and bundling shrubs (*buti*) to bring home.

Khodaydad, aged about ten years, showed and explained to his younger brother Walidad (two and a half) how to put *buti* together: He made up a small pile while Walidad squatted next to him and watched. Tying them together, he explained how to do it. Then he untied the bundle and bound it up again to show how it was done. Walidad then wanted to carry it home. His elder brother helped him shoulder it and his sister guided him home, and it was obvious that little Walidad was very proud of being able to accomplish the work. (Casimir 2010: 54)

To be sure, adults may intervene strategically in the learning process. For example, the 'knowledge gained from [Meriam] adults about the reef and how to forage remains limited mainly to what is edible and what is dangerous' (Bird and Bird 2002: 291). Bamana children may 'want to participate in the work done in the compound and the fields to a greater extent than they are able... they risk causing damage, for instance by using a hoe the wrong way or losing seeds' (Polak 2003: 126). Hence, parents must tactfully intervene to guide them to tasks that are within their grasp (Polak 2011: 104–5). For Warao boys learning to make canoes, the *sine qua non* of survival, 'there is not much verbal instruction... but the father does correct the hand of his son [and demonstrates] how to overcome the pain in his wrist from working with the adze' (Wilbert 1976: 323).

Girls may find that their freedom and opportunity to play is curtailed by their mother's need for a 'helper at the nest'. The mother becomes the model and supervisor of the girl's progress through the chore curriculum. As Riesman notes, by the time a young woman is pregnant, she has had years of watching her mother and others care for infants and she has herself logged many hours of child care under the watchful (and critical) eye of her mother and other senior female relatives (1992: 111). A Kpelle girl will accompany her mother to the garden, carrying a pail containing their lunch. At the field, she will watch as her mother hoes until given her own small hoe to try. She will match her mother's behaviour, learning the moves through repeated practice and observation (Lancy 1996: 144). If a Mazahua mother has a market stall, her daughter will 'pitch in' to assist her by trimming onions and tying them into bundles, using her mother's bundles as a model. She is eager to set up 'her' stand and once the mother's stand is established, does so using an abandoned piece of cardboard (Paradise and Rogoff 2009: 113).

It is rarer to find boys paired so closely with their fathers. Children are often considered too boisterous to serve as companions on fishing and hunting expeditions (Broch 1990:85; Puri 2005, 233). A Yanomami boy will not be welcomed on the hunt by his father until he is in his mid-teens and has already developed considerable expertise at tracking and knows the forest and its inhabitants intimately (Peters 1998: 90). Fathers are often absent from the homestead or the nature of their work, felling trees to clear land for a farm, precludes a youngster from 'pitching in'. However, there are a few cases where adult males (not necessarily the father) serve as critical role models. The boy or youth will be moved from the home to the exclusive company of men.

> When FulBe Mare'en boys... are old enough to herd... they no longer eat with their mother and sisters but with the men. Through explicit instruction, listening to conversations, and observation they learn about the general dietary needs of cattle, which types of grasses appeal most to cattle, the characteristics of each animal, the dominance hierarchy in the herd, and the genealogy of the herd. (Moritz 2008: 111)

As girls move out of the realm of everyday chores into more complex tasks, they may continue in the same mentoring relationship they have established with their mothers. Conambo mothers are very supportive of their daughter's fledgling efforts at ceramics, which is a chore in the sense that all women are expected to make pots. They sometimes give the girls well-formed pots and invite them to add minor painted designs or they take the daughter's ill-formed vessel, re-shape it and hand it back to the child to decorate. However, they do remain focused primarily on their own production (Bowser and Patton 2008). Köhler (2009, this volume) studied mother-daughter transmission of ceramic skills among the Nyarafolo. In her report, we see somewhat less engagement by the mothers, perhaps because pottery-making is optional. The onus is on the girls to take the initiative and mothers offer almost no verbal instruction even when doing so would accelerate the girl's mastery. In my study of the Kpelle, I found mothers even less involved in the sense that they seemed to take no responsibility for their daughter's learning to make textiles: at most they were willing to permit the daughter to work alongside and observe and copy their efforts. The attitude seemed to be that the child will learn the skill 'when she's ready' (Lancy 1996: 149). Yet another variation appears in a study of Dii potters: girls must endure a lengthy and demanding apprenticeship with their mother. It is significant that pottery-making is mandatory. In fact, 'to have an ungifted apprentice or potter in the family is a disgrace, and every potter is required to reach a certain level of expertise in order not to depart from the rest of the potter families' (Wallaert 2008: 187). The only 'teaching' consists in sharp verbal rebukes or directives: 'Stop wasting clay,' otherwise the girl learns the way she probably learned her other chores—through observation, imitation and much practice. At age ten, the process becomes even more restrictive.

> Initiative and trial and error are now forbidden; every gesture must follow the mother's pattern. Corporal punishments (spanking, forced eating of clay) are used to ensure that rules are respected, and verbal humiliations are very common. (Wallaert 2008: 190–1)

Dii pottery is somewhat unusual in that the child apprentices to a parent. In other societies it is far more usual that the child apprentices to a more distant kinsman or to a stranger. For example, 'Gonja believe that familiarity breeds contempt and that sons wouldn't show sufficient respect towards their fathers to learn from them' (Goody 2006: 254).

I want to conclude this section, however, by stressing, that despite the observed variability in the process of skill acquisition, the onus is on the learner not the model. Hence, Bolin's description of learning to weave in the Andes is probably normative. 'Children are not taught to spin or weave. Rather, *they observe family members who have mastered these crafts and imitate them directly*' (2006: 99, emphasis added). In other words, I think that the child likely draws on numerous models for guidance and inspiration, not just a single role model (see also Gosselain 2008: 153, Puri 2005: 280).

Progress in the chore curriculum

Two central principles of the chore curriculum are the motivation of the child, which propels them up the learning gradient, and the nature of the task environment, which reduces the severity of that gradient by offering 'steps' or stages. In this section, we will examine those stages and also consider what ensues when the child is not making the expected progress.

Herding is perhaps the most evidently staged 'chore'. The child first learns to care for a single, juvenile animal as a pet. She or he helps cut and gather fodder and mucks out the byre. The child's progress is monitored. 'Only after a boy has proved his reliability at herding goats is he preferred to the work of pasturing cattle' (Raum 1940: 200).The Tuareg boy progresses from a single kid (at three years-old) to a herd of goats (at ten) to a baby camel (at ten) to a herd of camels (fifteen) to managing a caravan on a trek across the Sahara (in their twenties, see Spittler, this volume).The Ngoni boy faces a challenging education in cattle lore.

> The Ngoni classified their cattle according to age, sex, coloring, size and shape of horns, whether castrated or not, whether in calf or not. Knowledge of the extensive series of names used for these 'classes' of cattle was part of a herd-boy's A.B.C. By the time he was old enough to be told to drive certain cattle out of the kraal, designated by their class, he knew exactly which ones were meant. He could also use the cattle terminology to be precise in telling an owner about a beast which has strayed or one that had a sore hoof, or one that was giving an exceptionally good or poor flow of milk. (Read 1960: 133)

Staging in agricultural production ranges from tasks as simple as chasing birds from the ripening crop (Grindal 1972: 29; Lancy 1996: 146) to ploughing behind a team of oxen (Polak 2011: 144). Children may be assigned their own garden plot as a gesture of encouragement, likewise they may be given their own scaled-down collecting calabash, hoe or machete. They will shadow an older relative who serves, as we saw, as a role model. They observe the model and emulate their behaviour, but the relative (usually an older sibling) also assists by keeping the child on task and preventing him or her from damaging the work of others (Polak 2011: 104–5). Some tasks are relatively easy to master, while others, such as learning to plant millet seeds, may take a couple of years and require an adult to demonstrate the correct procedure (Polak 2011: 84–6).

In foraging, there is a range of task levels corresponding to the difficulty of the terrain and the elusiveness of the prey. With respect to terrain, we might contrast the Ju/'hoansi (!Kung) with the Huaorani. In the former, the terrain is extremely difficult and foragers face the threat of predation. Children must be left behind in camp and do not begin their foraging careers until their late teens (Hames and Draper 2004; see also Kogel et al. 1983). The terrain, in the second case, is somewhat more benign and 'nothing is more cheering for a Huaorani parent than a three-year-old's decision to join a food gathering expedition' (Rival 2000: 116). Children on the island of Mer in the Torres Straits can collect edible marine life from the shoreline and shallows. They can be seen 'spearfishing with toddler-sized spears as soon as they begin walking, using them at first to spear sardines along the foreshore for bait' (Bird and Bird 2002: 262). However while some types of collecting can be mastered quickly at an early age, shellfish collecting takes more strength and mature production levels are achieved later in childhood (Bird and Bird 2002: 245).[4]

A précis of hunting development is available for the Western Apache. Children were kept from roaming beyond the camp until eight years old but then quickly learned to shoot small game with

---

[4] For a thorough discussion of the interaction of physical size and dexterity versus experience and learning in the child's movement through the chore curriculum, see Bock (2001).

sling or bow and arrow. They joined enthusiastically in communal quail drives. At twelve their tracking and hunting prowess yielded prey that they were proud to bring back to camp. For his first deer hunt, at fifteen or sixteen, a boy would be permitted to accompany an older male relative who acted as role model. One earned the right to tag along (and observe) by fetching wood and water for the temporary hunting camp (Goodwin and Goodwin 1942: 475). The pattern with hunting seems to be one where boys may get an early start on using weapons, tracking and capturing small prey, but nevertheless, take many years to reach adult levels of competence (MacDonald 2007: 391). Despite this, the larger pattern is quite clear, children master most of the skills needed to function in their society at an early age.

The chore curriculum is remarkably successful in moving children from a state of dependency to one where they are both self-sufficient and contributors to the domestic economy. And, this is accomplished with little intervention from an adult 'teacher'. What happens when a 'student' pursuing the chore curriculum 'fails'? Families vary in imposing sanctions on 'laggards', with foraging societies being the most *laissez faire*. Penalties range from the very mild, as when Mayan family members speak critically of a child who is cast in the role of 'overhearer', listening to his or her behaviour being described critically (de León ND) to more severe variations. An Amhara adult may encourage a child to do its chores 'by throwing clods of dirt or manure at him' (Levine 1965: 266). Aka children who evade responsibility are denied food by their mothers (Boyette 2008). Many societies prescribe a beating for children who fail to do chores or do them poorly (Ainsworth 1967). A Sebei mother condemns a 'lazy' daughter who is not up to the mark by saying, 'I hope that you have stomach pains and dysentery' (Goldschmidt 1976: 259).

Overall, however, accounts of children eagerly doing chores are far more frequent than accounts of laggards,[5] but significant change in the chore curriculum can be anticipated.

The waning of the chore curriculum

Earlier we touched on the breakdown of the chore curriculum due to forces affecting village youth. Among these, schooling stands out. In the 1930s and 1940s, schools were first introduced to Sisala villages and the emphasis was on preparing a new elite to lead and staff the colonial and then later the post-colonial administration. This meant 'a relatively small body of educated Sisala gained easy access to a large number of prestigious government positions' (Grindal 1972: 92). The majority of children, however, continued to pursue the chore curriculum (for a parallel case in Papua New Guinea, see Pomponio and Lancy 1986). The increasing monetization of the village economy and the consequent press to use schooling as a pathway to greater earning potential has, in recent years, forced parents to re-evaluate their dismissal of schooling (see Spittler, this volume). Government mandated universal schooling and the competition for scarce jobs has raised the bar in terms of the minimum level of education required to enter the labour force (Lord 2011: 102). Hence, schooling competes directly with the domestic economy for children's time and allegiance.

There are indirect threats to the chore curriculum as well. Chief among these is the loss of sibling caretakers or their transformation into 'teachers'. Mayan 'children who had been to school often tried the school model of teaching from a distance with much verbal discourse until they realized that that model was not resulting in the younger child's compliance in doing the task' (Maynard 2004: 530). Many villagers may remain ambivalent about the value of schooling.

---

[5]   Just as a boy may be forced to do 'girl's work' if sisters are unavailable, children may be forced to remain at a very menial level in the chore curriculum because that is the level at which their contribution is most critical.

In Fez, where there are a range of craft traditions that are still economically viable, schooling is seen as waste of time, or worse, that a
schooled child will not follow the strict dictates of his/her role model
in learning the craft (Schlemmer 2007: 114). The children are also
ambivalent and anthropologists report cases of children eager to
abandon what are seen as arduous and unpleasant chores for the relative ease of the classroom (Anderson-Levitt 2005: 988), as well as
cases where 'Staying at home or in the fields is preferable to the
despotic, sometimes boring, and often a bit cruel school reality...'
(Alber, paper for the conference). However, most communities try to
strike a balance, 'Family decisions in rural West Africa are based on
the notion that it might be wise to send some of the children going to
school and others to continue peasant's work' (Alber, paper for the
conference).

While the chore curriculum has retained its viability in many
villages, in another sector of society, it has disappeared altogether.
There has been a flood of studies recently of children's chores or
contributions to the household among middle-class families.

- In West Berlin 'parents alone are responsible for... the reproduction of daily life... the child is the recipient of care and services'
  (Zeiher 2001: 43; see also Wihstutz 2007: 80).
- In case studies from Los Angeles, a parent spends a lot of time
  cajoling/guiding a five-year-old into making her bed. It becomes a
  big dramatic production after she initially refuses, claiming
  incompetence. In a case from Rome, the father does not even
  bother trying to get his eight-year-old daughter to make her bed,
  he does it himself, while complaining that her large collection of
  stuffed animals and decision to move to the top bunk make his
  task much harder (Fasulo, et al. 2007: 16–18).
- In a related study in Los Angeles of 30 families 'no child routinely
  assumed responsibility for household tasks without being asked...
  the overall picture was one of effortful appeals by parents for help
  [who often] backtracked and did the task themselves... [a father

becoming, in effect] a valet for the child' (Ochs and Izquierdo 2009: 399–400).

- Genevan children 'use the vociferous defeat strategy. They comply with what is asked of them but... cry, scream, bang doors, lock themselves up in their rooms to sulk and so on... Some... agree to submit if their parents can prove their demands are well-founded... [some] agree to render a service to their parents in exchange for permission to go out... One boy mentioned employing a kind of "terrorism"' (Montandon 2001: 62).

In contrast to these cases, Orellana's research on Central American migrant families in Los Angeles shows children—in particular girls—making a large contribution to the care and well-being of the household (and attending school). Not only do they do household chores, they do odd jobs and bring in needed cash, unlike middle class white children whose earnings are not shared with the family (Bachman, et al. 2003: 301), and assist their parents and older relatives around the barriers of culture and language (Orellana 2001).

Contemporary society is not supportive of the chore curriculum. When children become cherubs rather than chattel (Lancy 2008: 77, 99), parents and society at large no longer view them as helpers, contributing significantly to the domestic economy. And children absorb these values trading a willingness to emulate and assist for an eagerness to express needs and preferences. The culture is no longer an open book; much of what is important to learn is hidden, because it is valuable, dangerous or complex. Teaching has all but replaced observation and imitation as the primary means of transmitting culture to the descending generation. School learning is highly staged but it is extremely difficult for the child to proceed from level to level at her own pace, without explicit instruction. The immediate feedback afforded by mastering the small steps leading to competent work is now very elusive. The child must be content with often meaningless ('Good Job!') praise, grades and smiley faces. The role model is unable to instruct via demonstration alone. Indeed, when the child tries to emulate a desired activity (cooking, carpentering, driving) it may be rebuffed because the possibility of damage to the child, the materials, the project or the tools is great. Toy tools are unsatisfactory because you cannot make anything truly useful. Where the chore curriculum thrives, it is a thing of beauty fitting the maturing child into its society like a key into a lock.

References

Ainsworth, Mary D. (1967): *Infancy in Uganda. Infant Care and the Growth of Love.* Baltimore, MD: Johns Hopkins Press.

Anderson-Levitt, Kathryn M. (2005): The Schoolyard Gate. Schooling and Childhood in Global Perspective. In: *Journal of Social History* 38, 987–1006.

Aronson, Lisa (1989): To Weave or Not to Weave. Apprenticeship Rules among the Akwete Igbo of Nigeria and the Baulè, of the Ivory Coast. In: Michael W. Coy (ed.): *Apprenticeship. From Theory to Methods and Back Again.* Albany, NY: SUNY Press, 149–162.

Bachman, Jerald G., Deborah J. Safron, Susan Rogala Sy, and John E. Schulenberg (2003): Wishing to Work. New Perspectives on How Adolescents' Part-Time Work Intensity Is Linked to Educational Disengagement, Substance Use, and Other Problem Behaviours. In: *International Journal of Behavioral Development* 27 (4), 301–315.

Balikci, Asen (1970): *The Netsilik Eskimo.* Garden City, NY: The Natural History Press.

Basedow, Herbert (1925): *The Australian Aboriginal.* Adelaide, Australia: F. W. Preece and Sons.

Binkley, David A. (2006): From Grasshoppers to Babende. The Socialization of Southern Kuba Boys to Masquerade. In: Simon Ottenberg and David A. Binkley (eds.): *Playful Performers. African Children's Masquerades.* London: Transaction Publishers, 105–115.

Bird, Douglas W. and Rebecca Bliege Bird (2002): Children on the Reef. Slow Learning or Strategic Foraging? In: *Human Nature* 13, 269–397.

Boas, Franz (1901): The Eskimo of Baffin Land and Hudson Bay. In: *Bulletin of the American Museum of Natural History* 15, Part 1, 1–370.

Bock, John (2001): Learning, Life History, and Productivity. Children's Lives in the Okavango Delta, Botswana. In: *Human Nature* 13, 161–197.

Bock, John (2004): Farming, Foraging, and Children's Play in the Okavango Delta, Botswana. In: Anthony D. Pellegrini and Peter K. Smith (eds): *The Nature of Play. Great Apes and Humans.* New York: Guilford, 254–281.

Bolin, Inge (2006): *Growing Up in a Culture of Respect: Child Rearing in Highland Peru.* Austin, TX: University of Texas Press.

Bowser, Brenda J., and John Q. Patton (2008): Learning and Transmission of Pottery Style. Women's Life Histories and Communities of Practice in the Ecuadorian Amazon. In: Miriam T. Stark, Brenda J. Bowser and Lee Horne (eds.): *Cultural Transmission and Material Culture: Breaking Down Boundaries.* Tucson, AZ: University of Arizona Press, 105–129.

Boyette, Adam (2008): Scaffolding for Cooperative Breeding among Aka Foragers, paper presented at the annual meeting of The American Anthropological Association, November 19th–23rd, San Francisco, CA.

Broch, Harald B. (1990): *Growing up Agreeably. Bonerate Childhood Observed.* Honolulu, HI: University of Hawaii Press.

Campbell, John K. (1964): *Honour, Family, and Patronage. A Study of Institutions and Moral Values in a Greek Mountain Community.* Oxford: Clarendon Press.

Casimir, Michael J. (2010): *Growing Up in a Pastoral Society. Socialization Among Pashtu Nomads.* Köln, Germany: Kölner Ethnologische Beiträge.

Clark, Gracia (1994): *Onions are My Husband. Survival and Accumulation by West African Market Women.* Chicago: University of Chicago Press.

de León, Lourdes (submitted): Socializing Attention. Directive Sequences, Participation, and Affect in a Mayan Family at Work. Submitted to *Ethos*, March.

Dyer, Caroline, and Archana Choksi (2006): With God's Grace and with Education, We Will Find a Way. Literacy, Education, and the Rabaris of Kutch, India. In: Caroline Dyer (ed.): *The Education of Nomadic Peoples. Current Issues, Future Prospects.* Oxford: Berghahn Books, 159–174.

Edel, May M. (1957/1996): *The Chiga of Uganda*, 2nd ed. New Brunswick, NJ: Transaction Publishers.

Einarsdottir, Jonina (2004): *Tired of Weeping. Mother Love, Child Death, and Poverty in Guinea-Bissau.* Madison, WI: The University of Wisconsin Press.

Ember, Carol R. (1973): Feminine Task Assignment and the Social Behavior of Boys. In: *Ethos* 1, 424–439.

Evans-Pritchard, Edward E. (1956): *Nuer Religion.* Oxford: Clarendon Press.

Fasulo, Alessandra, Heather Loyd, and Vincenzo Padiglione (2007): Children's Socialization into Cleaning Practices. A Cross-Cultural Perspective. In: *Discourse & Society* 18, 11–33.

Fortes, Meyer (1938/1970): Social and Psychological Aspects of Education in Taleland. In: John Middleton (ed.): *From Child to Adult. Studies in the Anthropology of Education.* Garden City, NY: The Natural History Press, 14–74.

Gaskins, Suzanne (In Press): Pretend Play as Culturally Constructed Activity. In: M Taylor (ed.): *Oxford Handbook on The Development of Imagination.* Oxford: Oxford University Press.

Goldschmidt, Walter (1976): *Culture and Behavior of the Sebei.* Berkeley, CA: University of California Press.

Goodwin, Grenville, and Janice Thompson Goodwin (1942): *The Social Organization of the Western Apache*. Chicago, IL: The University of Chicago Press.

Goody, Esther N. (1992): 'From Play to Work: Adults and Peers as Scaffolders of Adult Role Skills in Northern Ghana.' paper given at 91st Meeting, American Anthropological Association, San Francisco, December.

Goody, Esther N. (2006): Dynamics of the Emergence of Sociocultural Institutional Practices, In: David R. Olson and Michael Cole (eds.): *Technology, Literacy, and the Evolution of Society*. Mahwah, NJ: Erlbaum, 241–264.

Gorshkov, Boris B. (2009): *Russia's Factory Children. State, Society, and Law 1800–1917*. Pittsburgh, PA: University of Pittsburgh Press.

Gosselain, Olivier P. (2008): Mother Bella Was not a Bella. Inherited and Transformed Traditions in Southwestern Niger. In: Miriam T. Start, Brenda J. Bowser, and Lee Horne (eds.): *Cultural Transmission and Material Culture. Breaking Down Boundaries*. Tucson, AZ: The University of Arizona Press, 150–177.

Grindal, Bruce T. (1972): Growing up in Two Worlds. Education and Transition among the Sisala of Northern Ghana. New York: Holt, Rinehart, and Winston.

Grinnel, George B. (1923): *The Cheyenne Indians. Their History and Ways of Life,* 2 Vols. New Haven, CT: Yale University Press.

Hames, Raymond, and Draper, Patricia (2004): Women's Work, Child Care, and Helpers-at-the-Nest in a Hunter-Gatherer Society. In: *Human Nature* 15 (4), 319–341.

Harkness, Sara, and Charles M. Super (1985): The Cultural Context of Gender Segregation in Children's Peer Groups. In: *Child Development* 56, 219–224.

Harkness, Sara, and Charles M. Super (1986): The Cultural Structuring of Children's Play in a Rural African community. In: Kendall Blanchard (ed.): *The Many Faces of Play*. Champaign/ Urbana, IL: Human Kinetics, 96–103.

Henry, Paula Ivey, Gilda A. Morelli, and Edward Z. Tronick (2005): Child Caretakers Among Efe Foragers of the Itruri Forest. In: Barry S. Hewlett and Michael E. Lamb, *Hunter Gatherer Childhoods. Evolutionary, Developmental, and Cultural Perspectives*. New Brunswick, NJ: Aldine Transaction, 191–213.

Hirschfeld, Lawrence E. (2002): Why Don't Anthropologists Like Children? In: *American Anthropologist* 104, 611–627.

Hogbin, H. Ian (1969): *A Guadalcanal Society. The Kaoka Speakers*. New York: Holt, Rinehart, and Winston.

Honwana, Alcinda (2006): *Child Soldiers in Africa*. Philadelphia, PA: University of Pennsylvania Press.

Katz, Cindi (1986): Children and the Environment. Work, Play and Learning in Rural Sudan. In: *Children's Environment Quarterly* 3 (4), 43–51.

Katz, Richard. (1981): Education is Transformation. Becoming a Healer among the !Kung and the Fijians. In: *Harvard Education Review* 51, 57–78.

Köhler, Iris (2009): *Es sind die Hände, die die Töpfe schön machen. Töpfernde Frauen und Töpfernlernen bei den Nyarafolo*. Berlin: Lit Verlag.

Kogel, Amy, Ralph Bolton, and Charlene Bolton (1983): Time Allocation in Four Societies. In: *Ethnology* 22, 355–370.

Lancy, David F. (1980a): Becoming a Blacksmith in Gbarngasuakwelle. In: *Anthropology and Education Quarterly* 11, 266–274.

Lancy, David F. (1980b): Speech Events in a West African Court. In: *Communication and Cognition* 13, 397–412.

Lancy, David F. (1996): *Playing on the Mother Ground. Cultural Routines for Children's Development*. New York: Guilford.

Lancy, David F. (2007): Accounting for Variability in Mother-Child Play. In: *American Anthropologist* 109, 273–284.

Lancy, David F. (2008): *The Anthropology of Childhood: Cherubs, Chattel, Changelings*. Cambridge: Cambridge University Press.

Lancy, David F. (2010a): Learning 'From Nobody'. The Limited Role of Teaching, In: Folk Models of Children's Development. In: *Childhood in the Past* 3, 79–106.

Lancy, David F. (2010b): When Nurture becomes Nature. Ethnocentrism in Studies of Human Development. In: *Behavioral and Brain Sciences* 33, 39–40.

Lancy, David F. (2011a): 'Why Anthropology of Childhood? A Short History of an Emerging Discipline.' Keynote Speech for: Towards an Anthropology of Childhood and Children. Ethnographic Fieldwork Diversity and Construction of a Field. Institute of Human and Social Sciences, University of Liege (Belgium) March 9–11.

Lancy, David F. (2011b): 'Apprenticeship. A Survey of Ethnographic and Historical Sources.' Paper presented at the Fifth International Conference of the Society for the Study of Childhood in the Past. Theme: Child Labour in the Past: Children as Economic Contributors and Consumers, Oct. 1st.

Lancy, David F., and M. Annette Grove (2010): Learning Guided by Others. In: David F. Lancy, Suzanne Gaskins, and John Bock (eds.): *The Anthropology of Learning in Childhood*. Lanham, MD: Alta-Mira Press, 145–179.

Lancy, David F. and M. Annette Grove (2011): Getting Noticed. Middle Childhood in Cross-Cultural Perspective. In: *Human Nature* 22 (3)

Leavitt, Stephen C. (1998): The Bikhet Mystique. Masculine Identity and Patterns of Rebellion among Bumbita Adolescent Males. In: Gilbert Herdt and Stephen C. Leavitt (eds.): *Adolescence in Pacific Island Societies*. Pittsburgh, PA: University of Pittsburgh Press, 173–194.

Levine, Donald N. (1965): *Wax and Gold: Tradition and Innovation in Ethiopian Culture*. Chicago, IL: University of Chicago Press.

Lord, Jack (2011): Child Labor in the Gold Coast. The Economics of Work, Education, and the Family in Late-Colonial African

Households, c. 1940–57. In: *Journal of the History of Child-hood and Youth* 4 (1), 86–115.

MacDonald, Katherine (2007): Cross-Cultural Comparison of Learning in Human Hunting. Implication for Life History Evolution. In: *Human Nature*, 18, 386–402.

Marlowe, Frank W. (2010): *The Hadza. Hunter-Gatherers of Tanzania.* Berkeley, CA: University of California Press.

Martini, Mary, and John Kirkpatrick (1992): Parenting in Polynesia. A View from the Marquesas. In: Jaipaul L. Roopnarine and D. Bruce Carter (eds.): *Parent-Child Socialization in Diverse Cultures.* Norwood, NJ: Ablex, 199–222.

Mead, Margaret (1928): Samoan Children at Work and Play. In: *Natural History* 28, 626–636.

Maynard, Ashley E. (2002): Cultural Teaching. The development of Teaching Skills in Maya Sibling Interactions. In: *Child Development* 7, 969–982.

Maynard, Ashley E. (2004): Cultures of Teaching in Childhood. Formal Schooling and Maya Sibling Teaching at home. In: *Cognitive Development* 19, 517–535.

Messing, Simon D. (1985): *Highland Plateau Amhara of Ethiopia.* New Haven, CT: Human Relations Area Files.

Montandon, Cleopatre (2001): The Negotiation of Influence. Children's Experience of Parental Educational Practices in Geneva. In: Leena Alanen and Berry Mayall (eds.): *Conceptualizing Child-Adult Relations.* New York: Routledge, 54–69.

Moritz, Mark (2008): A Critical Examination of Honor Cultures and Herding Societies in Africa. In: *African Studies Review* 51, 99–117.

Ochs, Elinor and Izquierdo, Carolina (2009): Responsibility in Childhood. Three Developmental Trajectories. In: *Ethos* 37, 391–413.

Ohmagari, Kayo, and Fikret Berkes (1997): Transmission of Indigenous Knowledge and Bush Skills among the Western James

Bay Cree Women of Subarctic Canada. In: *Human Ecology* 23, 197–222.

Orellana, Marjorie F. (2001): The Work Kids Do. Mexican and Central American Immigrant Children's Contributions to Households and Schools in California. In: *Harvard Educational Review,* 71 (3), 366–389.

Ottenberg, Simon (1968): *Double Descent in an African Society. The Afikpo Village-group.* Seattle, WA: University of Washington Press.

Paradise, Ruth, and Barbara Rogoff (2009): Side by Side. Learning by Observing and Pitching In. In: *Ethos* 37, 102–138.

Park, Robert W. (2006): Growing up North. Exploring the Archaeology of Childhood in the Thule and Dorset Cultures of Arctic Canada. In: *Archaeological Papers of the American Anthropological Association* 15, 53–64.

Peters, John F. (1998): *Life Among the Yanomami. The Story of Change Among the Xilixana on the Mucajai River in Brazil.* Orchard Park, NY: Broadview Press.

Platt, Katherine (1988): Cognitive Development and Sex Roles of the Kerkennah Islands of Tunisia. In: Gustav Jahoda and Ioan M. Lewis (eds.): *Acquiring Culture. Cross Cultural Studies in Child Development.* London: Croom Helm, 271–287.

Polak, Barbara (2003): Little Peasants. On the Importance of Reliability in Child Labour. In Hèléne D'Almeida-Topor, Monique Lakroum, and Gerd Spittler (eds.): *Le Travail en Afrique Noire: Représentations et Pratiques à l'époque Contemporaine.* Paris: Karthala, 125–136.

Polak, Barbara (2011): *Die Könige der Feldarbeit.* Unpublished Ph.D. dissertation, Kulturwissenschaftlichen Fakultät der Universität Bayreuth. Bayreuth: Germany.

Pomponio, Alice, and David F. Lancy (1986): A Pen or a Bush Knife. School, Work and Personal Investment in Papua New Guinea. In: *Anthropology and Educ. Qtrly* 17, 40–61.

Pope-Edwards, Carolyn (2005): Children's Play in Cross-Cultural Perspective. A New Look at the Six Culture Study. In: Felicia F. McMahon, Don E. Lytle, & Brian Sutton-Smith (eds.): *Play. An Interdisciplinary Synthesis*. Lanham, MD: University Press of America, 81–96.

Power, Thomas G. (2000): *Play and Exploration in Children and Animals*. Mahwah, NJ: Lawrence Erlbaum Associates.

Puri, Rajindra K. (2005): *Deadly Dances in the Bornean Rainforest. Hunting Knowledge of the Punan Benalui*. Leiden, Netherlands: KITLV Press.

Raum, Otto F. (1940): *Chaga Childhood*. Oxford: Oxford University Press.

Read, Margaret (1960): *Children of their Fathers*. New Haven: Yale University Press.

Reynolds, Pamela (1991): *Dance Civet Cat. Child Labour in the Zambezi Valley*. Athens, OH: Ohio University Press.

Riesman, Paul (1992): *First Find Yourself a Good Mother*. New Brunswick, N.J.: Rutgers Univ. Press.

Rival, Laura (2000): Formal Schooling and the Production of Modern Citizens in the Ecuadorian Amazon. In: Bradley A.U. Levinson (ed.): *Schooling the Symbolic Animal. Social and Cultural Dimensions of Education*. Lanham, MA: Rowman & Littlefield, 108–122.

Ruiz, Luisa F. M. (2011): Coffee in Guatemala. In: G. Kristoffel Lieten (ed.): *Hazardous Child Labour in Latin America*. London: Springer, 165–189.

Sánchez, Martha A. R. (2007): 'Helping at Home'. The Concept of Childhood and Work among the Nahuas of Tlaxcala, Mexico. In: Beatrice Hungerland, Manfred Liebel, Brian Milne, and Anne Wihstutz (eds.): *Working to Be Someone. Child Focused Research and Practice with Working Children*. London: Jessica Kingsley, 87–95.

Schlemmer, Bernard (2007): Working Children in Fez, Morocco. Relationship between Knowledge and Strategies for Social and

Professional Integration. In: Beatrice Hungerland, Manfred Liebel, Brian Milne, and Anne Wihstutz (eds.): *Working to Be Someone. Child Focused Research and Practice with Working Children.* London: Jessica Kingsley, 109–115.

Spittler, Gerd. (1998): *Hirtenarbeit. Die Welt der Kamelhirten und Ziegenhirtinnen von Timia.* Köln: Rüdiger Köppe.

Tucker, Bram, and Alyson G. Young (2005): Growing Up Mikea. Children's Time Allocation and Tuber Foraging in Southwester Madagascar. In: Barry S. Hewlett and Michael E. Lamb: *Hunter Gatherer Childhoods. Evolutionary, Developmental, and Cultural Perspectives.* New Brunswick, NJ: Aldine Transaction, 147–171.

Turnbull, Colin M. (1965): *The Mbuti Pygmies. An Ethnographic Survey.* New York: American Museum of Natural History.

Wallaert, Hélène (2008): The Way of the Potter's Mother. Apprenticeship Strategies among Dii Potters from Cameroon, West Africa. In: Miriam T. Start, Brenda J. Bowser, and Lee Horne (eds.): *Cultural Transmission and Material Culture: Breaking Down Boundaries.* Tucson, AZ: The University of Arizona Press, 178–198.

Weisner, Thomas S. (1989): Cultural and Universal Aspects of Social Support for Children. Evidence from the Abaluyia of Kenya. In: Deborah Belle (ed.): *Children's Social Networks and Social Supports.* New York: Wiley, 70–90.

Wenger, Martha (1989): Work, Play and Social Relationships among Children in a Giriama Community. In: Deborah Belle (ed.): *Children's Social Networks and Social Supports.* New York: Wiley, 91–115.

Wihstutz, Anne (2007): The Significance of Care and Domestic Work to Children. A German Portrayal. In: Beatrice Hungerland, Manfred Liebel, Brian Milne, and Anne Wihstutz (eds.): *Working to Be Someone. Child Focused Research and Practice with Working Children.* London: Jessica Kingsley, 77–86.

Whiting, Beatrice B., and Carolyn P. Pope-Edwards (1988): *Children of Different Worlds. The Formation of Social Behavior*. Cambridge: MA Harvard University Press.

Whiting, John W.M. (1941): *Becoming a Kwoma*. New Haven, CT: Yale University Press

Wilbert, Johannes (1976): To Become a Maker of Canoes. An Essay in Warao Enculturation. In: Johannes Wilbert (ed.): *Enculturation in Latin America*. Los Angeles: UCLA Latin American Center Publications, 303–358.

Wileman, Julie (2005): *Hide and Seek. The Archaeology of Childhood*. Gloucester, UK: Tempus Publishing.

Wober, Mallory M. (1972): Culture and the Concept of Intelligence. A Case in Uganda. In: *Journal of Cross-Cultural Psychology* 3, 327–328.

Zeiher, Helga (2001): Dependent, Independent, and Interdependent Relations. Children as Members of the Family Household in West Berlin. In: Leena Alanen and Berry Mayall (eds.): *Conceptualizing Child-Adult Relations*. London: Routledge, 37–53.

Zelizer, Viviana A. (1985): *Pricing the Priceless Child. The Changing Social Value of Children*. New York: Basic Books.

Zeller, Anne C. (1987): A Role for Children in Hominid Evolution. In: *Man*, 22, 528–557.

Children's Work in a Family Economy:
A case study and theoretical discussion

Gerd Spittler

Family economies, including children's work, have always played
and continue to play an important role in Africa. The family economy has proved successful not only during periods of dynamic
expansion, but also as a survival strategy in times of crisis. This is
true not only in agriculture but also for the urban population, since a
large part of the so-called informal sector consists of domestic or
family economies which offer services or produce goods. The case
study in part I deals with children's work in the family economy of
the Kel Ewey Tuareg (Niger). I begin with an account of working
and learning in goat and camel herding, before going on to discuss
the introduction of the school and its reception by the local population. Part II offers a theoretical discussion of different types of
family economies and their implications for children's work.
Children's working and learning is conditioned not only by the
family structure but by their outside contacts as well. Depending on
their relation with the larger economy, we may distinguish between
closed, open and subordinated family economies. In the case of
family economies within the capitalist system children may be more
or less included in the work process, or included in different ways.

A case study: The family economy of the Kel Ewey Tuareg

The Kel Ewey Tuareg have lived in Niger, in the Aïr Mountains of
the Sahara, for centuries. Their economy is based on caravan trading,
camel and goat herding, and horticulture (Spittler 1993, 1998). Their
economic centre is the Timia oasis. Even though they obtain
products like milk, cheese and meat directly from their camels and
goats, they have always paid for millet, their staple food. Tea and
sugar are also bought, as are clothes. These products are obtained as

part of a system of long-distance trade that stretches 600 kilometres to the east and 1000 kilometres to the south.

Although the caravan trade covers an area the size of Germany, it is operated entirely by families, rather than by big merchants. When the caravans arrive in Bilma and Dirkou to buy salt and dates after 600 dangerous and demanding kilometres in the desert, they deal with men and women from family economies (Spittler 2002). With these goods, the caravan then travels 900 kilometres south to Kano, in Nigeria. In Hausaland they sell the salt and dates in local markets to the end consumers (farmers and herders).

Of all the goods which the Kel Timia acquire in the south, millet, their staple food, has the highest priority. It is bought directly from the farmers immediately after being harvested and is stored at the place of purchase. Other goods are bought only after this has been accomplished. All goods are not for resale, but are destined for individual households. Although the caravaneers engage in long-distance trade, they do not see themselves as traders, but rather as members of a household who are engaged in its upkeep.

Children's work in the family economy of the Kel Ewey

The work of goat herding is done mostly by women, while the men take care of the camels. Children's work plays an important role in the Kel Ewey economy. Very early on, young boys and girls playfully imitate the work performed by their elders. A toddler who can hardly walk often beats a bush with a blade of grass, in imitation of its mother using a long stick to knock down fruits from the trees for her goats. When the child is older, it will make a rope out of blades of grass, or build a small frame for a well and pretend to irrigate a garden.

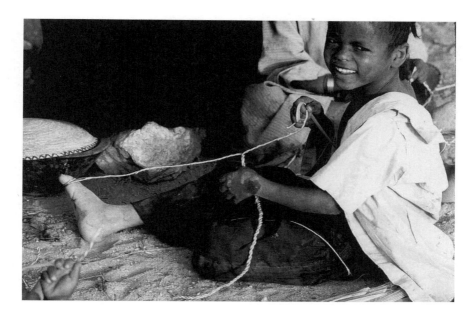

Six-year-old boy playing rope making (photographs by Gerd Spittler)

In addition to playing, children work from an early age. From about three onwards, they can help in the camp by keeping the goats out or driving them away. At about seven years old, both boys and girls go with an older brother or sister to watch over the goats while they are grazing. In this way they become familiar with the plants growing in the pastures. Not only can they identify the different types of trees and plants and their names, but they also know when they flower and when their fruits ripen, which plants are preferred by the goats, and their fodder value. A further important step is taken a few years later. At the age of about ten, a girl takes on the task of herding goats and leads them to grazing grounds on her own for the first time. When she does this, she takes on sole responsibility for the whole of the family herd, and so must be able to endure solitude, and not be afraid of wild animals or spirits.

Nine-year-old Makhmudan and six-year-old Minata milking a goat

By now, the young herdswoman is capable of carrying out the routine chores involved in tending goats. Helping goats to drink from a deep well requires physical strength, and this takes several years to develop. There are some qualifications that only a few herders acquire, such as knowledge and skills relating to goat diseases and their treatment, birth assistance when the kid is in a difficult position in the womb, or the therapeutic value for humans of certain herbs. These skills are not part of the tasks that every herder must learn (chores, see Lancy, this volume), and are acquired only by those who are particularly interested in learning them.

A ten-year-old herder or herdswoman makes an important contribution to the family economy, but is in many respects still a child. Children remain silent in the presence of adults, do not ask questions, nor do they participate in their conversations. But in many situations, children are treated as adults and they are proud of this. At nearly ten years of age, boys and girls are generally capable of observing their surroundings well. They look at the appearance of a camel, its markings, and in what direction it is moving. A herder who is looking for his camel will ask a child just as earnestly as if he were an adult. At the same time, just as an adult would, the child recounts what he has seen or heard, what he is sure of and what is merely supposition. This style of questioning is known as 'testifying', as in a courtroom: the child is then a witness who is taken seriously.

Herding camels is men's work. Tending a herd of camels is more challenging because camels tend to stray; they may also damage farmers' fields; or they may be stolen. Moreover, for most of the year they are not kept in their home area in the Aïr, but instead are taken in search of pastures to other places, sometimes even to another country (Nigeria). Consequently, camel herders bear greater responsibility and face more difficulties than goat herders in the Aïr. At the age of about ten, most boys give up herding goats. Instead they travel with their fathers and the caravans to the south. They stay away from home for a long time (six months) and travel great distances (600–900 kilometres). This separation from their mothers continues even after their return. They are only allowed to spend a few days with their mothers, so that they do not become accustomed to the comforts of home again.

While away from home, boys play with Hausa children and learn to speak their language fluently. The work of ten-year-old boys consists of helping with cooking and watching camel foals.

Ten-year-old Akhmed pounding millet

Akhmed tying up a camel foal

Still, the foals mean far more to them than just work: they are their
most important, and sometimes their only, playmates. An older
herdsman described the way children interact with foals in the
following manner:

They catch them and mount them.
They give them food to eat.
They tie them up.
They fight with them.
They mount them and run races.
They stroke them.
They are like the foals.
They lead them to the well and let them drink.
They lead them back to the camp and tie them up.
That is their work; that is their play.

At the age of fifteen, the boys may be given a camel herd to guard. By now the mixture of play and work has come to an end. Camel herding is a big responsibility, as it not only involves leading the herd to good pastures, but also protecting the farmers' fields from damage. The boys are proud to be given so much responsibility, and they quickly learn to master these tasks by themselves. In a society where children are silent in the presence of their elders and have to obey them, it is also a means of gaining freedom from social constraint.

The most important and most difficult thing for the boys to learn is tracking, in other words, reading the prints left behind by camels. This is important because camels stray and often get lost, and it takes many years to learn how to identify the prints of each camel in a herd. Some herd boys never acquire the skill, as it is difficult to learn tracking through trial and error alone. Clearly it is much easier if someone points out the important characteristics of a print to them. However, fathers rarely teach their sons, and it is more common for a cousin or maternal uncle to give them advice.

Kel Ewey boys take part in a Bilma caravan for the first time at the age of about sixteen. No special knowledge is required, but strength and stamina are necessary because they have to walk for 16 to 18 hours every day without a break. Over a period of several years, the boys learn how to orientate themselves in the desert. Yet only a few, those who have the necessary ability and interest, later become heads of caravans (*madugu*) themselves, and assume responsibility for leading a caravan through the desert.

As a consequence, it takes about ten years for a caravaneer and herder to learn how to carry out the routine chores: preparing meals, tending the goats and camels, as well as the other work associated with the caravans. In all of these areas, there is a broad range of tasks to be performed. In addition to tending to the needs of the goats, the herders also learn how to milk them and make cheese, and how to slaughter them and process the skin to make water sacks.

There are great differences between individuals and families, not only in respect of the different knowledge and skills, but also in strength, energy and motivation. A good herdswoman for instance avoids contact with other herdswomen and concentrates entirely on her goats. She knows where to find the best pasture at a particular time of the year, and she determinedly leads her herd there. Similarly, a good herdsmen stays with his camels all day, rather than just seeing to their needs in the morning and the evening. He observes each of his camels and knows which are sick or healthy.

The Kel Ewey are tolerant of children's individual differences. They expect some children to be naturally more sluggish (*amalghon*), and accept that these children will carry out their tasks with less energy than others. They also understand that some children work less, not because of their nature, but because they are lazy (*amallalu*), and they interpret this as a character deficiency. Families differ in the ways they react to this: some are very tolerant, while others try to teach such children to work harder. The differences between families depend mainly on the extent to which the parents support the work they do. If a woman lives with her daughters in the pastures, girls generally work harder than they would if she lived in Timia. Similarly, a father who regularly visits his sons in the camel camps encourages them by showing an interest in their work through his visits.

Capitalism, state and school

The caravan trade is still practised in Timia today, as is keeping goats and camels. However, the political and economic context has changed over the last fifty years, and this has affected both the family economy and children's work. Although the Kel Ewey still operate a family economy, today they live in a capitalist world. The goods that the Kel Ewey sell have to compete against products manufactured by capitalist companies. For a long time now, imported sea salt has replaced cooking salt from Bilma. Yet in the course of the 20th century, livestock levels and the resulting demand for cattle salt from Bilma have considerably increased, so that overall the demand has risen. In addition, the Kel Ewey's dates from Timia and Bilma compete with those from capitalist plantations in North Africa. Furthermore, whereas trucks were unable to compete with camel caravans in the extreme conditions of the desert for a long time, now they put pressure on the prices, as they are frequently subsidised by development aid. The profitability of the salt trade is best expressed by the terms of exchange between salt and millet, which were subject to great fluctuations throughout the 20th century. Overall, the terms of exchange worsened during the second half of the 20th century for the caravaneers, and Kel Ewey traders now receive less millet for the salt they supply (Spittler 2002).

Today, many young men work as migrant labourers in Algeria and Libya. They spend some months or years there before returning to the Aïr mountains. This leads to pressure on the traditional workforce from the caravan trade, camel herding and horticulture. Fathers or brothers who are left behind have to work harder in order to compensate for missing family members.

The introduction of a school also had far-reaching effects on the family economy of the Kel Ewey. In fact, it led to more important changes than those arising from migration and capitalist competition. In 1961, shortly after Niger became independent, a school was founded in Timia. Initially, no one was willing to send their child to the school voluntarily. Recruiting pupils was referred to as 'pupil-catching', comparable to 'soldier-catching'. On the basis of census lists, the state made it mandatory that each family send one child to school. If a child left school, he or she had to be replaced by another child from the family. Recruited children were mainly boys, as girls were only sent to school if there were no boys in the family. Neither the parents nor the children wanted children to remain at school for the full six years. This led some parents to order magic charms from Islamic clerics in the hope that bad results at school would lead to their child's expulsion.

This was the situation when I began my research in Timia at the end of the 1970s. I wanted to know what the reasons for rejecting the school were. Was it simply an obstinate refusal to accept something modern and foreign? Or were there more plausible reasons? Did the long working hours, and the distances between the pastures and the school, mean that the life of a herder was incompatible with schooling? This would partly explain the great resistance among the Kel Ewey to the idea of sending their children to school. School was actually interpreted as a coercive institution similar to a prison or military service. On the whole, it was the wealthy and influential people in Timia who were most likely to refuse to send their children to school. Alhaji Mussa, at that time the wealthiest and most powerful person among the Kel Ewey, once told me that he understood why poor people, with no camels or gardens of their own, sent their children to school, as it would help them find work later on. Yet anyone who owned camels had better things to do with his children's time.

The fact that children's work is important in the family economy of Timia does not fully explain the resistance to schooling. Some boys attend an advanced Koran school for several years, and during this period they are unable to work for the family. The resistance to schooling is thus also a rejection of a school system that has been influenced by the French since the colonial period. Knowledge of the Koran and other religious texts is highly respected by the Kel Ewey, not only because of the religious training, but also due to practical issues. Anyone who is familiar with the Maliki Risala not only knows how the law of inheritance works, but also how many other norms function which regulate everyday life. This cannot be said of the knowledge contained in the school books. Additionally, there are further reasons for preferring the Koran school to the French one. Attending a Koran school is voluntary, and pupils determine the speed at which they learn. An additional contrast is the time schedule in basic Koran schools: They leave children much more time for other activities.

One might assume that many people would send their children to school with the hope that they may obtain an attractive occupation later on. Yet completing six years of primary education in Timia scarcely opens up any employment opportunities outside the traditional occupations. In order to do so, it would be necessary to attend a middle school (CEG), a grammar school (*lycée*), or even a university, all of which are outside Timia. This would mean leaving the area for many years, and most parents find it hard to accept this idea. In the case of boys, they point out that no one can know whether they or their son will die during this time; and that there is no guarantee that he will get a good job after completing his education. People call those who leave for school 'lost'—*anakaw*—and this is the same word used in Timia for camels that have strayed and cannot be found. Even those who do find employment are very unlikely to do so in Timia. Young men frequently migrate to Nigeria, Algeria or Libya in order to seek work, although it is rare that someone leaves the oasis on a permanent basis. Almost all men marry women from Timia, and the women are even less willing than the men to move away.

The arguments outlined above can also be found in other regions and countries, although they were more frequent in the past than the present. However, there are other factors working against schooling. In school, the children have to sit on benches and at tables: for the Kel Ewey this is an ordeal, not only for children but also for adults. A typical household in Timia neither contains chairs nor tables, and this applies equally to wealthy and poor households. The people sit or lie on mats, and constantly change their positions; sitting on a chair is viewed as unnatural. Besides, apart from the schoolchildren, no one stays inside a closed room, except during cold periods in the winter.

In addition to this, teachers discipline their pupils with a stick. Among the Kel Ewey, children are very rarely beaten, and it is unthinkable that someone from outside the family would beat a child. The fact that a teacher can do so with impunity shows that he has been invested by the state with powers greater than those of the family. Yet even without a stick, the teacher-pupil relationship represents a power situation that is unusual for the Tuareg. While children traditionally learn to work independently by imitating and observing, and by trial and error, in school teachers determine what and how the children should learn, and assess the results.

Finally, there is the fundamental argument that children acquire knowledge at school, which not only helps them gain employment later on, but also helps them understand the world in more profound ways than if they were to remain 'illiterate'. This is not evident to the Kel Ewey, as during their time at school, pupils are shut in a classroom and have to learn what the teacher tells them. Unlike their friends of a similar age, who work as herders and caravaneers, they are cut off from the real world. They do not learn about trees and grasses in the pastures of the Aïr, their ripening cycle and their uses for animals and humans. They do not become familiar with the wide world of the Hausa, 800 kilometres from Timia, its different landscape, its agricultural economy, its markets, customs and, last but not least, its language which serves as a lingua franca in large parts of West Africa. They do not gain experience in tending and loading camels, or how to hunt for a lost camel, and to negotiate with farmers when the camels have caused damage. Instead they are in a situation of dependency, and remain subject to the will of the teacher. They neither learn to assume responsibility for the family, nor to make an economic contribution to its well-being. School children, unlike working children of a similar age, are far from being able to understand the world or act practically in it.

Up until now, we have seen what the people of Timia think about schooling. To what extent are their ideas based on prejudice, and to what extent on experience? In order to answer this question, let us take a look at what has become of the 21 boys and girls who made up the founding class from the school in Timia in 1961. The year in which we made our enquiries was 1985. By this time, the former pupils were about 25 years older. Many of them had returned to traditional occupations after leaving school and had largely forgotten what they had learned there, including their knowledge of French. Three of them had died, and four were working as labourers in Arlit or Agadez. The two girls were living and working like the other women in Timia. Five boys had continued their studies after completing primary school: two of them became teachers, and three were still students in 1985, studying in Dakar, Canada or Germany. Since then they have all completed their studies. Today, two of them have high posts in the state administration, and the third one is a director of an NGO. They live in Agadez or Arlit, but they have all married women from Timia and keep up close contact with this oasis town. They are not 'lost', as people feared they would be. On the contrary, it is the students and former students who are most interested in the history and traditions of Timia today.

About ten years ago parents had become more willing to send their children to school, and today there are even parents who voluntarily send their daughters to school. Yet there are high dropout rates in schools and at the university, and those who complete their studies do not always find suitable employment. However, there are some examples of successful careers in Timia, and the world has changed so much for the Kel Timia that many people now consider school education to be indispensable. Today, it is not only poor people who send their children to school; the rich do so as well. This also goes for those who do not take up a modern career, but remain in the domestic economy: there are grave disadvantages for caravaneers who undertake their far-reaching and cross-national tasks without proper schooling. This is the case as caravaneers are constantly involved in conflicts with police, soldiers and customs officials who require written documents and knowledge of the French language. After two rebellions against the government, first during the 1990s and the second from 2006 to 2009, it became clear that rebels who had been to school had a greater chance of obtaining a job in the state administration after the conclusion of peace. Saharan tourism came to a stop during the rebellions, but in times of peace it offers employment opportunities to many young men who speak French. The same applies to the development projects that have flourished in the Aïr at different times.

This case study of the family economy of the Kel Ewey forms the basis for the following general discussion of different types of family economies and their implications for children's work.

Theoretical discussion

Closed, open and subordinated family economies

What is a family or domestic economy? In today's Western capitalist countries, family economies play a very minor role in economic terms, and academic interest in them is correspondingly slight. Yet a hundred years ago they were at the heart of important theoretical debates, and it is worth referring to the discussions carried on at that time (Spittler 2008). I distinguish between three types of family economy: closed, open and subordinated. Although they frequently occur in mixed forms, it is useful here to regard them as ideal types.

A famous theory formulated by Karl Bücher presented the concept of the *geschlossene Hauswirtschaft* (closed domestic economy) (Bücher 1893/1901).[1] Since in a closed domestic economy the household must satisfy all of its own needs, its essential characteristic is not simplicity but diversity. Besides agricultural activities, many different kinds of productive work are necessary if all needs are to be met. 'All this leads to a diversity of employments, and, because of the primitive nature of the tools, demands a varied dexterity and intelligence of which modern civilized man can scarcely form a proper conception' (Bücher 1912: 91). This closed domestic econ-

---

[1] The official English edition (Bücher 1901/1912) translates *geschlossene Hauswirtschaft* as 'independent domestic economy'. I prefer the literal translation 'closed domestic economy'.

omy is an ideal type, a construction.[2] Even in pre- and non-capitalist economies, such domestic units are engaged in local and regional exchange relations. In addition to the closed domestic economy, it seems useful to distinguish between two other types: first, open domestic economies which have economic exchange relations with other domestic economies; and second, domestic economies which are subordinated to a capitalist system and a state. I shall return later to the first type, which has been neglected by theorists.

There has been, and continues to be, much theorising about the second type. As in the case of the closed family economy, the basic positions in this debate were formulated at the turn of the 19th and 20th centuries. In 1899, Karl Kautsky, the leading German socialist theorist after the death of Karl Marx and Friedrich Engels, argues that in the long term agriculture will follow industry, and that large capitalist enterprises will replace peasant families.[3] Be that is it may, this process is very slow, and the peasant family economy is able to compete with capitalist enterprises for three reasons: overwork (*Überarbeit*), underconsumption (*Unterkonsumption*), and greater care (*größere Sorgfalt*). Through self-exploitation, the peasant family can often produce less cost-intensively than capitalist agriculture. The peasant not only forces himself to work, but also his whole family, including women, old people and children. Instead of sending his children to school, he sets them to work. As for consumption, he eats less and is dressed worse than an agricultural labourer. Despite this, it is only the third factor that gives the peasant

---

[2] There are not only historical, but also current ethnographic examples that come close to this type. Descola's study of the domestic economy of the Achuar in Ecuador (Descola 1986) shows the great variety of plants that are needed in a garden for a functioning domestic economy. This makes working in the garden a complex task which is only fully mastered by the woman who owns the garden. Kramer (1986) shows the great variety of jobs carried out by children in an almost closed domestic economy among the Maya.

[3] *Die Agrarfrage*. An English translation was published nearly 100 years later in 1988.

real superior productivity: the greater care with which he performs his work, as compared to the agricultural labourer.

In Kautsky's theory, the peasant family can survive, but is by no means the dynamic market force suggested by Alexander Chayanov, a Russian agricultural economist who was a political opponent of socialist and communist theorists such as Kautsky and Lenin. In his synthesis (Tschajanow 1923), he brings together the different insights of Bücher and Kautsky, and adds new elements to them.[4] Peasant economies, as long as they are similar to the closed family economy, have a very complex level of organisation because they produce most of what they need. There are many different tasks to be performed, in contrast, market-oriented peasant economies only specialise in a few types of product. At the beginning of the 20th century, Russian family farms were based around a mixture of subsistence and market production. By comparing two farms, one with very limited and one with strong market integration, Chayanov showed that the subsistence-oriented farm was more complex. This type of economy produces most of its food and drink, as well as most of its clothes, and in these work processes, there are many tasks which are adaptable to the abilities of children.

Family farms can compete with capitalist agricultural entrepreneurs for several reasons: they can work more, or they can restrict their consumption. Chayanov here takes up Kautsky's arguments, but goes further and argues that care and intensification in agricultural work gives the family farm an advantage over the capitalist farm which employs labourers. However, peasant economies often become subordinated to capitalist traders (vertical integration):

Kautsky and Chayanov describe the peasant economy under the conditions of a capitalist system in Europe. However, they do not

---

[4] His most important work, *Die Lehre von der bäuerlichen Wirtschaft. Versuch einer Theorie der Familienwirtschaft im Landbau* (1923) [Theory of the Peasant Economy. An Attempt at a Theory of Family Economy in Agriculture], was followed two years later by an expanded edition in Russian. It was only in 1966 that the book was translated into English (Chayanov 1966).

discuss the existence of open family economies that interact with other family economies outside of a capitalist system. Nevertheless, these relations were quite common in non-capitalist societies in Africa and other parts of the world, but for information on them we will have to turn to anthropological theory. When we think of long-distance trade, we primarily think of professional traders. But here we are interested in another form of long-distance trade, in which local needs and the procurement of goods are not separate phenomena concerning different groups of people, but are united within one group. As end consumers, households organise the procurement of goods themselves from far-off places. In the anthropological literature, this form of long-distance trade is referred to as an *expedition*. The caravans of the Kel Ewey are good examples of such expeditions.

The classic description of a system of long-distance trade is provided by Malinowski's account (1922) of intertribal trading in the *kula* ring, but he did not make any systematic economic analysis of this kind of expedition. This was left to Richard Thurnwald (1932: 145–149), whose ideas were taken up by Karl Polanyi in 1944 (1957). Unfortunately, these authors were so focused on long distance trade that they failed to consider the family economy, which is basic to both the people who undertook the expedition and their trading partners. It also creates particular kinds of relations which have special consequences for children's work.

How children work and learn in a family economy

What can be said about children's work in the light of these theoretical considerations? In order to answer this question, we first concentrate on domestic economies that act largely outside of state and capitalist influences. How is the knowledge acquired that is needed to run a family economy? How do children develop the necessary manual skills and perseverance, when there are no textbooks, no apprenticeships, no teachers and no schools? Learning depends in the first instance on the child, who observes, imitates, experiments and gradually gets used to performing different tasks. Children are observant at a very early age; they see what their older siblings and adults do, and they try to imitate them. They not only copy others, but they try things out for themselves. It is rare for children to ask how a particular task is performed, or why something is done this way and not otherwise. Asking questions plays a minor role, compared with observation, imitation, help and experimentation. The older role models are not teachers in the sense that they have been specially trained and devote their whole time to teaching children how to work. They correct and advise children in passing, while carrying out their own daily tasks. More often than not, they do not have the time to instruct children, precisely because they have to get on with their own work.

Older siblings and adults intervene actively by demonstrating to the younger ones how something is done. This complements the children's own observations and imitation. Yet as a rule, learning begins not with being shown how to do something, but with copying or trying something out on one's own. Verbal communication and explanation play a very minor role, not only for the learner but also for the instructor. Few questions are asked and very little is explained. Firstly comes the activity of the learner: imitation or experimentation; then perhaps demonstration; and only after this, speech and explanation. When I asked how a herder learns to herd camels, Adunguju gave me a succinct answer: 'He has to watch the others. He does what the others do. They show him, they tell him, what to do. One day, when he has learnt enough, he goes out alone.' (Spittler 1998: 246)

Asking questions and giving explanations are of greater importance in tasks where demonstrating or copying is not enough. In herding camels, this applies for instance to one of the most important tasks, namely hunting for lost camels by identifying and following their tracks. Work processes which cannot be learned by imitation alone are found everywhere—for instance Polak describes the way the Bamana sow millet as such a task (Polak, this volume).

However, situations in which it is necessary to resort to questions and explanations are the exception. As a rule, learning and teaching take place without the need for many words. The difference between this and our system is not that we are dealing with a written culture on the one hand, and an oral one on the other. Instead, the written and the oral are both of lesser importance here.

It is not possible to make any general statements about how much work is performed by children in family economies, because this depends very much on the situation: the demography; the nature and variety of the tasks to be performed; and the season. Chayanov analysed the relation between demographic structure and work in the family cycle. When there are many dependents in the family, more work is performed. But most family cycles are not as normal as they appear in average calculations. How is the work organised, for example, when there are only sons or only daughters? I have studied such cases among the Kel Ewey. For instance in a family where there were five daughters but only one son, keeping camels was scaled down or abandoned, while the daughters took turns to tend the goats, with a different girl going out each day. In the opposite situation, when a family has no daughters, they give up keeping goats. To compensate for a shortage of labour, it is also possible to 'borrow' relatives from families with an 'excess' number of workers. This is not a stable solution: I observed several times that girl herders from related families among the Kel Ewey abandoned their work unexpectedly, either because they did not like it, felt they were being treated badly, or because they were needed at home.

There are different ways of compensating for demographic imbalances in the family structure. A long-term solution is adoption; however, this is only rarely practised among the Tuareg, although it is common among the Hausa. Fostering children is widespread in West Africa (Alber, Martin, this volume), but it is rare among the Kel Ewey. The most common solution is to temporarily employ workers from outside of the family. Among the Kel Ewey this is practised particularly in the caravan trade and in garden work, but only if the economy is sufficiently productive, as it is difficult and expensive to recruit young men as workers when there are more attractive alternatives such as migration.

An obvious solution for the problem of demographic imbalances would be to give up the gender-specific division of work. Girls could then do the work of boys, and vice versa. Among the Kel Ewey there are cases where girls do accompany their fathers on the Hausa caravan and help to look after the camels, but as soon as they reach a marriageable age, they refuse to join the caravans. Conversely, in the absence of girls, boys could tend goats, work which all boys learn when they are small. Yet after a certain age, when other boys have started to tend camels, they refuse to continue doing this work no matter how great the need of the family. Thus, division of work and family composition are only harmonious in ideal situations. In reality, there is often friction.

In agriculture, the amount of work available depends on the season. Yet in livestock, the situation is different: the goats of the Kel Ewey must be tended all year round, but the work is different at different times of the year. In the rainy season, the goats graze close to the camp and drink by themselves from the water holes. This means they only have to be watched over. Whereas in the dry season, a herdswoman has to travel many kilometres with them in order to find suitable pastures. If necessary, she has to beat leaves and fruit down from trees with a long stick. Wells are generally far away, and so water has to be drawn up from a great depth.

In drought years, work is even harder (Spittler 1993). A herdswoman has to struggle up hillsides to find grass left over from the previous year. Water holes are even further away, and even deeper than normal. There may be no grass available in the valleys and plains, and so herdswomen have to climb trees and break off the branches covered with leaves. In years such as this, young camel herders avoid the Aïr and stay in Hausaland which is generally less affected, but they remain constantly on watch to prevent their camels from damaging crops. In better years, they let their camels graze

freely in the Aïr, and only go out to look for them every few days.
Furthermore, the herders also face large seasonal differences. The
strenuous caravans from Hausaland back to the Aïr require great
endurance, even on the part of the young boys, who have to walk
long distances and help with cooking and keeping the camels
together. In comparison, the work in a camel camp in the Aïr seems
easy.

Chores and more

From the point of view of modern society based on divisions of
work, the qualifications required for routine tasks in family economies are low. Domestic economies are characterised by a 'diversity
of employments' (Bücher). Each individual task is less skilled than
in a complex industrialised society. However, in very different areas
there is a greater variation of tasks than in a complex society. This
also applies to children: a ten-year-old girl among the Kel Ewey will
not only be capable of performing all household tasks, but she will
also have acquired the most important skills needed for tending
goats. In view of the variety of tasks that have to be learned, it is
impossible to expect that great expertise will be acquired in every
area.

In a society with a less strict division of work, each individual
worker performs a broad variety of tasks, but many workers, if not
all, can be said to have the same occupation. The uniformity of the
work, with very little division of labour, stands in contrast to the
various abilities and skills of the workers. Even without aspiring to
discover all the different passions related to work, as did Charles
Fourier who counted 810 (Spittler 2008), everyone will agree that
people differ considerably in their interests and abilities. 'Aghalak
wer olan'—people are not all the same—as the Kel Ewey say. On the
other hand, the same work is required of everybody, and in the case
of the Kel Ewey, women cannot choose whether they want to
become goat herders or not. In contrast, the men at least have a
choice between becoming a gardener, or becoming, a camel herder

and caravaneer. Many men practise both of these occupations during the course of their lives. But there are also many individuals who specialise depending on their own inclinations and abilities: one brother may spend all his life working in the garden, while the other works exclusively as a herder and caravaneer.

In comparison to a capitalist industrial society, with its complex occupational structure, the choices here are small. If people have varied characteristics and abilities, what effect does this have on performance at work? Among the Kel Ewey, performance is very unequal. There are excellent herdswomen who not only work very hard, but also possess an exact knowledge of the plant world because they find it highly interesting, whereas others are satisfied with knowing only the most important trees and plants. Similarly, there are camel herders who can identify not only the tracks of their own camels, but also those of many others, yet some herders cannot even follow the tracks of their own camels. Additionally, only very few caravaneers become caravan leaders; and only a small number of herders are skilled in the diagnosis and therapy of camel diseases, even though these occur in every herd. These specialists are then consulted by others.

On the basis of comprehensive ethnographic evidence, David Lancy speaks of the 'chore curriculum' in traditional societies (Lancy, this volume), in which children learn to perform the chores necessary in their milieu in stages. They learn a given particular task quickly, and mostly by imitation, observation and experimentation. Lancy argues that the 'chore curriculum' is universally applicable to pre-capitalist societies, perhaps with the exception of hunter-gatherer societies. While this curriculum may cover routine chores, it does not take into account the great differences in competences. In family economies with little social division of work, only minimal demands are made on each person. In cases where everybody has to do the same work, top levels of performance cannot be expected from all, as the differences between people are simply too great. Despite this, there is always a minority that does perform excellently, and these people are often vital to the success of the economy (such as good trackers or caravan leaders among the Kel Ewey). Such excellent achievements require an unusual interest on the part of the learner, and frequently also teaching by experts, even if this cannot be equated with a formal apprenticeship.

There are also great differences in work performance with regard to the ordinary chores. These can be carried out by anyone, but the individual's motivation and the amount of energy invested in the work vary considerably. As we saw above, the Kel Ewey tolerate the fact that some people are sluggish, while others are energetic. They also accept that people are different, not only in their abilities, but also in their motivation and their diligence.

Children's work in a subordinated family economy

In family economies that operate within a state and a capitalist system, the conditions related to children's work change. When family economies compete with capitalist enterprises, there is pressure on prices, exemplified by the salt trade of the Kel Ewey. Often families make up for this by working harder, and this frequently means children are expected to work more, either by starting at an earlier age or by doing extra work.

Chayanov found that Russian peasants are frequently integrated into a trade system in which their position comes close to that of dependent labourers. Today, peasants in Africa often depend on organisations that determine not only the prices but also the work. This is particularly true in respect of irrigation systems (Katz, this volume). Here too, children's work has changed. Katz observed that following the introduction of a state irrigation system in Sudan, only two crops were cultivated (groundnuts and cotton), instead of the previous variety. Additionally, children's working hours were longer and the work became more intensive. Similarly, the former variety of tasks, which had always included playful elements, had been replaced by work-intensive monocultures; and the fact that they had to work, meant some children were unable to attend school.

Reynolds, Pamela (1990): *Dance Civet Cat. Child Labour in the Zambezi Valley*. London: Zed Books.

Spittler, Gerd (1993): *Les Touaregs face aux sécheresses et aux famines. Les Kel Ewey de l'Aïr (Niger) (1900–1985)*. Paris: Karthala,

Spittler, Gerd (1998): *Hirtenarbeit. Die Welt der Kamelhirten und Ziegenhirtinnen von Timia*. Köln: Köppe.

Spittler, Gerd (2002): Die Salzkarawane der Kel Ewey Tuareg. In: *Geographische Rundschau* 54 (H.3), S. 22–29.

Spittler, Gerd (2008): *Founders of the Anthropology of Work. German Social Scientists of the 19th and Early 20th Centuries and the First Ethnographers*. Berlin: Lit.

Thurnwald, Richard (1932): *Economics in Primitive Communities*. Oxford: Oxford University Press.

Tschajanow, Alexander (1987 (1923)): *Die Lehre von der bäuerlichen Wirtschaft*. Frankfurt: Campus.

Verlet, Martin (2005): *Grandir à Nima (Ghana). Les figures du travail dans un faubourg populaire d'Accra*. Paris: Karth.

Peasants in the Making:
Bamana children at work

Barbara Polak

Anthropological studies of children in peasant and nomadic house-hold economies have been reproached for romanticizing children's conditions of work or for not even conceiving their activities as work. This criticism appears reasonable in view of the growing corpus of studies of abusive or harmful working conditions for children especially in the wage labour sector. However, it is not productive for understanding the daily life of peasants' or pastoralists' children because it defines an ideal childhood as excluding work. By contrast, a perspective that conceives of work as essential for growing up offers insights into children's life-worlds, which challenge current stereotypes of child work (Bourdillon et al. 2010: 88-107). In this paper, I will do so based on my ethnographic research in the everyday work-life of Bamana peasants' children in Mali.[1] This paper contributes to the ethnographic study of child work in the context of family economies in nomadic or peasant societies. In particular, it addresses the common understanding of child work as a result of pressure exerted by adults, and as a form of exploitation.

Researching peasant children's work

Crossing a millet field in northern Ghana in the 1930s, ethnographer Meyer Fortes unwarily trampled on some plants. The Tallensi

---

[1] Largely funded by the German Research Council (*Deutsche Forschungsgemeinschaft*, DFG) in the context of the graduate program 'Cross-Cultural Relationships in Africa' at Bayreuth University, I spent 18 months in several villages of the Bèlèdugu region (*cercles* of Kolokani and of Banamba) in central Mali between 1993 and 1998.

farmers' children who were accompanying him snapped at him with indignation that he better pay more attention since it was these plants that they were living from (Fortes 1938:11). In many West African peasant societies, children still regularly perform agricultural work. Regarding the Bamana ethnic group from central Mali, this is the case for the large majority of children. As for the encounter between farming people and clueless ethnographers, my experiences with Bamana children were similar to those of Fortes with Tallensi children. In an adult's tone of address, they patiently explained to me steps and sequences of work and specified details about the crops they cultivate. By asking, however, whether they enjoyed performing this or that work task, or rather preferred to do something else, I provoked a sort of silence that seemed to speak of a lack of comprehension on their side of what I was thinking of at all. It took some time for me to understand why my specific questions seemed so absurd to them. What I realized quite quickly, by contrast, was the general difficulty for an adult stranger to interview children in a foreign society.

Yet, there *are* methodological approaches to get over this so-called double strangeness. Most of the participatory research methods to do 'research *with*, rather than, *on* children' (Christensen and James 2008:1; italics in the original) presented by Pia Christensen and Allison James have been developed in European settings and are based on Western societies' patterns of communication. Their focus on verbal communication is hardly productive with Bamana and other African children, who are not accustomed to talking to adults for various reasons. First, from an early age, children learn to see adults as persons of respect, to whom it is not appropriate to talk on equal terms (see Diarra 1979). They can always *listen* to adults' conversations, yet they are urged not to interfere by posing questions or expressing opinions. Second, much of what they want to learn in their everyday social environment is acquired more easily and simply by observing or participating in the concerned activity. This is particularly true for agricultural work.[2] It thus seemed more appropriate for me to follow the children and participate in their work rather than talk about it.

My temporary participation in children's work was not difficult to realise. During my research among Bamana peasants, everybody asked me to participate in whatever was currently in progress on the millet, sorghum and peanut fields; I was always offered a hoe to learn how to sow, to weed, etc. And my research interest in agricultural work would not have appeared plausible to the farmers had I not accepted these invitations to engage myself. Participation thus represented an obligation inherent to the social situation rather than an exclusive privilege.

Because of my lack of skills in most steps of cultivation, I was often assigned the role of a child in the groups of joint agricultural work I took part in. That is, I was assigned tasks the performance of which only required a minimum of skills. My obvious clumsiness further added to the fact that I, in contrast to other adults, be they locals or foreigners such as, for instance, development workers, did not represent a person of authority to the children. For instance, they loved to include me in their usual competition against each other in work tasks, because I used to lose so reliably all the time. In the context of our joint working in the fields, my presence thus did not decisively alter their behaviour. I was able to observe their activities and listen to their conversations from a socially comfortable and methodologically advantageous position, that is, undisturbed and, even more importantly, non-disturbing.

---

[2]   For adults, too, it is hardly necessary to talk about their work. Visual and tactile perception is much more important to eventual problem solving than is verbal expression. Generally, routine activities tend to be low in verbalization. In his essay on radical participant observation or 'thick participation', Gerd Spittler (2001) thus argues for a decidedly multi-sensual engagement that goes beyond what is usual in ethnographic fieldwork.

An important aspect of observing children at work is the perspective, which is different when working bent over in the field in
comparison to standing upright on the margins. In the field, I was
close to the action and could observe which work-steps were hard to
perform for the children and how they tried to master them. I could
thus follow in detail the process of learning complex activities such
as sowing millet (Polak 1998). Another aspect of my temporary
partaking was crucial. I personally experienced how much practice it
takes to master a certain movement or how strenuous it is to walk
slowly bent down while working with the short-handled hoe. Only
then, based on my own experience, could I observe the solutions or
workaround strategies that children and adults apply to, for instance,
alleviating backache or preventing overstrain and fatigue (Polak
forthcoming).

In short, while the double—both cultural and generational—
strangeness often encountered in the anthropology of child labour
raises methodological problems, it does not necessarily preclude
productive research. Temporary participation in the children's
working activities, for instance, turned out to be an ethnographically
efficient approach to my own study. The insights I gained from such
participation are explored in the following example of three Bamana
boys helping their mother to weed her peanut field.

Case study

In the later part of the morning, Koriya calls me to accompany her to
her peanut field. She has just finished cooking the *to*, the traditional
Bamana luncheon. Arriving at the field at about 11 a.m., her three
sons Fase (aged 11), Samba (7) and Sumaèla (5) are already busy
there. Koriya calls them to take a break and have lunch together.
Like adults I have observed many times in the same situation, the
three boys do not come at once. In spite of Koriya's repeated calls,
they continue weeding for a while to demonstrate their diligence.
Then we have lunch together in the shade of a tree. Twenty minutes

later at around 11.30 a.m., when everybody is ready after eating, Koriya and her sons get up to work.

Koriya and eleven-year-old Fase are using hoes of nearly equal size and of the same type, called *daba*, the main tool for weeding, which is quite large and heavy. The handle of Samba's *daba* is half of the normal length, it is much lighter, and its blade is much smaller and blunt compared to those of his mother and his older brother. Samba's is a worn-out hoe that used to belong to his parents. It was not discarded completely, however, but is held ready for use by small children.[3] Five-year-old Sumaèla is using a different type of hoe, called *falo*, which is used for digging small holes in the sowing process, for instance. It is much smaller and lighter than the *daba*, which makes it easier to work with. Moreover, Sumaèla's old *falo* is quite blunt.

Koriya and her sons all do the weeding in the same manner. They move forward in a bent-over position along a furrow, and hoe up tufts of grasses and weeds. After shaking clods of earth out of these tussocks—still bent-over and continuously moving forward— they throw them away backwards through their own feet. Fase, aged eleven, works as speedily and vigilantly as his mother does until 2 p.m., that is, two and a half hours; the only difference is that he takes more rests lasting a few seconds at the end of the furrows, which are about 30 m in length.

The two little ones, by contrast, behave differently. They know how to handle the hoe and are able to hoe up weeds with roots, but they do not bring up the strength and concentration to care continuously for the whole length of a furrow. Seven-year-old Samba often stops hoeing somewhere in the middle of the turn, while his younger brother Sumaèla rarely accomplishes more than five to ten meters at

---

[3] This hoe's handle and hilt are so worn that they had to be reduced. Working with an overly short hoe is unnecessarily toilsome, since you have to bend down lower than usual; and a small hilt only takes a small blade which does not move much soil or weed. While using such a hoe is thus inefficient for adults, it might be perfect for children.

a stretch. They then take longer rests, which are more frequent and extended with Sumaèla than with his older brother Samba. Sometimes they pause in their weeding and watch the others working, have a talk or hunt for mice. During these activities they stay near their working-place, the rows they are working on. When they take up work again, they approach the furrow that they worked on before. However, only Samba cares to find the actual spot he was at before and thus sees to a seamless continuation of the work process. By contrast, little Sumaèla rather has an eye for staying as close as possible to his brother Samba.

While hoeing, they frequently cry of joy in a manner typical of young Bamana men when surpassing competitors in the context of work contests. The two boys are probably inspired by such a 'work-party' that took place in the village two weeks ago. The longer they try to imitate these cries, the more enthusiastic they become. Fase from time to time participates in the shouting. Mostly, however, he sings or hums to himself. Koriya, too, often sings while hoeing.

Sumaèla once hoes up a beanstalk inadvertently. Samba notices the mistake and calls Sumaèla's attention to it in a reproachful tone. Then together they start to replant the tendril. When Fase and I approach the situation, Fase tells me: 'He is not yet capable of it [weeding]!'

One and a half hours later, at around one p.m., the two little boys are charged with a new task. Their mother Koriya sends them back home to fill the empty can with fresh water. They set off in a merry mood. This is my opportunity to gain more experience in hoeing: I take Samba's hoe and try to do some weeding in the rows, which Sumaèla did not finish. At 2 p.m., I take a rest together with Koriya and Fase. Whereas Koriya did not repose at all after lunch the other days that I had accompanied her, today she takes three quarters of an hour's rest. She immediately falls asleep in her sitting position and I have a conversation with Fase.

Koriya wakes up when the boys return to the field with the refilled water containers. They were away nearly two hours; buzzing

tive activity, which often also implies a change of settings.[4] Children's participation in agricultural work is thus not necessarily characterized by their mastering the situation and finishing the task.

Yet, when children's behaviour in work and play can be identical, the questions arise whether they themselves distinguish both settings, and if so, how. According to my observations, children differentiate insofar as they take up tasks according to their own skills. As long as they have not yet learned to handle the hoe, they explore weeding at the field's margins with the help of a stick; when they have mastered the hoe, they stop using sticks as a replacement. That is to say, the more skills children have acquired in relation to a certain work task they can perform in the field, the less they are interested in the options for more playful action at the edge.

In the example given above, the relation between skills, work and play was realized, for instance, in Sumaèla and Samba's hike to refill the water container. Concerning this activity, in contrast to weeding, they are already fully skilled: they know their way back home to the village, they know where and how to best fill the canister with fresh water, and they are sure about being able to carry the load and find the way back again to the field. It is characteristic of the skilful performance that they know, even though they insert a break, that they do not drop out from their task as they did with the weeding. The all too interesting distraction of the kid's birth does not finally keep them from returning to the field and fulfilling the task.

When Samba and Sumaèla are charged by their mother with going to fill the water container, they look pleased. Obviously, they do not at all regret that they thus are restrained from further playing. To the contrary, they rather seem to be proud of the opportunity to help the others with some relevant contribution.

---

[4] Katz gives another example of this relationship in her description of two children who continuously change from sowing sorghum to hunting birds, and back (Katz 2004:84–86). In this situation, it was not obvious to the researcher whether they took a break from planting while snaring, or the other way round, or both (Katz 2004:86).

As the analysis of the five- and seven-year-old brothers' activities has shown, it is implausible to conceive of the peasant children's work and play as two distinct, mutually exclusive domains. Work and play for them rather constitute overlapping fields of action that require different levels of skill, which enable them to interact with their environment to different degrees. Exactly because playing at the margin of the field is mostly about agricultural work, and because children already learn many essentials of various work tasks through observation and mimesis in the play setting, they do not experience the change from the margin into the field, and into the work setting, as a discontinuity. Rather, they act in a continuum of increasing options for appropriating more and more skills, which enable them to take on tasks in some work areas while still 'only' exploring in others.

The freedom to explore work tasks, which Bamana children enjoy, is not a matter of course. It depends, first, on the adults' tolerance of the children's desire to participate and try out work activities, and, second, on the adults actively supporting the children's exploration by providing the spatial and material framework. Peasant woman Koriya, for instance, grants much freedom to her five- and seven-year-old sons and does not interfere even once in their frequent moving back and forth between work and play settings. She neither tells them off when, in the course of weeding, they suddenly cut short their serious efforts, nor does she urge them to keep on working consistently. She does not inhibit their play. Moreover, she even consciously facilitated the boys' exploration in that, earlier in the morning, she told her older son Fase to look for appropriate hoes. Concluding from Samba's and Sumaèla's proud way of demonstrating their early skilfulness in hoeing, it was not that they were called upon to do so by their brother, but rather that they followed their own commitment. This is to say, Bamana children are afforded much scope for explorative action, and they make use of it. Neither are they urged to try out a task or a tool, nor are they kept from doing so—as long as they do not produce serious damage.

It is a particularity of peasant family economies that they afford good prospects for the probably universally valid desire of children to participate in the adult world. Children usually want to join their parents and older siblings in what they do. Yet, in many social contexts, they rarely get the opportunity to join everyday work-life. In contrast to peasant family economies, it is even often hardly possible for them to be present at all at their parents' workplace, not to speak of exploring the activity area and tools or even participation. Yet, the context of agricultural work per se does not suffice to explain the Bamana peasants' way of dealing with the child-work relation. The children's participation, from observation and exploration to performing complex work tasks, is based on the precondition of the adults' explicit enhancement. As I will show in the following section, the younger and less experienced a child is, the larger is the effort to be invested by the parents in order to facilitate his or her participation.

Integrating children into the work cycle: the adults' role

The problem for adults or adolescents responsible for their children or younger siblings is that children wish to participate in all of their parents' activities as early as they are physically able. They want to participate in work to a much greater extent than they are able to. This is the case, for instance, with Koriya's younger boys. She permanently has to keep an eye on their activities, since there is a high risk of them causing damage.

Five-year-old Sumaèla's skills include handling a hoe without hurting himself or somebody else, plus a certain consistency in tracking a row, i.e., he does not haphazardly switch between arbitrary points in the field. However, his commitment and attention as a rule is stable only for short periods. He thus often cuts short hoeing somewhere in the middle of a row. Moreover, his knowledge about plants is still inchoate. For instance, he chopped out a beanstalk, because he was unable to distinguish it from weeds. This is of some concern to his mother Koriya, and to eleven-year-old Fase, who

alone is responsible for his younger brothers in the morning. He must
never lose sight of low-skilled Sumaèla and always be able to intervene immediately in case he makes a mistake. They have to focus
(and remember) the exact spots where Sumaèla started a row,
because later they will have to pace out those rows again. They will
want to inspect them with regard to, for instance, crops chopped out
mistakenly or root balls of weed that were removed correctly but
only inefficiently cleared from clods of topsoil, which otherwise
would quickly enable it to take root again with the next rain.

Sumaèla's activities not only amount to an increase in the time
his mother or older brother need to invest in supervision, but also
imply a specific mode of organizing the work according to the boy's
low level of skill. For instance, they need to work closely to
Sumaèla; staying nearby and permanently keeping an eye on the boy
in order to reach him immediately in case of necessity. However,
observing children is not only a matter of repairing, but also of
preventing damage or harm. Perceiving signs of exhaustion allows
one to charge the child with another, lighter task. In other instances,
a child might indicate dissatisfaction with how little is demanded,
which also often results in a change of the task he or she is charged
with.

Koriya sent Sumaèla and Samba for water at a critical moment,
when a lack of variety had led to the boys to become bored with
working in the field. They had started to play instead, yet seemed
even more interested in doing something more related to work. To
Koriya and Fase, this was helpful both by providing water to drink
and by freeing them from the task of supervision. Koriya's change in
the organization of work thus shows a good sense of timing.

Seven-year-old Samba's participation in weeding causes relatively little extra work. In using the hoe, he is more experienced than
his little brother, he has more stamina, and he is more knowledgeable
about plants, and can distinguish most crops (not only millet) from
weeds. The last becomes obvious when he brings Sumaèla's attention to his mistake of digging out a beanstalk. Moreover, Samba acts

more systematically: after a break, he resumes hoeing at exactly the spot where he had stopped. Because of his greater skills, Koriya and Fase need to invest little effort in monitoring the rows he weeds, and there is no need always to stay close to him and provide supervision. It is true that he still lacks the endurance to weed the complete length of a field in a continuous run. Koriya and Fase thus need to be aware of (and remember) Samba's position in the field in order eventually to finish a row that he started but left incomplete.

This analysis of examples demonstrates that in the Bamana peasants' family economy, adults do almost everything to allow even young children with few skills to take part in work activities in the fields. It is insufficient, however, to characterize this as an expression of mere tolerance of their children's desire for action and inclination to explore. The peasants also accept the extra workload that inevitably comes with young children's participation. And last but not least, they develop and apply considerable skill in the division and organization of work tasks, oriented by careful observation and the will to regard the individual children's skills plus the ever-changing actual situational circumstances in much detail (see Polak 2004; forthcoming).

Mostly, the extra workload caused by participating children is out of proportion to the immediate returns. For instance, Koriya and her older son Fase would have worked more quickly and easily the couple of meters weeded by young Samba and Sumaèla if they had been on their own. At this point, it becomes obvious that Bamana peasants do not prioritize effective production when integrating their children into work-life. Correspondingly, it is not an eventual pressure for productivity and possibly related over-exertion or annoyance on the side of the children that confronts Bamana peasants with daily problems, but, on the contrary, they are much more frequently challenged by the children's high spirits and enthusiasm for joining the work process. The focus on wage labour, which is characteristic of the larger part of studies in child labour, seems to somehow blind the analytical eye for the possibility of other criteria than productivity that guide the inclusion of children in work-life in the context of family economies.

Yet, when it is not maximizing effective production, what is it that makes Bamana peasants act as they do? Why do they invest so much effort into supporting their children's participation? The first answer is that being in the work-life without necessarily taking the responsibility for the results of what one does allows the children to learn to perform all relevant work tasks perfectly and naturally.

Developmental psychologists in industrialized societies propagate as one of their most important findings that children should be able to enjoy as much time, space and material as possible to explore their immediate environment. They would not tell Bamana peasants much that is new, but rather confirm their experience. It is not any environment that Bamana children explore; largely, it is their parents' workplace. This context affords the exploring to support learning peasant work through observation and 'guided participation'. This is Barbara Rogoff's term, acknowledging the parents' contribution, who first organize, divide and delegate work with regard to their children's desire to participate and, second, accept the extra task of supervising this participation in the work process (Rogoff 1990; 2003). The advantage of this process lies in that the parents do not have to care about the learning as such. It is the children, who bring with them the impetus to observe, explore and imitate, and it is they, who control the intensity and tempo of their activities. Only exceptionally is it necessary to inspire or instruct them (see Polak 1998). This phenomenon is the rule in non-industrial societies, as David Lancy (2010; this volume) has demonstrated compellingly.

Nevertheless, the Bamana way of treating their children is not of mainly pedagogical or otherwise idealistic intention. Rather, the peasants are pragmatists. What is the utility of the children's initiatives to learn when the extra task of supervision keeps the adults from working on their own? If the adults would give in to every little skilled child's wish to engage in the work process, they would be busy preventing damage during the larger part of their work-time instead of producing. Unrestricted access is not in the adults' interest, as the analysis of the selection of tasks and degree of involvement that is afforded to low-skilled children clearly shows. For instance, Koriya does not allow her youngest son, age three, to join the weeding but leaves him with her ten-year-old daughter, who cares for the little one and performs housework in the compound. He was granted participation, however, with other work tasks. When I joined Koriya and her children in harvesting beans some weeks later, the three-year-old boy was with us and was allowed to participate to some extent, which was limited, for instance, by the small capacity of the old lid that was given to him to collect the beans (see Polak 2003).

Two girls—aged ten and five—pick beans in between peanuts

Reliability versus productivity

In the context of a pragmatic understanding of the peasants' relation
to early child work, the question arises as to what are the criteria for
the decision to take (or not to take) a child to the field and trust him
or her with some task or tool. With respect to little boys or girls and
their participation in agricultural work, I often heard remarks like 'he
is not yet capable of it', as for instance in the above example, when
eleven-year-old Fase comments on his younger brother's mistake of
chopping out a bean stalk. Such statements seem to indicate that the
activity of small children with little skill is not taken very seriously.
Accordingly, adults in interviews did not mention their sons' and
daughters' cooperation in work tasks such as sowing, weeding or
harvesting, which start to be performed from an age as early as three
or four years. Most adults, by contrast, expressed the opinion that
leading the draft oxen (with an adult steering the plough) is the first
task to be delegated to children. This task is quite challenging, however. Children perform it at an age of six or seven years at the earliest. Realizing that there is a gap between this information of Bamana
adults about the first working task of their children and my observations of the little peasants, I sensed that I had probably posed the
wrong questions. Having already given up talking with children
about their work, I thus soon stopped trying to talk about child work
with adults, too. Yet, how are we to explain the gap between Bamana
peasants' verbal statements and everyday activities concerning their
children's cooperation? In order to answer this, it is worth describing
and comparing the tasks that I often observed small children actually
performing, on the one hand, and the task that children would start
with according to the adult peasants' statements.

There is one fundamental difference between leading a span of
oxen, on the one hand, and hoeing, sowing, and harvesting, on the
other: only one individual at a time can perform the task of leading
the draft animals. Because of the indivisible responsibility, a performing child has to be fully skilled. By contrast, individuals can join
in performing and sharing the responsibility for work tasks such as

sowing, weeding, and harvesting. This allows for integrating less skilled children in the context of these work tasks, since one can isolate easier steps or parts of the work procedure from more challenging ones. You thus could give the easier parts (of the job) to smaller children while allotting the more difficult ones to older children or adults. Even children with very little skill can thus participate and contribute without creating uncontrollable risks of damage or hindering the workflow.

This question of divisibility or non-divisibility of tasks and responsibilities is related to another difference. When a child is leading the oxen, older children or adults, who are experienced in leading the oxen, are present, but they are fully engaged in another task such as steering the plough, and thus are not available immediately when something goes wrong with leading the draft oxen. This is different from sowing, hoeing or harvesting, when children and adults are performing a task together, and the adults as a rule can easily engage with any upcoming problem their children are facing.

One can conclude from this comparison that Bamana peasants *speak* of work only when the activity is fully productive in the sense that its performance does not imply supervision. Equally interesting from the perspective of an anthropology of work, is to state that peasants regularly delegate work to their children even if the outcome in terms of productivity is low. No abstract criteria such as age or level of skill are critical for children's participation in agricultural work. It rather is a matter of how far parents can rely on their sons and daughters not to cause damage in the field.

A bundle of various skills is a prerequisite to each work activity. It would appear that in the first place parents pay attention to whether their child has acquired these or not. However, it is not the question of skills alone that is decisive in delegating an activity or parts of it to a child. It is also a matter of the amount of supervision that is necessary to prevent the child from doing damage and to guarantee that the child performs the task waiting to be done, or the part that it is charged with. Not to cause damage in an activity, to ease the workload of others, or to make an own contribution to the work process, means cooperating with one's social environment. I speak of the criterion of reliability in order to address exactly this context.

Reliability in respect of a particular activity becomes manifest in a child's specific skills, by means of which he or she cooperates with other children or adults. The cooperative function, however, is never acquired independently, but always as an aspect of a skill, because the child's increasing acquisition of specific skills means a decrease in the need for supervision by adults. Less supervision means that the child offers more cooperation to its social environment.

Why exactly is the criterion of reliability so pervasive in the context of a family economy? Every Bamana peasant household depends on its own means of production. No household can run the risk of having a tool, such as a hoe, damaged by allowing someone to use it who does not know how exactly to handle it. Seed, too, is limited and must not be wasted. Every loss of harvest means smaller stores for the coming year. If parents gave in to their children's urge for activity, they would spend the better part of their time supervising them and preventing damage. The children, for their part, would not cooperate with their social environment, but on the contrary, would considerably impede the activities of others. Therefore, parents take into account to what extent their children are reliable before entrusting them with the full sequence of operations of a particular work cycle, or a part of it, or only with an object like a hoe.

An eight-year-old boy carefully leads a span of draft oxen

The reliability of their sons and daughters is central to Bamana peasants' interests for another reason: each household works on its own account and the mode of agriculture is labour-intensive. Thus, each family member able to work is needed in the fields or in the compound. The more members there are who are reliable in respect of one or more agricultural tasks, the more likely it is that the livelihood of the household will be secured. An unreliable member means economic loss. He or she cannot be replaced: every household has to care for non-reliable members. Neither the extended family nor the village community is able to compensate for them economically or personally. Thus, Bamana peasants are anxious that their children acquire skills that will enable them to cooperate with any member of the household in agricultural activities.

According to the measure of cooperation, one can distinguish various degrees of reliability, which are nicely shown in the example of the weeding undertaken by Koriya's three sons. Eleven-year-old Fase is fully reliable in weeding, since he does not need to be supervised any more. Moreover he has acquired further skills to a degree that his performance equals that of an adult. For instance, his tempo at weeding is the same is his mother's and the total duration of his input this day even surpasses hers by one hour at least. Seven-year-old Samba is reliable in weeding at least insofar as nobody has to permanently stay close enough to look after him. Concerning the walk for water, he is fully reliable. Five-year-old Sumaèla, by contrast, is not yet capable of weeding reliably, since his work generally has be controlled and repaired. Yet he is already reliable in handling the hoe. He does not do harm to himself or his workmates, nor does he damage the tool. So, since he neither has the attentiveness nor the strength to perform much weeding, his supervisors simply let him go ahead.

The smaller boys' work performance in particular demonstrates that Bamana peasants do not primarily aim to increase productivity. If this were the core criterion, then Koriya would have only taken the oldest boy with her to the field. The little one's contribution is ridiculously small in terms of economic output. It is essential, however, for the peasants to commit themselves fully to their own tasks. It is thus of great advantage to them to have the care their children combined with their own work performance. This, however, can only turn out well when the children even in their earliest explorations neither do much damage nor keep their fellows from efficiently performing their own tasks.

However, it is not only the adults who gain from the children's reliable action. The little agents themselves profit, too. Making part of the working adults' life-world—as small as the contribution may ever be—seems to be an experience of great meaning to the children. This probably relates to the social esteem that the children acquire when they cooperate through their skills with their social environment. It begins with adults being responsive to their desires and ends with charging them with complex tasks. From a child's perspective this means that social esteem as a rule comes along with his or her experience of being capable of something particular. Positive responses always relate to specific actions. This stands in contrast to the context of industrialized societies, where abstract competencies or contents are mediated in schools, but are applied only much later.

Indirectly, this social esteem also results in work motivation. The experience of being excluded from particular activities because of a lack of skills, while older mates are already able to perform these very tasks, encourages the younger children to catch up and appropriate the respective skills. It seems sufficient for the young children to feel motivated to simply observe older children, youths or adults at performing tasks from which they themselves are excluded (cf. Lancy and Grove 2010; Gaskins and Paradise 2010). For the case of West African peasants, this connection between (in-)activity, observation, and motivation is clearly emerging from Guinean peasant Alphonse Sara's impressive childhood memoirs, when he reports how, as a young boy, his watching male youths performing in work contests not only made him admire them, but also raised his incurable desire to join them (Gessain and Sara 1981). Similarly when Koriya's younger sons, Samba and Sumaèla imitate the shouts of glee that are so typical of competing peasants in the heat of performance, they indicate that they too long for the day when they will be able to join in the work party. The children, as well as the adults, seem not to count success in terms of economic output, but in

social participation. Surprisingly, research in child work only rarely
considers alternative orientations beyond productivity, neither
concerning the adults' nor the children's perspectives, even when the
'wealth of children' is explicitly addressed from anthropological
(Nieuwenhuys 2005) or economic (Cigno and Rosati 2005)
approaches.

Resumé

'Most work undertaken by children has for a long time been
explained away as socialization, education, training and play', writes
Nieuwenhuys (1996:247) in an influential review article. According
to my research, this is exactly true: observing and participating in
Bamana child work in central Mali suggests that child work in this
context indeed amounts at the same time to socialization, education,
training and play. It is a kind of privilege. It is a basic experience,
which many children in other societies than those characterized by
family economies do not enjoy. One can often clearly see the joy that
Bamana children feel when they perform the tasks they are charged
with. Their desire to participate in the adults' work-life—which is at
the core of their life-world—is overwhelming.

I have never seen any children complaining, resisting or being
sad about leaving the compound in the early morning to go into the
fields. On the contrary, I often observed children begging to be
allowed to join the workers in the morning instead of being taken
along only at noon, when their mothers join the party in the field
after having prepared lunch. During daytime, when almost everybody is off, the village seems to be a boring place to the children
rather than an attractive playground. From a Bamana child's
perspective, the widespread assumption that work is not an occupation suitable for children, and that children participate mainly
because they are pressed to do so from early on, is absurd.

African peasants are usually depicted as being interested
primarily in employing their children as part of the work force as
early as possible. Bamana peasants' ways of dealing with their chil-

dren contradicts this view. They simply support their children's desire to participate in the adult life world, for instance by providing tools that match the children's size, strength and skills, by charging them with suitable tasks and supervising their performance. The peasants try not to overstrain the children. They do so not only for the children's sake, but also for pragmatic reasons. Children at work are busy, which allows the adults to perform their own lot, and acquire skills by themselves. Allowing them to work thus saves the extra workload that childcare and tuition otherwise would demand.

References

Bourdillon, Michael F.C., Deborah Levison, William E. Myers, and Ben White (2010): *Rights and Wrongs of Children's Work*. New Brunswick: Rutgers University Press.

Christensen, Pia, and Allison (2008): *Research with Children. Perspectives and Practices* (2nd ed.). New York, NY: Routledge.

Cigno, Alessandro, and Furio Camillo Rosati (2005): *The Economics of Child Labour*. Oxford: Oxford Univ. Press.

Diarra, Tieman (1979): Un aspect de l'éducation par la communauté en milieu traditionnel Bamana du Beledugu. In: *Etudes Maliennes* 1, 39–42.

Fortes, Meyer (1938): Social and Psychological Aspects of Education in Taleland. In: *Africa*, Supplement to Vol. XI, 5–64.

Gaskins, Suzanne, and Ruth Paradise (2010): Learning Through Observation. In: D.F. Lancy, J. Bock, and S. Gaskins (eds.): *The Anthropology of Learning in Childhood*. Lanham, MD: Alta Mira Press, 85–117.

Gessain, Monique, and Alphonse Sara (1981): Souvenirs d'enfances Coniagui. In: *Journal des africanistes* 51 (1/2), 277–290.

Katz, Cindi (2004): *Growing up Global. Economic Restructuring and Children's Everyday Lives*. Minneapolis: University of Minnesota Press.

Lancy, David (2010): Learning 'from nobody.' The Limited Role of Teaching in Folk Models of Children's Development. In: *Childhood in the Past* 3, 79–106.

Lancy, David F., and Annette M. Grove (2010): The Role of Adults in Children's Learning. In: D. Lancy, J. Bock, and S. Gaskins (eds.): *The Anthropology of Learning in Childhood.* Walnut Creek: Altamira Press, 145–180.

Nieuwenhuys, Olga (1996): The Paradox of Child Labor and Anthropology. In: *Annual Review of Anthropology* 25, 237–251.

Nieuwenhuys, Olga (2005): The Wealth of Children. Reconsidering the Child Labour Debate. In: J. Qvortrup (ed.): *Studies in Modern Childhood. Society, Agency, Culture.* Basingstoke: Palgrave MacMillan, 167–183.

Polak, Barbara (1998): Wie Bamana Kinder Feldarbeit lernen. In: H. Schmidt; A. Wirz (eds.): *Afrika und das Andere. Alterität und Innovation.* Hamburg: LIT-Verlag, 103–114.

Polak, Barbara (2003): Little Peasants. On the Importance of Reliability in Child-Labour. In: Hèléne Almeida-Topor, Monique Lakroum, and Gerd Spittler (eds.): *Le travail en Afrique noire. Représentations et pratiques à l'epoque contemporaine.* Paris: Karthala, 125–136.

Polak, Barbara (2004): Verlässlichkeit als Kriterium der Arbeitsorganisation. In: Kurt Beck, Hans P. Hans, and Till Förster (eds.): *Blick nach vorn. Festschrift für Gerd Spittler.* Köln: Köppe Verlag, 224–234.

Polak, Barbara (forthcoming): Aus Kindern werden Bauern. Kinder-, Frauen- und Männerarbeit in Mali.

Rogoff, Barbara (1990): *Apprenticeship in Thinking. Cognitive Development in Social Context.* New York, NY: Oxford Univ. Press.

Rogoff, Barbara (2003): *The Cultural Nature of Human Development.* Oxford: Oxford Univ. Press.

Spittler, Gerd (2001): Teilnehmende Beobachtung als Dichte Teilnahme. In: *Zeitschrift für Ethnologie* 126, 1–2.

Learning and Children's Work in a Pottery-Making Environment in Northern Côte d'Ivoire

Iris Köhler

Introduction

The small village of Sangopari in northern Côte d'Ivoire is a centre for pottery, which supplies its products to customers mainly via markets located within a radius of 30 kilometres of the village. A major part of the village's female population is able to make pottery. The social organisation of the Nyarafolo living in Sangopari is segmentary, as it is in other Senufo groups. In addition, society is divided according to a system of age classes. This could lead to the assumption that competence in pottery, and authority and control in the acquisition and transmission of knowledge, are associated with powerful senior women within the context of the family. Yet empirical data show that young girls and women work with clay on their own for themselves, and not only for the older women.

According to Sieni, a Nyarafolo woman in her forties, 'An intelligent girl watches her mother creating pots and thus is able to do it herself.' Sieni lives in Sangopari and works in pottery. Her youngest daughter, who still lives with her, is also learning the craft. Like many other women Sieni sells her products in the markets located around the village. Pots are generally produced for sale in the region, with only a small number made for domestic use. The pots are mainly used for traditional medicine, storing grain, and to look after items in the women's houses.

Sieni's statement, that an 'intelligent' girl learns ceramics by watching her mother, is both exemplary of the opinion among the Nyarafolo potters, and illustrative of the potters' and the society's basic understanding of learning. Sieni's statement could be interpreted as meaning that learning starts in childhood, takes place non-verbally, and that observation plays a considerable role. But is this really the case? Do children really play with clay and in doing so gain relevant experience of pottery at an early age? If this is the case, what about other ways of learning in Sangopari, such as gaining experience through repetition or helpful verbal instruction? In addition, how important a factor for learning is acting as an assistant, and performing specific tasks for the potters?

Like a young girl from the village watching her mother, I also watched and tried to learn to make pots by myself. Yet I soon realised that in order to make pots the way in which the Nyarafolo do, observation alone is simply not enough.[1] For instance, I was unable to observe completely each of the small steps undertaken in the pottery-making process. This difficulty became particularly clear to me when I started making pots by myself. In doing so I learned something the hard way, something that I had already known in theory right from the start. Yet it was not until I began making pots by myself that I actually accepted that pottery requires more than just eyes and hands, instead, all of the senses are involved. Learning in this case requires more than mere observation and imitation.

In this chapter, I describe how children as newcomers find their way into pottery, and the way in which the transmission of knowledge within this handicraft is organised in Sangopari. In doing so, the following questions arise. First, how do children learn to make pots? Second, how do they learn to make a *good* pot? Finally, how are these newcomers to pottery involved in the daily work and routines of the potters themselves?

Some ethnographic remarks about the Nyarafolo and pottery

The Nyarafolo are a sub-group of the Senufo and live in the city of Ferkessédougou and in the area to the north east of it. Sangopari is 30 kilometres away from Ferkessédougou, and its residents are farmers. Agriculture is characterised by a mixture of subsistence

---

[1] I gained many years of experience in pottery, but have no formal apprenticeship.

farming, production for national markets, and to some extent for international markets. Most farmers grow maize, millet, yam, rice, peanuts, tomatoes and spices; and they do so generally without the help of a plough. As a consequence of the social unrest which began in 1999 and the ensuing civil war and division of the country in 2002, the villagers have faced a number of economic changes: for example growing cotton has ceased; the risk of theft by groups of thieves has risen; and markets and trade routes have become more insecure.[2] Yet the role of women has hardly changed. Women remain primarily wives and mothers who work in the fields, gardens, houses, and compounds. The women involved in pottery are not professionals or full time workers, and instead they only work with clay during their free time to earn money for themselves.[3] Although pottery is made throughout the year, production declines drastically during the rainy season.

Nyarafolo villages are rural conglomerations, not enclosed within walls, but with most doors facing towards an imagined centre of the compound. The various compounds are not visibly separated from each other and there are no fences or walls between them.[4] Most daily work takes place in the open air and anyone can watch. This enables children to become familiar with the ways adults work in their daily lives: children are present when adults work in public; they hear adults speaking about numerous topics; observe them when they rest; and watch them make pottery.

---

[2] Between 1996 and 2000, I carried out ethnographic research lasting 16 months in and around this small settlement. I present this study as a snapshot of the relatively calm times before the division of the country. For further information see Köhler (2008).

[3] Strictly speaking there are no potters in Sangopari, because this term was only used in the past.

[4] For more details on the spatial arrangement of the compounds, see Rödiger (1999).

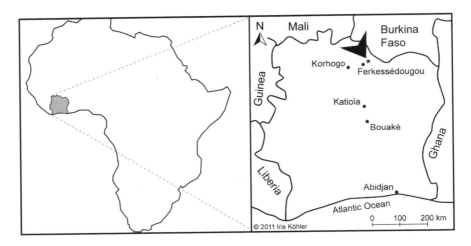

Map of Côte d'Ivoire showing the area in which the fieldwork took place.

Sieni's statement above also indicates that the actors involved in making pottery are exclusively women: pottery is a female affair. In addition, women working with clay do not separate themselves from women who are performing other activities. Potters are not only watched by their own children or relatives. Anyone may watch, and this is made even easier by the fact that in this small village, and with the exceptions of the clay pits outside the village and the area used to fire the pots on the edge of the village, there are no specific places in which pottery is carried out. Pottery is therefore performed in public spaces, just like any other daily activity, and the products and skills of master potters can be observed just as easily as the work of novices.

Making pottery: the past and the present

Yet if everything about pottery is observable and anyone is able to watch, then the following questions arise. First, can any woman access this work? Second, if this is the case, is it possible for any girl or woman to work in ceramics? Third, does having access to pottery mean that girls and women have to produce pots?

When old women talk about the past, they state that making pottery used to be in the hands of the older women. Young women merely assisted the older women by performing small tasks. This also was the case among the endogamous Kpeenbele Senufo potters (see Spindel 1989), and this division of tasks and labour corresponds to the organisation of society. Traditionally, Senufo societies are organised according to a system of age classes, and every class has its own rights and tasks assigned to it.

Women working with clay in their compound.

In Sangopari too, access to making pottery used to be restricted. For instance, women who were sexually active, menstruating, breast-feeding, or pregnant were not allowed to perform certain pottery tasks. This made it difficult—if not impossible—for young women to be continuously involved in pottery and acquire certain skills. Some older women say they only began making pots after the master potter they worked for had died. Nowadays numerous young girls are involved in pottery. My interviews with older women show that today newcomers begin learning at an earlier age than they did in the past. In addition, today the old restrictions are often ignored: young women now realise that they will face no consequences for disregarding them; or simply do not view the restrictions as important.

It could be argued that people in general always interpret bygone times as better, and complain about the way previous restrictions are ignored in current society. Be this as it may, apprenticeship systems, where newcomers only take on assisting roles and gain very little direct experience of their own, enable established potters to preserve their own competencies. In contrast, young girls today are no longer merely acting as assistants; instead they are directly involved in making pottery themselves. They produce pots, sell them on the markets and are able to keep the profits. Some of the villagers argue that this commercialisation is one of the reasons behind the changes occurring among the potters. They argue that pottery has now become a trade, and as no one should be allowed to prevent another person from earning a living, it is no longer possible to prevent certain women from becoming involved in pottery.

A parallel development can also be observed in other parts of this society, and I touch on it briefly here. Whereas the number and importance of 'private' gardens is increasing, collectively cultivated fields are becoming fewer in number. These fields are being replaced with fields used for personal consumption and sale. It is argued that this change directly results from independence in 1960. During this time young people placed strong emphasis on political freedom, and this led to a feeling of personal freedom and independence from older people. Consequently, individualism has risen, as has the pursuit of personal benefit. Although commercialisation is then one cause of change among the potters, the changes occurring among them can also be linked to growing individualism.[5]

Today competence in pottery and the transmission of knowledge in Sangopari is no longer tied to age, nor is it necessary to belong to a specific endogamous social group to take up pottery, as is often the case in West Africa.[6] Instead, pottery is open to everyone in Sangopari, including members of other ethnic groups. The small village of Sangopari is the only village within a radius of 30 kilometres where women work with clay. About 30 to 40 years ago, there were some other settlements involved in pottery; whereas pottery gradually died out in other villages, in Sangopari it is expanding.[7]

Making pottery or doing other work?

In Sangopari pottery also has to compete with other types of work. The villagers understand pottery to be an *additional* form of work for everyone who is involved in it, since the family economy is based on work undertaken in the fields, and everyone has his or her own tasks to complete. Additionally, women are responsible for nearly all of the tasks in the households and the compounds, and girls are expected to help them. Their tasks include fetching drinking water, cooking, washing, preparing meals, and taking the food they make to the men working in the fields and gardens. Additionally women are also expected to collect wood, and clean the house and compound. Women also take on specific tasks, in both farming, such as sowing

---

[5]   In her study of Maya women, Greenfield (2004) describes the processes of intergenerational knowledge transmission in weavers. She identifies an erosion of age-based authority and related signs of change, while linking different cultural models of learning to different ecologies, and to commercialisation.

[6]   For more information, see Frank (1998) on the Mande. Barley (1994) gives a broad overview of pottery in Africa. Fruitful research on cultural transmission and material culture has been done in ethnoarchaeology, as an example see Stark et al. (2008), where the studies by Bowser & Patton, Gosselain, Wallaert, and Herbich & Dietler are particularly important.

[7]   To explain all the reasons behind this development goes beyond the scope of this paper. For more details see Köhler (2008: 278ff).

seeds, harvesting crops and removing weeds; and during the construction of houses. Men are expected to provide household members
with staple, 'solid' foods, for instance maize and millet. In contrast,
women provide the 'liquid' part of the meals, and so plant or buy the
ingredients they need for sauces. Daily work varies throughout the
course of the year and people's lives, but it is also dependent on
family size.

It is only after women have undertaken the tasks that secure
their own and their family's means of survival, that they make
pottery. Nevertheless, it is in their personal interests to make pots
and sell them for profit, as the women spend their money on soap,
kerosene, medicine, sugar, and on clothes or items for their children.
Additionally, they regularly buy ingredients for the sauces such as
oil, spices, peanuts, and tomatoes. Unmarried girls, who do not have
to perform this role, spend the money they earn from pottery on
items for themselves such as cheap jewellery and clothes.

This situation forces potters to plan and organise their work:
they have to find enough time to make, finish, and sell their pots.
This often proves difficult since girls are still expected to do as they
are told by their elders. This means they have far less freedom to
organise their own time. If for instance, an older man from the
household were to tell one of the girls to wash his laundry, she would
have to comply. This could mean she would have to change her plans
for the next two days. As a consequence, pottery competes with other
work.

In contrast to everyday work, school plays no role in Sangopari:
I only know of two children who attend school. As the nearest school
is about two hours' walk away, someone must be found to provide
accommodation for the child in the village—or in the case of
secondary school the city—in which the school is located. Additionally, if a child does go to school, he or she leaves the village and is
no longer available to perform his or her daily tasks. Furthermore,
farmers in Sangopari do not like sending their children to school.
They argue that in years with bad harvests, they would be unable to

pay for the child's schooling, and this would not only mean removing the child from school, but also losing their entire investment.

In the case of girls, there are further arguments against schooling. Nyarafolo society is organised patrilocally. In such societies women move to a different compound to marry and have children, and in many cases this compound is located in another village. Importantly, women remain obliged to send one girl away to work in her old compound, or to someone in her family. In most cases the first or second daughter is given away. Maybe an older person in the woman's family asks for help, sometimes even only temporarily. This causes the families an obvious problem: by giving one girl away and sending another to school, there may be no girls left at home to help with the work.

Whatever the situation, working and learning the tasks necessary to secure the family's livelihood clearly come first. Other income-generating activities are merely of secondary importance. In contrast to learning the daily tasks which children are expected to perform, learning pottery is optional. Consequently, there is no punishment for girls who are unable to learn, or who are uninterested in pottery. Although pottery cannot feed a family, it is still the best possibility for women in Sangopari to earn money for themselves, and this is a great stimulus for learning to do so.

Learning pottery

There are two groups which learn pottery in Sangopari: women who lived elsewhere and came to Sangopari as adults, mostly through marriage; and children who were born, grew up or live temporarily in the area. This article focuses on the latter group. Compared to adults, children have the disadvantage that their motor coordination needs to develop before they are fully able to perform certain tasks. Despite this, they benefit from the fact that from a very early age they spend a lot of time with women carrying out their daily work. Even very young children learn a lot from their environment, although this need not necessarily imply that they understand everything they see.

Throughout Sangopari, women and girls of different ages can be readily observed making pottery: but what about learning?

The *process* of learning itself cannot be observed, but its *results* can. The learning process gives rise to certain observable changes. A craft such as pottery provides us with a medium through which the results of learning can be directly observed: when the pots no longer fall apart in production; when they start to become more regular in shape; when production speeds improve and become a matter of routine; and when the pieces produced are larger than the small bowls made in the beginning, it is clear that learning has taken place.

It has been frequently observed in the literature that in family economies, children learn within the family unit. Thus a young girl learns everything that is necessary for her everyday life directly from her mother. This includes skills such as cooking, fetching water, collecting wood, but also other activities such as producing charcoal, shea butter or pottery. Unlike everyday work within the family economy, pottery in Sangopari does not have to be learned at a certain age. It is not part of the repertoire of everyday tasks which must be undertaken, and instead it is an option, or in Lancy's terms, it is not a chore (this volume). Nevertheless it is learned within the everyday context.

But let me first describe what the children do.

Children participate in pottery just as they participate in daily life. So for instance, girls go alone, in groups or with women to the stream to fetch water needed for the household and for pottery—water is the most important resource needed to make pots after clay. Girls also accompany their mothers or other relatives to the clay pit outside the settlement, where older girls extract the clay and others carry it to the village. Older girls are also involved in collecting the wood needed to fire the pots. In addition, girls of all ages assist in smaller ways, such as fetching small amounts of water, or a tool such as a scratcher from inside the house. Girls also help transport the pots after they have been fired on the edge of the village.

In Nyarafolo society, younger people are expected to help older ones. For example, when they go together to the stream or clay pit, it is the younger ones who have to take on the burden of carrying the large enamel bowls full of tools, so that the older ones may walk unhindered. The only exception to this is when the pots are fired: the girls do not normally assist in this, and instead the potters do this work by themselves as it is regarded as particularly arduous. During the time I was there, I only observed one girl arranging the firewood for firing, she did this for her mother, who is nearly blind, but is still able to produce pots. In this case, the woman relies on her daughter to point out the parts of the pots that still need working on.

In Sangopari, children as well as young married women are more or less involved as learners in the different stages of pottery. Children play with clay, but they also play a role in the manufacturing process itself. Despite this, learning and the sedimentation of knowledge does not correspond to the sequence of production found in the manufacturing process. Children may learn to build up pots without mounting coils, or to scratch the bottom of the pot into a hemispherical shape and polish the interior, but they will not be able to decorate a pot's leather-hard surface, and they almost never fire the dried pots. In addition, girls may take on assistant roles in work such as transporting clay into the village, and selling the pots at the markets, yet they are still unable to produce pottery completely by themselves: I would hardly describe a nine-year-old child's first attempt at decorating pots as a real embellishment. This girl in particular was able to polish pots and prepare them for firing, but could not form the typical rim or embellish the pots with their usual patterns. Despite this, girls not only lend a helping hand, they also carry out the individual steps which make up the pottery-making process itself, and some of these steps can be learned earlier than others.

As a matter of course, young girls are not paid for the assistance described above, but there is one special case in which girls are able to earn their own money. Girls or young married women often go to the market in Ferkessédougou. This is 30 kilometres away, and they do so on behalf of potters who are unable to leave the village for the two days needed to attend the market. In such cases, potters take the earnings made from the pots sold at the market and produce pots for the next week. The girl or young woman takes pots to the market once more, and she is allowed to keep these earnings for herself. This enables the girls to buy small items such as earrings which would otherwise not be possible, or save for new clothes. The unmarried girls who make pots themselves do so as advanced learners and sell them independently. Yet they do not do this as a means of subsistence, but instead generally keep the earnings for themselves.

By assisting in this way and participating in the daily lives of pottery-making women, children learn the basics of pottery. They learn which materials are needed; where to find the necessary tools; and something about the order in which the process is undertaken. Consequently, this enables newcomers to learn for instance, how long pots must dry before another step can be carried out; where pots can be sold; and how much they can earn by selling them.

The ways of learning

In the introduction I quoted Sieni as saying that intelligent girls watch their mothers, and this enables them to create pots by themselves. Sieni's statement refers to two of the basic ways of learning in Sangopari: *learning through observation* and *learning by imitation*. I observed small girls, and even some small boys or men, who were able to perform some of the special movements required to form clay, although nobody 'taught' them how to do so. Children who gain experience with making pottery from their early childhood learn a lot about it and possess a broad knowledge of the craft. Children who do not grow up with or close to pottery-making women, generally neither know which utensils are needed during each step, nor do they have a clear understanding of the process itself. There are also *learning by repetition* and *learning by assisting,* and this includes the small tasks such as pounding clay or carrying water mentioned above.

When children join women who are working with clay, they often do so voluntarily and because they are interested in adult affairs. They watch them, play with the clay, and in this way gain their own first experiences with the material without playing a leading role.[8]

This kind of learning takes place in very different informal situations, it occurs on a daily basis, and without prior arrangement. In the following I describe one such situation in detail.

Case study: Three children learning to make pots

Sangopari, one afternoon in February. A young woman called Wariba, is making pots in the shade between her house and a granary at the edge of the compound. She is scraping surplus clay out of the interior of well-constructed pots to reduce the thickness of their walls. Yele, an eight- or nine-year-old girl from the other part of Sangopari is sitting next to her.[9] Yele joined Wariba perhaps after running an errand or because she was playing in this part of the village. The young girl's mother does not know how to make pots herself. In fact, in Yele's compound only one woman knows how to do so, and she only makes pots very rarely and for her own needs. This means Yele has very few opportunities to observe pottery-making in her own compound.

Yele takes a piece of clay which the woman has scraped out from a pot and starts shaping a bowl directly on the ground. The woman tells her not to work on the bare ground, and gives her a

---

[8]   Lancy illustrates adults' view of 'play as learning' with various examples in this volume.

[9]   Yele lives in the part of Sangopari in which there are very few women who are able to make pottery. The first potters in Sangopari, the oldest women's master potters, all lived in the older part of Sangopari and there are far more potters living there today than in the area where Yele lives. This is explained further below.

piece of clay from an old fired pot to work on. Such pieces are used by learners as well as potters to construct small pots. The young girl begins shaping a small pot and the young woman shows her which parts have not been finished properly, pointing out the cracks and unevenness. The potter instructs Yele to use more water and to move out of the sun, but does not explain the reasons behind her advice. Experienced potters know that if the clay dries too fast or unevenly, cracks may arise.

Girls playing with clay and learning to shape pots in the presence of a young pottery-making woman.

Yele appears nervous, she does not know what to do or how to finish her piece. In contrast, Wariba continues working on her own calmly. She urges Yele to keep on trying, saying that if anything is not perfectly shaped, she will fix it later on. The young girl hesitatingly tries to shape the rim of her pot with a piece of cloth, wringing the cloth out and then wetting it again. The child folds the cloth, but not the way that experienced potters do. She asks Wariba to form the rim for her, but the potter says she will do it later, and continues working on her own pieces. Yele takes another lump of clay, forms it and hollows it out with two fingers.

In the meantime, Fatima, Wariba's two-and-a-half-year-old daughter has appeared. She was sleeping and begins to whine. Wariba interrupts her work and breastfeeds her daughter. Yele carries on working on her pot, and begins using coils of clay. The potter encourages her to do so, promising to rework the piece later. Yele starts speaking with Tene, another girl from her part of the village. She also wants to learn pottery and begins to form some clay. Yele, who has noticed a small crack in her pot, asks for a piece of an old calabash to form and repair it. She tries to form its special rim with her fingers, but the rim tears open. Yele mocks Tene, who has already damaged her own work twice. Yele then asks the potter if she would finish the pot for her and fire it with her own ones. Now Fatima also wants to make pots. She knows that she needs clay, and a piece of gourd to form her pot and so tries to reach the container of water. Fatima is now very keen to learn and participate in women's work, and she is very proud of being allowed to do so. Fatima wants to help in other situations too, such as when her mother pounds or winnows grain, and she loudly tries to get her own way.

Fatima also wants to form Yele's pots, but Yele refuses, and claims the little girl would only damage them. Instead Yele tells Fatima to watch her own mother. Yele kneads one of her pieces of clay and forms it into a lump. Each of the girls has produced some kind of work, although Fatima's pot more resembles a lump of clay. She declares she is finished and places her 'pot' in the sun to dry. Despite this she continues adding more and more water to it with a piece of cloth, and even begins adding water to the other girl's pieces. A short quarrel ensues.

After the dispute has been settled, Tene shows Yele how to form a small pot. She says that she wants 'to eat the money of the

clay'. Tene means she wants to learn to make pots and buy food from
the money she earns. It is unlikely that she will be able to do so.
Firstly, no potter makes a living by selling pots alone. Second, the
young girl is disabled. Her legs are not straight, and she may need
assistance in adulthood, although this will depend on how well she is
able to walk.

A young boy arrives to pick up Tene. She washes her hands,
places her pot in the sun and leaves. Yele also puts her pot away and
leaves. Little Fatima continues observing her mother and points out
the places which need improvement. Then Fatima takes the only pot
which Yele made that turned out well. She breaks one side of the
small pot, before demolishing the whole piece. Only Tene's work
remains untouched. Fatima loses interest and begins throwing clay
and dust around, before pounding small pieces of clay on a stool with
a piece of calabash.

Nothing produced by the learners survived the end of this
session, as the children were either unable to construct a pot, or the
pots they made were destroyed afterwards. In addition, the smallest
child added so much water to her own piece of clay and to the other
pieces that they all fell apart.

Although the three girls worked together with a pottery-making
woman they played no significant role in the situation. Nobody
forced them to join in, and so everything they did was voluntary.
Clearly, the pottery-making woman wanted to get on with her own
work, and complained that the girls' lively behaviour and bickering
disturbed her. The girls learned by themselves, and did so because
they were interested. They watched the woman and imitated her
playfully: they performed the steps they had observed, or repeated
those they already knew. Furthermore, their actions were corrected
by the young woman both verbally and non-verbally. So for example, instead of explaining what she was doing, at one point the
woman took the small pieces and improved them herself.

There are other situations where skilled potters sit together with
learners, with the clear aim of transferring their knowledge. In such

situations, they too normally work on their own pots. Yet such situations are rare, as competent potters generally do not pay attention exclusively to learners, and rarely exclusively actively 'teach' them. Instead, experienced potters are more likely just to continue working on their own pots by themselves. Situations where young girls make their own pots are then important in providing the experience needed, even if this occurs without the help of an experienced potter. Furthermore, girls who are by themselves are more likely to try out different techniques than when they are together with a competent woman, as she may regularly intervene and correct the learners. In such cases experienced individuals take over the situation and take charge of the learner intensively, even if this only occurs for a short period of time.

Apart from *learning by assisting*, the situation described above also illustrates several other ways of learning: observing as active behaviour; playful imitation; trying to do something by oneself; gaining one's own experiences; learning through repetition; and finally, being corrected, in other words profiting directly from the experience of the competent woman.

What I call here the ways of learning, are referred to by Gaskins and Paradise (2010) as 'learning strategies'. They focus on learning through observation as part of daily life and as a universal learning strategy. The two key characteristics they describe certainly apply to Sangopari: participation in meaningful activities, which refers to children being embedded in everyday life; and active participation on the part of the learner. Children in Sangopari are present at and take part in daily tasks. They take the initiative in learning, and the girls themselves are responsible for learning how to make pottery. These girls are highly motivated, as was the case with the youngest girl in my example. Whether Gaskins and Paradise's third characteristic of observational learning, 'open attention', is also applicable to Sangopari will need to be examined in a future study.

The Nyarafolo understanding of learning

Sieni's statement that 'An intelligent girl watches her mother creating pots and thus is able to do it herself', is illustrative of the Nyarafolo and their understanding of learning, and reflects their assumptions about the ways in which children should learn in general. The Nyarafolo consider watching and copying as the fundamental basis of learning. So for instance, a girl watches her mother, another close family member, or neighbour and imitates that person. A young man in Sangopari explained this in the following manner: 'The small brother walks like the big brother does.' Furthermore, he pointed out that there was simply no time to sit down and explain things. This attitude is also typical of the Nyarafolo and may certainly be applied without reservation to the process of pottery production.

A girl scratching and polishing pots under the guidance of a young pottery-making woman.

In Sangopari, children are expected to adopt the normative behaviour of adults, which is perceived as being 'correct' behaviour. Adults are then assumed to be the ones who know what is right, and how things are done. Although knowledge is also transferred when sitting around the fire, in descriptions of times gone by, or by passing on proverbs and myths, this is of secondary importance. In the case of pottery, no one at all sits down intentionally to pass on knowledge about the manufacturing process itself, and instead experienced women simply act as role models. They demonstrate how pottery should be done and they often do so without comment. They work on pots that have been started by someone else, even without asking, and intervene if they believe a pot would otherwise collapse.[10]

Verbal transmission of knowledge, if it takes place at all, is situation-dependent. Verbal communication consists of short instructions, such as which step in the process should be carried out next. Learners are not told *how* to do something, but *what* has to be done. Furthermore, *why* something should be done is also rarely explained, for instance when the pots are moved out of the sun to prevent them from drying too fast or irregularly.

However, Sieni's statement goes even further, as it contains an emic concept of intelligence. Sieni states that only an *intelligent* girl is able to make pottery. This means that it is necessary to have the required skill, will, or understanding in order to make pottery. I argue that this plays a role in how the children see and develop an awareness of what is good, how something should be done, and how they are to meet other people's expectations. This leads children to learn how to work in the right way. Consequently there is more than mere observation involved in the Nyarafolo attitude to learning: learning is also linked to the concept of intelligence, as is our understanding of

---

[10] In this case the question of authorship is clear. The one who began the pot, i.e. the one who shaped the basic form, is the creator and the owner of the work. In contrast, I did not like it when others worked on pots which I had tried to make by myself. I felt they were no longer mine. Yet in Sangopari it seems it is considered more important that the objects are finished successfully.

being gifted or talented. There are women in Sangopari who are unable to make pottery; this may be due to the fact that they come from other settlements, but in some cases women have tried to learn, and were not able to. When asked why she did not do pottery, one woman, for example, explained that she was too stupid for that kind of work.

From small raw pieces to larger and more elaborate pots

In general, learners begin by producing small bowls, pulling them directly from a small cylinder of fresh clay. To do so they only use one technique, and their small bowls, which are also made by experienced women in a larger form, are not built up with coils, nor are they decorated. This stands in contrast to the bigger pots made by the experienced women and advanced learners. Learners often do not yet use the more complex methods of treating the clay using a spring from a bicycle saddle, a snail shell, a pebble or a piece of gourd for decoration. Instead they are likely to use more simple processes such as polishing their pots with a smooth pebble. Their pieces are generally uneven and asymmetrical. These very simple pots are not usually kept or fired unless they can be used in the household or sold at the market; consequently people attach little value to them. Occasionally after a learner's pot has been left to dry, it is forgotten and may even be damaged by rain. This makes it quite difficult to identify and find such pieces.

The pots made by beginners are likely to be of lower quality than those made by experienced women. This leads to the assumption that they will be less durable than 'normal' pots. However, small pieces of a certain shape may have a longer life span, as they may be used less frequently and they are thicker in relation to their size than the other pots.

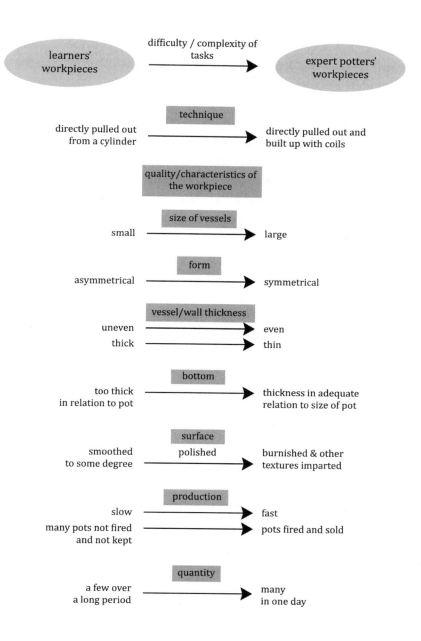

difficulty / complexity of tasks

learners' workpieces → expert potters' workpieces

technique
directly pulled out from a cylinder → directly pulled out and built up with coils

quality/characteristics of the workpiece

size of vessels
small → large

form
asymmetrical → symmetrical

vessel/wall thickness
uneven → even
thick → thin

bottom
too thick in relation to pot → thickness in adequate relation to size of pot

surface
smoothed to some degree → polished → burnished & other textures imparted

production
slow → fast
many pots not fired and not kept → pots fired and sold

quantity
a few over a long period → many in one day

Some characteristics of pots made by learners and experts.

Who is involved in learning?

It is clear that actors in a learning process can be divided into two groups—those who 'learn' and those who 'teach'. Yet in Sangopari, fixed models of schooling similar to those found in Western forms of schooling and apprenticeships do not exist.[11] Instead, the roles are variable, and actors are not divided into fixed or strictly defined groups. It is the relationship between experience, skill, and competence that counts when dividing individuals into learners and 'teachers'. Depending on the specific situation, a young woman can be a learner at one time, and a 'teacher' at another. Even young girls may 'teach' others who are less skilled during playful situations, and this occurs without regard to age, as we have seen in the example above. The transmission of knowledge is always an interaction between more skilled and less skilled individuals, making it difficult to describe as a standardised process.

Although Sieni's statement suggests that young girls mainly learn from their mothers, by questioning the potters themselves we come to a different conclusion. My research shows that 34 per cent of the women learned pottery from a mother-in-law, while only 20 per cent learned the craft from their mothers. The rest of the women had learned pottery from other relatives, in-laws, friends, or neighbours. Since women do not primarily learn how to make pots from their own mothers, Sangopari differs from most family-based economies. We now need to ask why this is the case, and what importance it may have.

These two questions can be answered by looking at the group of women who learned from a mother-in-law. Of these 17 women, only four had mothers who were able to make pottery themselves. Consequently, most of the women who learned from a mother-in-law did not have the opportunity to learn from their own mothers. If we look closely at other women who learned the craft from someone other

---

[11] David Lancy identifies a concept corresponding to Western apprenticeships among the Kpelle blacksmiths in Liberia (see for example Lancy, 1980 & 1996).

than their mother, a similar pattern occurs: most of these women's mothers were not potters, and there was no opportunity to pass on knowledge of the craft from mother to daughter.

However, most of the women born in Sangopari did learn pottery from their mothers, and those who were born elsewhere were mostly taught by a mother-in-law. Furthermore, all of those who gained their knowledge from a friend were born outside of Sangopari. Consequently girls and women generally learn from someone that is spatially, temporally, or socially close to them.

In Sangopari, the ability to pass on knowledge does not depend on a person's skills in imparting knowledge. Women who are experts in making pottery are therefore also competent in the transferral of the necessary knowledge. The ability to pass on knowledge is a question of competence, and not necessarily of age. Yet importantly, women who have been producing pots for a long time are normally older than those who have just begun to learn. Who then is competent and responsible for passing on the necessary knowledge? Although several women were shown how something was to be done properly, other women were unable to name the particular woman from whom they had learned pottery. This does not mean that no one was responsible for passing on knowledge, but instead that many people were involved in doing so.

Passing on knowledge in Sangopari is an open and dynamic social process. Learning takes place in public spaces in the sphere of pottery-making women, and this means many women contribute towards learning. Certainly, as individuals, they are aware of their responsibility towards ensuring a daughter, daughter-in-law, or friend is able to learn pottery. Yet, there is no single person or group of people who are understood as having the sole competence or responsibility for passing on knowledge. Instead, each person's contribution, will, time, and ability is required.

The conditions necessary for learning: growing up in a pottery-making environment

Learning pottery relies on a number of conditions to be fulfilled. These include good health and physical ability, a certain talent, which corresponds to the Nyarafolo concept of intelligence, and motivation. These conditions relate to the learner as a person. Furthermore, novices, whether women or girls, also need the opportunity, and this includes access to at least one competent potter. Similarly they need to have the time it takes to learn through practice. One woman told me: 'A young girl or a woman who wants to learn how to make pottery doesn't wait until a master potter tells her to start. She seeks the proximity or company of pottery-making women, she watches and observes, and at some point she will begin to try it herself by imitating the others.' The initiative is taken by the children themselves, and as I have already shown, they learn through self-motivation. This quote also highlights the basic factors necessary for learning: *place* and *time*.

The first factor, place, can be quite small. Even within a village such as Sangopari with only about 350 inhabitants, learning depends on the compound in which a girl grows up, as potters are not evenly spread throughout the settlement. This means that newcomers to the craft have different chances of experiencing this work close at hand, as was the case with the three girls in my example above.

The second basic aspect is time: learners, whether children or young women, must have enough time to gain their own experience of making pottery. This is difficult because a young wife is generally burdened with work in the household by her mother-in-law. This leaves her with neither the time nor the energy needed to make pots. Apart from newcomers to the craft, this is also applicable to women who were born in Sangopari and are already able to produce different types of pots. The numerous tasks expected of young married women, and unmarried girls, from fetching water to work in the fields, have already been mentioned above. An old woman recounted that her master potter, her mother-in-law, told her, 'You are tired—

go and cook!' This meant she was unable to begin producing her own pots until after the death of her master potter. Furthermore, she was unable to profit from the advice of an experienced woman, and so was denied this way of learning. In addition to the conditions mentioned so far, a certain continuity is also needed if a person is to learn a craft: creating pots requires practice.

Generally speaking, learning can result from experience, and experience comes from practice—with all the senses. Consequently, learning how to create pots cannot be achieved by thinking alone. One has to touch things in order to comprehend them. In German this can be expressed even more clearly using the terms *greifen* (to grab or take hold of something) and *begreifen* (to understand or comprehend something—see Förster 2001).

I argue that women potters have the finished pot in mind and learn how to produce or reproduce that image.[12] This would mean that novices not only learn how to make pottery in general, but instead they learn how to create special types of pots.[13] A potter has to imagine the pot while working with the clay. From my own experience and the women's comments, I know that while working on the inside of a pot, it is also necessary to look at its outside, so for instance to ensure that the belly of the pot takes on the desired form. Consequently, the women almost exclusively reproduce certain types of pots, and although innovative designs are possible, they are not actively encouraged. Learning in Sangopari is then aimed at reproduction, not innovation, and if production of a certain type of pot were to cease, novices would no longer learn how to produce it. Women are not trained to use their tools to make other types than those they already know, nor do most of them have the self-

---

[12] This is comparable to what Makovicky found out with Slovak lace-makers: 'a lace-maker monitors the effect—the weave—rather than the movements used in creating it' (2010: 79). See also the other contributions in Marchand (2010).
[13] See also for example Wallaert-Pêtre (2001), and 2008 in Stark et al. (2008). Wallaert-Pêtre has done very interesting research on the transmission of knowledge in pottery, for instance on the transmission of style.

confidence to try. Importantly, the statement recounted by Sieni implies that young girls can *only* learn what their mothers or other skilled potters show them.[14]

All the women I asked told me that people learn the type of work that is typical of the place in which they grow up. I have already mentioned that novices learn from those who are spatially, temporally or socially close to them. There are some tendencies here which can be summed up using the term *dichte Erfahrung* (thick experience). This refers to the fact that social and spatial proximity supports the transfer of knowledge in making pottery over generations. The advantage of living in the vicinity of potters is clear. Obviously, being close to other women potters is important: learning is shaped by such thick experiences. I have borrowed and modified this concept from Gerd Spittler's *dichte Teilnahme* (thick participation—1998), which itself refers to Clifford Geertz's 'thick description' (1983). Both of these terms describe ethnographic methods which are used during and after academic research. Spittler emphasizes the importance of *active* participation, of experience gained in a social situation involving all of the senses. I argue that this concept can be applied to learning in Sangopari, and that experience as knowledge obtained through perception plays an important role in the learning process. Perception which relies on all of the senses may result from active participation, but also from merely being present. This *dichte Erfahrung* in social and spatial proximity to the pottery-making women while growing up facilitates access to pottery, and learning the craft. Consequently, I would refer to the Nyarafolo understanding of learning as expressed in Sangopari, to be one of 'growing up in a pottery-making environment'. It could also be called 'being involved in the milieu of pottery-making women'. As I have shown, children gain experience informally by accompanying

---

[14] Only occasionally do individual potters try to produce new types of pots that for example they have seen on the markets. I only noticed one pair of small clay figurines in the context of a sacrifice. During the time of my research, no such figurines were made.

their mothers, but the *dichte Erfahrung* becomes less relevant the further away girls are from pottery-making women, whether socially or spatially.

The claim by the women that people learn the work which is typical of the place where they live, is not only applicable to Sangopari and its surrounding villages, it can also be applied to the compounds *within* Sangopari itself. In one part of Sangopari there are very few pottery-making women, and so the children there cannot benefit from *thick experience*. I did not observe any girls learning to make pottery in this part of the village. Furthermore, I traced back the oldest knowledge of making pottery in Sangopari to seven women, all of whom had lived in the part of the village that still has a high density of pottery-making women. It seems that the need for close contact and the immediate vicinity of women working with clay is responsible for the irregular distribution of pottery-making women and learners.[15]

Conclusion

Children in Sangopari participate in making pottery in every-day situations. Much of what they learn is learned informally, first by simply playing with the clay, but later on more intentionally. Their knowledge grows by playing, by gaining their own experience, and then through repetition and from being corrected. Their work changes: they begin with small pots before proceeding to bigger and more elaborate ones, and they are guided throughout by non-verbal communication. Girls learn how to make pots within the context of the family economy as a matter of course, just as they also learn other kinds of everyday work. Their learning is self-motivated, and they are actively engaged in the process themselves. Even small children learn a lot just by being close to their mothers, but there is

---

[15] In other patrilocal societies proximity also plays a special role. There too, pottery-making women tend to live and work in close vicinity to each other. For instance see Herbich and Dietler (1991) on the Luo in Kenya.

one significant difference: making pottery is optional, it is an additional work. No girls have to make pots, nor do they have to learn the skill by a specific age. Despite this, the financial benefits provide a strong incentive to learn pottery at an early age, since it provides women with the best possibility of earning their own income. Even small children realise this early in their lives, and so making pots for pleasure or tradition is certainly of secondary importance. What I have referred to as *'dichte Erfahrung'* or the special importance of proximity to practitioners, characterises learning and the transmission of knowledge in making pottery today, and it is this which enables learners to become familiar with the different aspects of this kind of work.

References

Barley, Nigel (1994): *Smashing Pots. Feats of Clay from Africa.* London: British Museum Press.

Förster, Till (2001): Sehen und Beobachten. Ethnographie nach der Postmoderne. In: *Sozialer Sinn* 3, 459–484.

Frank, Barbara E. (1998): *Mande Potters and Leatherworkers. Art and Heritage in West Africa.* Washington, DC & London: Smithsonian Institution Press.

Gaskins, Suzanne and Ruth Paradise (2010): Learning through Observation in Daily Life. In: David F. Lancy, John Bock, and Suzanne Gaskins (eds.): *The Anthropology of Learning in Childhood.* Lanham: Alta-Mira Press, 85–117.

Geertz, Clifford (1983): *Dichte Beschreibung. Beiträge zum Verstehen kultureller Systeme.* Frankfurt: Suhrkamp.

Greenfield, Patricia Marks (2004): *Weaving Generations Together. Evolving Creativity in the Maya of Chiapas.* Santa Fe, New Mexico: School of American Research Press.

Herbich, Ingrid and Michael Dietler (1991): Aspects of the Ceramic System of the Luo of Kenya. In: H. Lüdtke, and R. Vossen (eds.): *Töpfereiforschung—archäologisch, ethnologisch, volkskundlich. Beiträge des internationalen Kolloquiums 1987 in*

Schleswig, Bonn: Habelt, 105-135. (= Töpferei- und Keramik-forschung 2)

Köhler, Iris (2008): *Es sind die Hände, die die Töpfe schön machen. Töpfernde Frauen und Töpfernlernen bei den Nyarafolo im Norden der Côte d'Ivoire*. Hamburg: Lit. (= Beiträge zur Afrika-Forschung 41)

Lancy, David F. (1980): Becoming a Blacksmith in Gbarngasu-akwelle. In: *Anthropology* 11, 266–274.

Lancy, David F. (1996): *Playing on the Mother-Ground. Cultural Routines for Children's Development*. New York & London: The Guilford Press.

Makovicky, Nicolette (2010): 'Something to Talk About'. Notation and Knowledge-Making among Central Slovak Lace-Makers. In: Trevor H.J. Marchand (ed.): *Making Knowledge. Explorations of the Indissoluble Relation between Mind, Body and Environment*. Oxford: Whiley-Blackwell, 76–94.

Marchand, Trevor H.J. (ed.) (2010): *Making Knowledge. Explorations of the Indissoluble Relation between Mind, Body and Environment*. Oxford: Whiley-Blackwell.

Rödiger, Iris (1999): Offenes Zusammenleben? Gestaltung und Nutzung von Haus und Hof bei den Nyarafolo im Norden der Côte d'Ivoire. In: *Iwalewa-Forum* 1–2, 35–48.

Spindel, Carol (1989): Kpeenbele Senufo Potters. In: *African Arts* 22/2, 66–73.

Spittler, Gerd (1998): *Hirtenarbeit. Die Welt der Kamelhirten und Ziegenhirtinnen von Timia*. Köln: Köppe.

Stark, Miriam, Brenda J. Bowser, and Lee Horne (eds.) (2008): *Cultural Transmission and Material Culture. Breaking Down Boundaries*. Tucson: University of Arizona Press.

Wallaert-Pêtre, Hélène (2001): Learning How to Make the Right Pots, Apprenticeship Strategies and Material Culture. A Case Study in Handmade Pottery from Cameroon. In: *Journal of Anthropological Research* 57 (4), 471–493.

Migration of Children and Youth in Mali: Global versus local discourses

Isaie Dougnon

In Mali as well as in many other African countries, child labour is just one phase of the long process in training and teaching future household workers[1]. Douglas Galbi (1997) has shown a similar process in his study of the role of child labour in training factory workers in the early English factories. As we will see in this paper, the different training phases are regulated by local lifecycle patterns. From the perspectives of young migrants, migration in the global labour market is just a new expression or form of the same pattern of training and learning. In particular, the trainees access global knowledge and goods that are unreachable in their home society. These socially valued global goods and knowledge explain why— through a ritualized migration—Malian children experience one or more of their lifecycle phases in the post-colonial urban centres, where they are more and more labelled by many human rights organizations (UNICEF, Human Rights Watch, Terres des Hommes, ILO etc.) as 'trafficked children'.

In Mali, lifecycle and labour training phases for the vast majority of children (those who have no possibility of going to school or attending village-based schooling) are defined in accordance with the cycle of education based on the ancestral initiation of children to local activities and knowledge. In Dogon society, there are two crucial phases of childhood in processes associated with work learning. The first phase is that of uncircumcised children (five to 12 years old): in this phase, the child is compelled to do all the unpaid

---

[1]   This article was developed from my two previous articles, Dougnon forthcoming b, and 2011. I use the term 'child labour' to cover all intensive work by children, without prejudice as to whether or not it is harmful to them.

work in the home, work including tough jobs like market gardening and cattle rearing. The second phase is post-circumcision: once a child has been circumcised, he could do all the jobs that an adult does or is supposed to do. In addition to these tasks, a circumcised child may be a member of the secret society of Masks, where his elders teach him the esoteric and practical knowledge of his society.

Although two factors—revealed religions and labour migration—have consistently reduced the role of secret initiation societies in the training of children, the lifecycle pattern which regulates children's training in labour still remains valid. An examination of the profiles of the waves of children who migrate to the urban centres confirms this ancestral pattern.

In this chapter, I show how the local lifecycle pattern contradicts the global discourse against rural youth labour migration using my ethnographic data collected in Dogon country. During my doctoral and post-doctoral research (1998–2005), I collected data from returned migrants in Dogon villages. In Ghana I worked (among Dogon communities) in five cities, Accra remaining the most important one. The great majority of the Dogon migrants in Ghana come from the cliff and plateau areas. I carefully photographed ancient objects brought back from Ghana: shoes, male symbols, hats, knives and lances. In addition, I talked to the country dwellers about the role of the imported objects in social ceremonies and new identity building. Children's labour cannot be reduced to cheap labour at the mercy of capitalistic exploitation. However, it is that image that human rights organizations[2] strive to convey to Africa and the rest of the world. At the same time, they urge African countries to take action, and to fight vigorously against child labour, considered the new human plague.

---

[2] See, Human Rights Watch Report (2003): *Borderline Slavery, Child Trafficking in Togo*, and Terres des Hommes Report (2004): *Kids as Commodities? Child Trafficking and what to do about it.*

Ans Kolk and Rob van Tulder (2002: 191) clearly pointed out the historical fight of human rights organizations against child labour in Europe and other continents, including Africa:

Since the early 20th century, the issue of child labor has been the subject of widespread regulatory and societal attention. After several industrialized countries had adopted laws that limited the minimum working age of children and their working conditions, international organizations were requested to advance similar measures worldwide.

In Africa, in contrast to Europe, we see a connection between the campaigns of human rights organizations and the migration policy agenda of developed countries. The fight against child labour in Sub-Saharan Africa goes hand-in-hand with the restriction of African youth migration to Europe and America.

In the following pages, I show that youth labour migration reflects the lifecycle pattern in rural activities, which provide livelihoods for up to 75 per cent of the Malian population. I point out how the local lifecycle model is perpetuated by paid labour in urban areas and the current growing rush of children towards traditional methods of gold extraction.

The same lifecycle model explains why numerous children are sent to the cities by their parents to work for their relatives. Ester Goody, in her book *Parenthood and Social Reproduction* (1982), overstressed the particular forms of fostering in which rural children and adolescents were sent to West African urban centres to be trained by relatives or others. According to her, children's spatial mobility, driven by the modern apprenticeship, was a response to the social differentiation which has taken place in many West African societies since the 1960s (Goody 1982: 188–192). In her wake, other scholars such as Serra (2009) and Kielland (2007) have emphasised how child fostering in urban African cities seeks at both the labour of the rural children and their schooling. As we will see, travelling far from the home village may be compared to modern educational institutions because it is so well organized and embedded in society that it introduces new social attitudes valued by the vast majority of society.

From 1960 to the mid-1970s, neo-Marxists highlighted the devastating impact of migration on African villages (Amin 1974, Meillassoux 1964). Many governments have taken measures to limit youth migration. However, for the last two decades the same governments contend that migration brings more cash to the local economy than development aid, and further that migration is the main factor behind qualitative and quantitative change in the villages.

However, facing economic crisis and terrorist threats, developed countries are no longer willing to admit African migrants. One of the measures aimed at restricting African migration is a sensitization campaign against illegal migration, which became popular because of the legal and physical barriers to legal migration. What are, in fact, the success stories of these measures; even coupled with the redefinition of youth migration as a result of trafficking in children?

How anti-migration campaigns discount children

It is easy to discern—through television, newspapers or radio—the risks that characterize the lives of young African migrants. It is more difficult to establish analytical categories relevant to the understanding of the essential significance of 'leaving' and 'being' far from the natal village in different African societies, as James Clifford has done regarding the concept of the diaspora (1994). Indeed, for at least a decade, we note that reflection concerning African migration is limited to flourishing literature on rural and urban poverty, as well as images of drowned migrants in the Atlantic and the Mediterranean. The media show dead migrants on landing strips, or devoured by lions on the Mozambique and South African border. Even more captivating are the images of migrants who desperately attempt to surmount the barbed-wired walls of Ceuta and Melina. Certain NGOs and frontier security agencies identify, on behalf of their Governments, the nationalities of migrants, the route they take, their countries of transit and final destination, as well as their strategies.

In parts of West Africa (Mali, Senegal and Guinea) we are witnessing a growth in co-development programmes and/or strategies of communication that work to dissuade young Africans from leaving for Europe or big African cities. These programmes are often financed by developed countries, supplementing the efforts of national governments in these areas. Various NGOs and local leaders have organized sensitization campaigns in African villages to awaken a consciousness in the heart of youth that migration is a dangerous and risky enterprise (they are exposed to horrible images of hundreds of drowned bodies in the Mediterranean and the Atlantic).

Despite speeches and policies, migratory flows are not declining and destinations are becoming more numerous. Facing these failures, questions arise such as: How do Africans themselves conceptualize the idea of leaving their homes for other places? Why do they travel against all odds? What is the real impact of this communication strategy, even when it is coupled with legal and physical barriers? In fact, we see that in spite of discursive campaigns against migration and small scale rural development projects to create job opportunities, youth migration from rural and urban Mali is intensifying and the destinations are becoming more diverse. This chapter tries to demonstrate that policy-makers' discourse on the danger of migration is, in fact, at the core of the Malian conception of travelling outside their community. In most Malian societies, the word 'migration' means a pilgrimage into the wilderness. How then, using the grassroots understanding of migration, will state policies be able to stop rural and urban movement towards European and African cities?

Before the colonial period, most African societies were characterized by sharply bounded communities, with members living amidst the environment and this constituted the integral part of humans' lived world. Any movement of individuals outside of this community and environment was understood in terms of a threat or danger to life. This ancestral conception of travelling has been extended by the challenges of colonial and post-colonial Africa with

various frontiers and border checkpoints. The most important aspect
of this conception is that the returning migrant is celebrated as a
hero. A return to the home village means that she or he has coped
with the wilderness and been victorious. The newly acquired qualities of this person, based on what she or he has learned or obtained
from the outside, may form a cluster of values that contribute to the
migrant's overall identity. Using the definition of the word 'migration' in several Malian national languages, I shall discuss the meaning of migration and migrants' discourse about crossing borders in
the colonial and post-colonial periods, as well as illustrate how
current migrants' strategies to overcome all types of barriers—even
when this means risking their lives—is rooted in their very definitions of migration to seek paid work or to discover the outside world.

Migration as a rite of passage

*The head of a migrant is like the handle of an axe, it must be thrown
where it breaks. A young boy should not be scared to see his head
broken (death) in the course of his migration* (Bambara proverb,
Mali).

Studying migratory dynamism in the long term within African
societies reveals that structural forms of migration cannot by themselves integrally define the historical and sentimental relations
between the paternal home and the external world. It is now some
years since politicians and academics felt the urgency to explore the
current dynamic of migration in Africa. But the question is, with
what approach? Should we start with the description of visible
consequences of African migration towards Europe and elsewhere?
Or should we stick to an analysis of local concepts by which the
migrants establish social, material, and cultural relations with the
outside world? In this chapter, I start with the latter.

Nevertheless, I acknowledge the importance of economic
factors in current African migration in and out of Africa as described
by many scholars and development experts. In my forthcoming paper
on migration in the Malian Sahel, I describe the transition from the

migration de prestige from the 1920s to the 1940s, when cultural values demanded short-lived imported items like umbrellas, clothes and perfume, to the survival migration of post-drought periods (1973 and 1984). In fact, during these three decades, many Malian migrants were searching for cash in order to invest in building houses, shops, or small workshops in big Malian cities and in motor-pump and other modern agricultural technologies for small scale irrigation in rural areas (Dougnon forthcoming a).

My point in this chapter is to show that migration is not a mere relation of individuals to property or earnings, but the realisation of young people's dreams and social aspiration. In Malian villages, one gains the soul of a migrant at a very young age. Boys, for instance, have to migrate if they are to be viewed as men, although they often do not know exactly what this task actually consists of. Just like 'voyage literature' (which provoked a tourism boom in Europe), seductive novels and songs about emigration have awakened the desire for travel among young people in these villages.

The migrant has foremost a taste for adventure, a taste origi-nating particularly from exposure to the accounts of those who come back from far and unknown countries. In familial conversations, they tell other young people about the particular experiences they made while discovering other countries. They influence young people who stayed in the village who then believe that the migrants participated in the creation of the country they visited and worked in (see the accounts of Malians and Burkinabe migrants on their role in the birth of the 'Ivory El Dorado' or the former Gold Coast, now Ghana). But it is not enough for the migrant only to have memories. He must expose other men to what he has brought back. In addition, to be complete, the stories demand many objects of prestige (clothing, money, and other items) and proficiency in foreign languages.

In this chapter, the focus is not on the visible consequences of migrations, but rather on local concepts through which the migrants establish their own relations with the external world. The analysis then turns to the way these relations are based on a series of morals that form the identity of the migrants who return to the village. To comprehend the recent intensity of migration in Africa, despite all the forms of barriers, we need to understand the significance of the word 'travel' and the collective imagination of migration through which rural youth in Mali experiment, interpret, and frame their voyages and relations with the outside world. To do so, this chapter begins with a socio-cultural approach—the idea that the meaning given by each Malian society to migration is associated with its migratory traditions and its current perceptions of life abroad.

My research in Mali has shown that the migrants have a clear conception of the problems invoked to persuade them not to travel. Indeed, migrants' stories incorporate—just as the (British and French) colonial reports mention on multiple occasions—the nature and consequences of young migrants' exploitation while in search of work. Migrants from yesteryear warn young prospective migrants of the dangers to which they are exposing themselves. Just like their elders in the colonial era, today's young migrants are conscious that to migrate is to venture into risks and perils. Several local songs interpret the dangers of leaving the home town.

This chapter also analyses two local terms collected among the Dogon migrants in Ghana and in Office du Niger in Mali (Dougnon 2007). These local concepts define the total reality of migration in its dangerous as well as its heroic aspects. For example, the Dogon have two expressions to define migration and the attendant risks. The first one is *bara nu* ('to flee into the wilderness').[3] *Bara* is at once, the locality and the wilderness that surrounds it, while the term *nu* signifies 'to flee'. The concept *bara nu* therefore refers to the person who

---

[3] Here, we use the dialect Tinkiu, the one spoken in the Plain zone of Dogon Country, known as Seno Region; particularly, in the communes of Pel, Koporo Pen and Koproro Na. Notice that the sense of the word 'migration' is identical in every Dogon dialect.

journeys beyond the land, someone who is neither socially nor geographically under the control of the village or community.[4]

The second expression, *bara gunu* ('to collect and place'),
defines the manner by which migrants on their way towards regions
known to have employment opportunities are approached by recruiters in their trucks. The recruiters propose a job and a compelling
salary. With the verbal contract concluded, migrants embark via the
truck and arrive in conditions of near-slavery at cacao or coffee
fields (from which they are eventually liberated by a third party or
run away). As we have witnessed, such risk is at the heart of the
terminology of young rural individuals regarding migration irrespec-
tive of space and time.

According to certain elderly Dogon migrants, in the 1920s and
1930s their voyage was so dangerous that it could take travellers
three days to travel 25 kilometres, the density of the vegetation and
the presence of animals such as lions, hyenas, and foxes slowed
down the pace of the travellers. In these early years of colonisation,
young recruits that ventured out for their military duty or service
would often be blocked on the road by lions or other dangers.

In Dogon country, the perilous nature of the voyage is compared to the struggle of a girl and a boy faced with a community
which opposes their relationship. In the migrant's novel, we witness
the narrow correlation between migration for love and the voyage to
an unknown world, a land where the two lovers will find the freedom
to live for their love. When two individuals love each other and the
community opposes their love, the two lovers must flee to live hap-
pily under other horizons. On the same level, a man has to migrate to
search for objects he desires but cannot find in his homeland, just as
this old popular song demonstrates:

---

[4]   In certain Bandiagara regions, migration is identified with the universe, the
global world. In these regions people use the term *ganda*. To describe the
migrants they say: *ganda oulembe* (literally, the children of the world, or those
who have seen the world).

Kidjè èju diguè ma so yai ma koye	*It is only getting lost in pursuit of good*
salamu siri le yana èju le dikè ma so yai	*Such a beautiful sword and a beautiful girl*
tinè éju digè ma so yai ma koye	*It is only getting lost by following a man of good spirit*
Ni pa suyi kèjè, yanan èju digè ma	*Even if it means crossing seven seas and seven streams.*
Olu yai ka su yai, yanna ine teke, nininri ine teke	*To migrate is to lose oneself: the women, the singers cry for the migrant.*
salamu birè digè ma so yai	*It is only getting lost searching for valuable objects.*

In this song, love and migration have the same value. They are as difficult to obtain as a snake's phlegm. The effort of the one who seeks to live his love in freedom is comparable to the effort of one who travels in faraway countries. The risks are numerous in both cases but it is a price that must be paid. The risks emerge from the fact that society does not provide any necessary means at the disposition of the migrant who faces these dangers. There is no specific preparation: when one decides to leave, he prepares himself for death. The migrant is alone in facing the immense wilderness full of misery, diseases and cruel men.

The voyage into the wilderness represents the first collective or individual experience of a man who desires to be considered equal among the mature. Weeks of walking through the forests, savannah, and soils reinforces his masculinity. No one knows how long the voyage will take. Everything depends on nature and the will of the migrant to face these dangers. In the past, secure roads did not exist and disaster could emerge at any time. Sacrifices and magic amulets were and still are a traveller's only guide and protection. Muslims and Christians attribute the success or disaster of their voyage to God, just as the Puritans interpreted the violent winds during their crossing of the Atlantic as an expression of power and glory of God (Cressy 1987: 137). Whatever the voyage event may be, it can be interpreted as the manifestation of God's will.

In recent novels, like those of the colonial period, the migrants make reference to disappeared or dead men. The dead—those that their colleagues consider glorious—were never discouraged and would never discourage future candidates. Those who fall are, in reality, torches in the sea or desert that will be raised again to be carried higher and farther. The characteristic young villager, never satisfied with his immobility in the village, always likes to travel—to know and gain more. This is the goal of all migrants.

Another notion, *jobo* (to flee) is always an act of temerity, because it is equated with a leap towards the unknown. The village/community cannot allow their sons to go on their own into peril. Their sons must consequently 'flee' or *jobo*. In other words, this is leaving without social authorization and thus living in the wilderness without the consent of their parents. Before it became an acknowledged part of 'local culture', migration in the sense of 'flee-ing' was a violation of village social regulations.

This is why the returned migrant is considered impure and must be purified before re-entering village life. He is comparable to a woman who is menstruating. Considered impure, when she is menstruating she must leave the village. On the seventh day, she is reunited with her family after purifying herself with water. The returning migrant must also be purified before entering the village. On the surface, a Dogon migrant is hypothetically impure. He might have eaten a type of meat which is forbidden for his clan or slept with casted women (such as the daughter of a blacksmith or shoe-maker, etc.). If he were to come back into the village and drink water from the commune ladle, all of these impurities would be transmitted to the village. The reparations for this would be too expensive for the village and his family.

Therefore, before entering the village, a returning migrant was required to signal that a 'stranger' was waiting to be received. To

announce this, he either blew a whistle that he had bought for the
purpose or opened a box of perfume and spilled a bit in order for the
smell to invade the village. Certain inhabitants, familiar with the
signal, would run in the direction of the sound of the whistle or
towards the smell of the perfume. Once the migrant had been identified, his parents would come to get his luggage. Then the 'purifier'
would come; this person was most often one of the village's religious
leaders. He ceremonially purified the returning migrant and served
him water to drink. The objects of purification were made up of a
band of local textiles, stalks of millet, and sacred water. After the
purification ritual, the returning individual first visited the *Hogon*
(religious leader) before being reuniting with his family. Anyone
contravening this required purification was punished by the religious
leadership or even by the village gods (Dougnon 2007).

By the 1960s, migration was so anchored in local culture that
the wilderness was no longer viewed as taboo or impure. On the
contrary, it became a new place of learning with which kids were
expected to familiarise themselves. Except for Koranic students,
young beggars, and children who assisted beggars, seasonal or
permanent migration became the goal of boys between the age of 14
and 30 and of girls between 13 and 18.

According to the Dogon conceptions of migration analysed
above, we see that young people need to migrate even if it means
risking their own life. Like their ancestors[5] who stood up to the
dangers of the forest and wilderness, they must surmount the legal
and physical barriers to reach Europe, Asia, or other African countries. If we do not take into consideration the cultural foundations of
migration, then even if we expose the intolerance in receiving coun-

---

[5]   The Dogon have elaborated heroic tales on the migration of their ancestors from
the Mande region, deep in the south of ancient Mali to the plateau of Bandiagara.
There are tales about the sufferings of some Dogon who undertook pilgrimages
to Mecca by foot at the end of the 19th century and the beginning of the 20th
century.

tries, the many expulsions, and the controls on airways or maritime frontiers, nothing will change the migratory wave.

Child trafficking or labour migration?

In 2000, Mali's Ministry for the Promotion of Women, Children, and the Family asked donors for 824,000,000 West African Francs (US$1.7 million) to fight child trafficking to neighbouring Côte d'Ivoire. The question of child trafficking quickly drew so much attention from state and privately-owned media that it submerged other issues, such as poverty or AIDS.

It is hard today to engage in debate over child trafficking in the poor countries of West Africa without referring to the different United Nations conventions on human rights, and especially the International Labour Organization's Convention 182 on the 'Worst Forms of Child Labour', adopted on June 17, 1999. This convention is one of the new legal instruments intended to eliminate the 'worst forms' of child labour in the same vein as the ILO's preceding Forced Labour Convention (1930).

How is child trafficking defined in these international legal documents? According to the Article 3 of the ILO convention, the worst forms of child labour are '(a) all forms of slavery or practices similar to slavery, such as the sale and trafficking of children, debt bondage and serfdom and forced or compulsory labour, including forced or compulsory recruitment of children for use in armed conflict; (b) the use, procuring or offering of a child for prostitution, for the production of pornography or for pornographic performances; (c) the use, procuring or offering of a child for illicit activities, in particular for the production and trafficking of drugs as defined in the relevant international treaties; (d) work which, by its nature or the circumstances in which it is carried out, is likely to harm the health, safety or morals of children.'[6]

---

[6]   http://www.ilo.org/public/english/standards/relm/ilc/ilc87/com-chic.htm

In addition to Convention 182, there is also the Convention on the Rights of the Child (1989), Article 35 of which condemns 'the abduction of, the sale of or traffic in children for any purpose or in any form'. Although 'trafficking in children' is left without explicit definition, the term is taken up in the UN Protocol to Prevent, Suppress and Punish Trafficking in Persons Especially Women and Children, supplementing the United Nations Convention against Transnational Organized Crime (2000). Its crucial article repeats the worst forms already mentioned in the two earlier conventions and in numerous other documents negotiated in international conferences.[7]

Whatever definition is provided in each of these documents, trafficking appears as a phase—and the most odious—of the cycle of exploitation of children as well as adults; and it demands urgent action by the international community. The phenomenon is declared to be a global one and no country is spared, whether as a source, transit point, or destination for trafficked children. UNICEF estimated in 2004 that trafficking in children affects approximately 1.2 million children each year.[8]

All the signatory countries of convention 182 are called upon to develop national programs aimed at eliminating the worst forms of child labour once and for all. Convention 182 specifies that these programs are intended to function in consultation with public institutions and employers' and workers' organisations, and if necessary by taking the views of other interested groups into consideration.

If this global discourse of child trafficking is produced and popularized from Geneva, here I examine how it is taken up by state officials in Mali. Is it applied mechanically or accommodated

---

[7] Trafficking is defined as 'the recruitment, transportation, transfer, harbouring or receipt of persons, by means of the threat or use of force or other forms of coercion, of abduction, of fraud, of deception, of the abuse of power or of a position of vulnerability or of the giving or receiving of payments or benefits to achieve the consent of a person having control over another person, for the purpose of exploitation.'

[8] *Trafficking in Human Beings, Especially Women and Children, in Africa*, UNESCO, 2004.

conceptually to local historical and social realities? How have the words 'traffic' and 'work' been translated into other languages? To what degree have concerned groups and interested parties—peasant parents of working children on the one hand and urban heads of households who are their principal employers on the other—been involved in the campaign, as called for by Article 3 of Convention 182? An ethnographic and historical approach to the relationship between domestic labour and paid labour in colonial and post-colonial polities in Africa may provide a way to answer these questions.

As soon as the debate was launched in Mali in 2000, child trafficking became the object of a moral condemnation so strong that few researchers have dared to examine it from a historical and sociocultural angle in the way that Hashim and Thorsen (2011) and Howard (forthcoming) have done in their recent work. Such an approach, however, can put into strong relief the disparity between the regional politics of applying formal international conventions on child labour and local ways of thinking about labour and the life cycle in rural Malian societies. In what follows, I do this while focussing on the villages and villagers of what is commonly known as 'Dogon country'. As scholars have done in other contexts, I bring out the double tension between the victims of trafficking (peasants and their children) and government officials—not only around the concept of child trafficking itself, but also, and especially, the question that bears on the social and moral responsibility of the anonymous traffickers and the impoverished parents as Christine J. Walley (1997) pointed out in her work on global debate about female genital operations in Africa.

In several notes of the ILO's International Program on the Elimination of Child Labour, Mali was targeted as one of the countries where child trafficking surpassed far more than what has been supposed, particularly if one compares Mali to neighbouring countries. According to several official documents, Mali presents all the economic and geographic conditions favouring trafficking on a large scale. Meanwhile, Mali's political context, characterized by a process of peaceful democratization, favours all debates that touch on human rights, particularly those of women and children.

The point is not simply to dismiss concern for child trafficking as paternalistic, but to enrich—as Lawrence Cohen (1999) has suggested—the contextual sensitivity to the situation of those who engage in the stigmatized activity. Economic indigence will not disappear due to a moral or legal norm, and the relative risks and benefits—including the question of available alternatives—must always be kept in view, as a considerable literature on 'trafficking' suggests.

But there is a crucial perspective on trafficking afforded by an approach combining ethnography and history. For demographic and historical reasons, there is no way to separate a discussion of the worst forms of child labour from the history of rural migration patterns. Only a few years ago, demographers were deeply concerned with the migration of the peasantry to towns but a concern with child trafficking has now taken the place of this focus.

Indeed, the movement of young Africans has reached Europe, in spite of physical and legal barriers erected against them. The debate about child trafficking is also inseparable from the problem of the rights of immigrant and undocumented workers, both on the African continent as well as in Europe and the United States. All so-called 'irregular' migration—whether major or minor—is likely to be understood as the product of a network of traffickers based on the Mediterranean coast and with far-flung connections to the countries of the Sahel (Mali, Mauritania, and Senegal). This justifies, in part, the hardening of measures of expulsion and imprisonment of 'irregular' migrants and the relentless pursuit of those who smuggle them. Mali appears to the European Union as the country where both elements are most prominent, as the recent creation of the Migration Information and Management Centre (CIGEM) attests. The connection between the fear of an invasion of workers from poor countries and the problem of child trafficking (or trafficking in general) is obvious. It is the reason, among other things, for the financing by wealthy countries of numerous social scientific studies that focus on the connection between trafficking and migration, on the premise that traffickers exploit the difficult conditions in which both child and adult migrants find themselves in their search for work.

What if such inquiries were to take account of the voices of migrants or children along the way? What version of the facts would they give? To be more specific, let us take the case of Dogon country, which according to official Malian documents is one of the zones most disposed to child trafficking. The ethnography of the rural exodus from the Dogon country, together with the history of labour organization in the colonial era, provides critical perspectives.

Ethnography and history as windows on child trafficking

The regions of Sikasso and Segu, and the Dogon country have been cited as zones disposed towards child trafficking. The Bamana, Senoufo, and Dogon ethnic groups are often cited as being affected by trafficking. Non-governmental organizations, government administrators and law enforcement agencies hold forums to discuss a solution to this scourge; a few peasants are invited to these conferences as well.

The Dogon country, according to the Ministry's findings, is the zone where child trafficking is the most intense. The *cercles* of Bankass, Koro, Douentza and Bandiagara supply 'bargain children' to the Côte d'Ivoire, Sikasso, Bamako, and Mecca in Saudi Arabia. According to the British consulate in Mali,[9] a documentary on child trafficking in Dogon country that was shown in the U.K. sparked the indignation of Malians living in London. Some of them swore that Mali's Dogon were not capable of such atrocities, particularly in relation to their own children.

---

[9]   According to the consul, the fight against child trafficking in Dogon country is the primary activity of the new British Embassy, which opened its doors in 2001.

To begin with, we must clearly define the object at the centre of our analysis: until what age is one a child, and what is it that we mean by the phrase 'child trafficking'? UNICEF experts, following the UNCRC and the Palermo Protocols, consider anyone under eighteen years of age as a child. And Mali's National Agency for the Promotion of Children and the Family gives the following definition of 'child trafficking'.

Child trafficking is defined as any act involving the recruitment, transport, transfer (fencing), or sale of children within national boundaries or abroad. Child trafficking has multiple results: sexual exploitation, adoption, labour, criminal activities, begging, armed conflict, sports, marriage, and organ trafficking.[10]

Civil servants and NGO workers have drawn donors' attention to the social and ethical aspects of the problem, arguing that child trafficking is a 'new form of slavery' and should be banned.[11]

To submit to donors a report entitled 'Child Trafficking in Dogon country' is to suggest that Dogon peasants take part in this traffic in one way or another. In any case, this was the case presented to the British public. But does a system of recruitment, transport, transfer, and the sale of children from the Dogon country to other Malian cities or to the Côte d'Ivoire really exist? If so, do Dogon peasants play a role in this trade? There is no historical evidence to support the argument that parents are involved in the sale of their children. The inadequacies of official definitions of child labour in

---

[10] See *'Le Trafic transfrontalier d'enfants'*, the report of the preliminary inquiry of the Ministry for the Protection of Women, Children and Families in the regions of Sikasso, Segu, Mopti, and Timbuktu (Document de travail du Ministère de la Femmes de l'Enfant et de la Famille, June 2000).

[11] The first seminar on child trafficking in Dogon country was held in Bankass, the *cercle* most affected by the problem, from 14-16 March 2002. It was financed by the British Embassy in Mali. Peasants from all the rural communes of Bankass took part. Behind the scenes, the representatives of the commune of Wangaro affirmed that they had been asked to come and stated that the girls from their village had been enslaved in Mecca, and that this trade in girls was organized by people from Wangaro whose wealthy employers are located in Mecca.

local contexts is due in part to the fact that in Malian villages, there is no distinction between domestic labour and the type of labour performed for wages in towns and cities, as Chandrasekhar (1997) demonstrates with reference to child labour in India. That being the case, why would a child who works in the village not do the same in town, or elsewhere?

Examining the question of child trafficking from a historical and anthropological perspective, while drawing on the testimony of migrants and on colonial archives, allows one to avoid making the same analytical errors as those who herald the return of barbarism to Africa. We should interrogate both the colonial past and the present with respect to migration, while scrutinizing the relationship between the cities and the countryside. In order to do so, I base my analysis on material collected between 2001 and 2003 with migrants from Dogon country in Ghana and in the vast irrigated zone known as the Office du Niger, among migrants who have returned to Dogon country after a sojourn in the cities of the sub-region, and among those who have never left the village. To the question, 'How did you come to sell your children?' peasants gave the following response:

No, there is no traffic in children at Bankass. It's the NGOs who say that there is a traffic and that they are going to help us to fight it. What we've known since the 'time of the Whites' (colonization) is the rural exodus, or the migration of the youth. If there is a traffic in children, it is in the country where our children go, and not here (*chez nous*).

This kind of NGO discourse, so common since the 1980s in regards to Africa, takes place in the context of the changing fashions of development projects: genital mutilation, organ trafficking, child labour, the rights of women and children, national solidarity programs, and so on. Richard Shweder has strongly criticized this kind of fashion calling it the return of cultural developmental thinking (Shweder 2003).

One could deduce from the United Nation's definition of 'child trafficking' quoted above that if a boy or a girl younger than 18 moves to a new setting more or less distant from his or her birth village, that this was due to trafficking.[12] But at 17 years old, is one really still a child in a Malian village?

As the Dogon lifecycle pattern in work training shows, seasonal or permanent migration is practised by young men of 14 to 30 years of age and by girls or young women from 13 to 18 years old. They themselves decide to leave. A peasant would have a hard time forbidding his son or daughter from taking part in what is considered to be a village tradition. Many family heads do not even know the destinations their children have chosen. They may have sought to dissuade them by telling them that they are leaving for regions where their predecessors were shamelessly exploited, and from which they returned poorer than when they left, but the young people leave all the same. Their parents have no power over them. One day, they simply leave, without informing anyone at all. Sometimes as many as 20 young people leave a village on the same day. How then can one talk about traffic in children in the zone of departure? In fact, many peasants were shocked to hear allegations that they were involved in the sale of their children to 'labour merchants'. According to the peasants, the very idea is an insult manufactured by certain NGOs in search of funding.

Conclusion

We retain from this analysis of youth and child migration two essential elements: (1) the rituals of migration and labour in colonial centres are reinterpreted, as a prestigious, 'initiatory', value-giving experience (Bouju 1984); (2) Through the channel of migration, young men from Dogon villages discover another world, acquire new knowledge and learn other types of work. As far as their friends and

---

[12] The incoherence of the discourse on child trafficking is apparent in the fact that the NGOs, the police, and the government all affirm that the sellers or 'traffickers' are difficult to identify. If this is the case, how can one prove that trafficking in Dogon children to Malian or Ivorian towns really exists?

relatives who remain in the village are concerned, the human nature of these men has changed: they are now reborn and have reached a higher grade. Their marvellous clothes on their clean bodies lend them the image of men who have reached the summit of perfection, something which used to be the unique preserve of water and bush spirits.

The experience acquired in crossing the wilderness is passed on from generation to generation. With so much experience in surviving to reach their destination, the African migrants have placed the experiences of their voyage at the centre of their stories. Almost all old accounts contain memories of dangers in the wilderness. The migrants narrate, with powerful details, the events that happened amidst the super powerful, fearful wilderness. In this rite of passage, the hand of God is often called upon, just like the courage or the temerity of the traveller. It is tempting here to cite the phrase of an English traveller to illustrate the novels of Dogon migrants from the 1920s: 'To have come so far, and to have endured so much, was surely a sanctifying and a winnowing experiences from which great things could be expected' (Cressy 1987: 176).

The generations from the 1970s and 1980s did not face the same experiences in the frightening wilderness. The roads were safer and transportation means more abundant. With the new policy of 'zero migration' adopted by certain European and African countries, the generation from the 1990s began to live the experience of the sea and the Sahara. They now take on adventure without preparation, only at God's mercy. Thousands of deaths and disappearances have also been counted. African and European states attempt to forbid the voyage or to warn that boats may be swept away by the tide. The multiplication of boat journeys is proof that this new generation has, in reality, lost nothing of the capacity of previous generations to undergo the rite of passage and has no fear of perishing in the ocean or the Sahara.

Despite numerous national programs of 'sensitization' in the departure states, the migrants appear unaware of the peril of travel that awaits them on the roads to Europe, or ignorant of the certain death that awaits them on illegal routes through the Sahara and across the Mediterranean and Atlantic. These programs appear simply as a 'new project' that will require funding. It is appropriate to caution against this 'mercantile' treatment of a problem that eventually leads to applying measures of an illusory character and a waste of material and human resources, all in the name of young men who ultimately leave to wherever, whenever they decide.

The failure of visa restriction measures and the control of the frontiers reveal a poor definition of the migratory problem. In its socio-cultural and socio-economic contexts, the evolving concepts of employment amongst African youth have not been sufficiently addressed in preliminary discussions between the EU and the US when they were elaborating a plan of attack against illegal migration. When we evaluate young migrants' attitudes vis-à-vis rural development projects we see that in addition to ecological causes, another cause for migration has appeared recently that we could call developmentalist.[13] The introduction of micro projects, such as the 'village perimeters', generate further rural debt. The solution remains migration, as it used to be during the head tax era. No specific study has been undertaken to answer the question of why the development activities presently being undertaken have not been able to solve the issue of migration.

Without a deepened study of cultural parameters and economic constraints, the struggle will be in vain. We cannot know what the future holds for the economic development of Africa or the migratory trends that will arise as a result. There is, evidently, one solution to the dilemma. African researchers need to be able to predict migratory trends both inside and outside Africa. To succeed, they will have to produce a large knowledge-base of certain facts and

---

[13] See my draft article not yet published, 'From the assistance to the development: The peasant participation in question, the case of the region of Timbuktu'. AEGIS Conference, London, from 29 June to 2 July 2005.

objectives from the past and the present of African migration (including forms, intensity, regions of departure and arrival).

Currently, all the policies working to limit migration are faced with failure. If migrants are driven away from one country, we simply find them (after a few months) in another African or European country—if they do not return directly to the country from where they were expelled. In the struggle against child trafficking, more than 500 children were repatriated to Dogon country. We know today that more than 90 per cent of these 'trafficking' victims came back after forced repatriations to their homeland[14]. This means that these young people, despite their difficult living conditions in the urban centres, have never been the objects of trafficking. In addition, with the interconnection of the world economy, we would need a global solution to migratory flows. Europe may close its doors but the interests are not exclusively there. The roads to migration are as numerous as the economic ramifications for the countries of the North. All of these examples show that without a clear and undistorted understanding of migration, we will not find a durable solution to the problems it causes.

References

Amin, Samin (1974): *Les migrations contemporaines en Afrique de l'Ouest*. Dakar: IDEP.

Bouju, Jacky (1984): *Graine de l'homme enfant du mil*. Paris: Société d'ethnographie.

---

[14] Amongst these illusory and ineffective measures we can cite the decree N° 01-534/ P. RM from 1 November 2001, which established a travel document to serve as evidence of permission for children from zero to 18 years of age to leave the country. This title of voyage is only valid for three months. It is delivered by the minister of security and civil protection. Security agents are authorized to return all children younger than 19 years old traveling without this title.

Chandrasekhar, C.P. (1997): The Economic Consequences of the Abolition of Child Labor. An India Case Study. In: *The Journal of Peasant Studies* 24, 137–179.

Cressy, David (1987): *Coming Over. Migration and Communication Between England and New England in the Seventeenth Century.* Cambridge: Cambridge University Press.

Clifford, James (1994): Diaspora. In: *Cultural Anthropology* 9, 302–338.

Cohen, Lawrence (1999): Where It Hurts. Indian Material for an Ethics of Organ Transplantation. In: *Daedalus* 128, 135–165.

Dougnon, Isaie (2007): *Travail de blanc, travail de noir. La migration des paysans dogons vers l'Office du Niger et au Ghana. 1910–1980.* Paris: Sephis-Karthala.

Dougnon, Isaie (2011): Child Trafficking or Labor Migration? An Historical Perspective from Dogon Country. In: *Humanity. An International Journal of Human Rights, Humanitarianism, and Development* 2, 85–105.

Dougnon, Isaie (forthcoming a): Migration as Coping with Risk and States' Barriers. The Case Analysis of Malian Migrants' Conception of Being Far from Home. In: T. Leedy and K. Abdoulaye (eds.). *African Migrations Today. Patterns and Perspectives.* Indiana University Press.

Dougnon, Isaie (forthcoming b): Comparing Dogon and Songhai Migrations towards Ghana. In: H. de Haas and M. Berriane (eds.). *African Migrations Research. Innovative Methods and Methodologies.* Africa World Press.

Galbi, A. Douglas (1997): Child Labor and the Division of Labor in the Early English Cotton Mills. In: *Journal of Population Economics* 10, 357–375.

Goody, Esther (1982): *Parenthood and Social Reproduction.* Cambridge: Cambridge University Press.

Hashim, Iman M., and Dorte Thorsen (2011): *Child Migration in Africa.* London & Uppsala: Zed Books & Nordiska Afrika-institutet.

Howard, Neil (forthcoming): Protecting Children from Trafficking in Southern Benin. The Need for Politics and Participation. In: *Development in Practice*.

Kielland, Anne (2007): *Modeling Choices of Children Labor Migration and Schooling. Incentives, Constraint or Agency. A Multinomial Logit Analysis*. Dissertation: Oslo.

Kolk, Ans, and Rob van Tulder (2002): Child Labor and Multinational Conduct. A Comparison of International Business and Stakeholder Codes. In: *Journal of Business Ethics* 36, 291–301.

Meillassoux, Claude (1964) : *Anthropologie économique des Gouros de la Côte-D'Ivoire. De l'économie de subsistance à l'agriculture commerciale*. Paris: Mouton.

Serra, Renata (2009): Child Fostering in Africa. When Labor and Schooling Motives May Coexist. In: *Journal of Development Economics* 88, 157–170.

Shweder, Richard (2003): *Why do Men Barbecue? Recipes for Cultural Psychology*. Harvard University Press.

Walley, Christine J. (1997): Searching for 'Voices'. Feminism, Anthropology, and the Global Debate over Female Genital Operations. In: *Cultural Anthropology* 12, 405–438.

Schooling or Working?
How family decision processes, children's agencies and state policy influence the life paths of children in northern Benin

Erdmute Alber

A case story

When I visited the Baatombu village Tebo in northern Benin in 2005, I was astonished to see 8-year-old Abaz leaving the village in the morning in old clothes, dressed for field work. Together with his father and his (foster) brothers, he went to the family fields to spend the day working there. The year before, during my last visit in Tebo, I had seen him every morning, dressed in the national school uniform, leaving the compound together with his sister Falli in order to go to the local primary school. I asked him what happened.

'I didn´t want to go to school anymore!!' he answered with a smile on his face. Considering that many village children in Tebo drop out of schooling because they do not like sitting there, being punished by the teachers, and having to speak French in the class-room, I imagined that it was just his unwillingness to go to school that led to the decision to drop out of school. I have come to know Abaz and his family very well over a period of about 20 years. Since I started sponsoring the school career of Abaz's half-brother Saka, I have been considered his foster mother, and thus, a family member. Therefore I feel somewhat responsible for the future of Saka and his siblings. This fact and my own, 'western' belief that children should be sent to school if at all possible, made me decide to discuss this with Abaz's parents, if there was a chance of encouraging him to continue his school career. I thought that it had been his decision to drop out of school.

My assumption was based on the knowledge about the hard-ships associated with the reality of schooling in Tebo and the region:

despotic and aggressive teachers, children having permanently to
copy what the teachers dictate to them, the content being uncon-
nected from the everyday reality of peasant children, as well as the
lack of chairs and desks that make classrooms places which are not at
all nice to spend time in. In the view of local peasant families, there
is a consensus that spending a day working in the fields or running
around is much more pleasant for children and gives them more
freedom than sitting in school.

This is at least what I came to understand from many conversations with Baatombu children or adults who had spent their childhood in the village.

This is even more the case as, due to the fact that all village
children are integrated into the working processes of the peasant
households, many school children have in sum more everyday obligations associated with work than those who do not attend school.
Before going to school girls maybe required to collect water,
whereas boys work in the fields on the week-ends or sometimes after
school. As a result, this combination of work and schooling in the
everyday-life of Baatombu school children means they are often
more loaded with work and occupations than children who do not
attend school.

For all these reasons, Baatombu peasants rarely use much
paternal pressure to encourage their children to continue going to
school no matter what the price. As the majority of them are illiterate, and they normally do not have the knowledge, and very often
not even the will, to help their children face the many difficulties
they are confronted with in public village schools.

On the other hand, the notion of schooling has changed since
my first visits to Tebo in 1992. Due to state-initiated schooling campaigns, increasing literacy among the parents and other reasons that I
will go into later in this chapter, the importance of schooling for the
future life chances of their children is increasingly being acknowledged by the people. Therefore, I thought it would be better for the
future of Abaz to speak with his parents and to see if it would be

possible to put some pressure on them to let him continue his schooling career despite all the hardship that would mean for the boy.

But to my surprise, Abaz's mother Dado answered me very quickly: 'He did not want to anymore, why should I force him to go?' I was astonished, since Dado is one of the few adult women of her generation in Tebo who went to school for 5 years. Consequently, making schooling available to her children has been a real concern for her. She even encouraged two of her younger sisters to do the same, and over the years she had taken them into her household and paid school fees in order to ensure they went to school. Nevertheless, her two eldest biological children (daughters) have never been to school. As many girls in the region, they grew up with foster parents, who very often do not send their foster girls to school (see Martin in this volume). In the cases of rural foster arrangements, it is quite difficult for biological parents to influence the schooling decisions of their children because they have to leave the full responsibility for the children with the foster parents (see Alber 2003). After that experience, Dado and her husband Mora had made it possible for their daughter Falli, their third child, not to be fostered by relatives but instead to be kept at home and sent to school. Actually, Falli is continuing her school career quite successfully in a secondary school in a village nearby. Thus, knowing Dado's attitude towards school, I was astonished that she seemed to readily accept Abaz, her fourth child and eldest son, giving up his school career so easily, and with it a chance of getting a formal job in the future.

Later on, I talked to Mora, Dado's husband and Abaz's father. Mora gave me the same answer: Abaz had not wanted to go anymore; he was a lazy boy who preferred the liberty of staying in the village and going to the field. Furthermore, according to Mora, Abaz had not been a good pupil.

Having in mind that among the Baatombu everybody tends to avoid speaking openly about conflict (Alber 2004), I felt that a part of the truth of the story had been missed in both Mora's and Dado's answers. I was especially mistrusting because I knew Mora, like his wife, was fully aware of the life chances schooling offers. Of the three children from his first and divorced marriage prior to Dado, he had two daughters who were fostered by relatives and were never sent to school. But Saka, the third child from that marriage and his first son, was kept with Mora. After finishing primary school in Tebo, I sponsored him and so he was sent by his father to secondary school in Parakou, the capital of the region. When Abaz dropped out of school, Saka was just doing his final exams and planned to continue his career at a national university.

Even among his three foster sons (his sisters' children who grew up in Mora's household) named Taairou, Kirikou and Mam Mam, Mora had sent one, Kirikou, to primary and later on to secondary school.

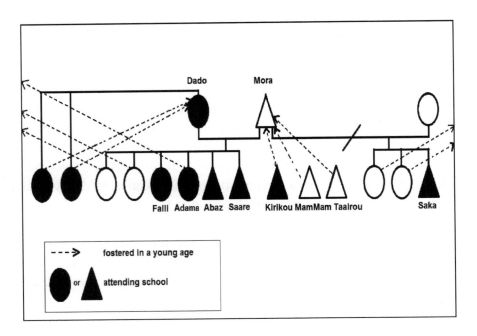

Picture 1: Mora and Dado's children

Knowing about their principal engagement for the formal education of their children, I doubted that Mora and Dado had told me the whole truth. Therefore I went to Parakou where I met Saka, and asked him what had happened with Abaz's school career. Saka told me that he was very angry about Abaz dropping out, and that he had argued with his father about what had happened. When he heard that Abaz had left school, like me, he had tried to convince his father to let him continue. And, he told me, Abaz had been a good pupil before leaving school.

'So, what happened in the end?' I asked. 'Look,' Saka told me, 'you know that after his daughters were no longer his responsibility and were growing up with foster parents, he was still responsible for six boys and two daughters. I was sent to school, and Kirikou was sent to school. But our two foster brothers, Taairou and Mam Mam, go to the fields with Mora. Once, Taairou even said to me that I could only go to school because he was working in the fields, providing food for the family and earning our school fees. Mam Mam, up to now, has not said anything. But he could start gossiping. And Mora was worried that the people in the village might talk about the fact that he was sending his biological sons to school, while his foster sons were working in the fields. In order to avoid that image, he took Abaz out of school. He thinks that Abaz should become a farmer, and as he is Mora's biological son, he should remain in the village to care for his parents when they grow old.' 'Well,' I asked, 'but why did Mora then send Abaz firstly to school and take him out later?' 'You see,' Saka answered, 'at that time it was not sure that I would do well in school. Mora was not sure if I would make it. But as I have done it now, he wants to ensure that one son stays with him.'

In this chapter[1], I take the example of Abaz in order to show how the life course, the schooling decision and the working career of a specific child is influenced by changing state politics, parental decisions and the agency of the child in rural northern Benin. I contribute to the general theme of this volume by demonstrating that one can no longer talk about children's work in Africa without reflecting on school and schooling. At the beginning of the 21st century, when the global model of schooling is reflected in different forms all over the globe, even in the hinterlands of northern Benin, an uncaptured peasantry which has not been influenced by the idea that children have to be sent to school no longer exists.

I aim to demonstrate, that even in times of massive schooling campaigns and a generalized model of a schooling childhood, a working childhood remains a real alternative option for parents and children. I discuss the reasons for local resistance to a globalized model that becomes visible in specific decision-making processes as is the case with Abaz's story.

In order to understand how peasants decide between schooling and non-schooling of their children, my hypothesis is that they have two kinds of childhood in mind: a working childhood and a schooling childhood. A decision between the two has to be made for every child.

The two models of childhood, a working and a schooling childhood, lead to two different options for adulthood and life chances. Despite the fact that real pathways to growing up could be much more complex than these two alternatives, they remain nevertheless the basis of the local decision processes. These models are also reproduced in state schooling policy as well as schooling campaigns. I now go on to describe these two models, then I come to the history of schooling in northern Benin, before finally coming back to my

---

[1]   My chapter is based on field research on child fosterage in northern Benin which I have undertaken since 1999. Thanks to Tabea Häbelrein and Jakob Treige for their critical reading of the paper, to Jeannett Martin for long discussions on child fosterage and to the editors of this volume for their comments and discussion.

case study which I analyse on the basis of the information provided above.

Two models of a proper childhood

The notion that it is in the best interests of a child to grow up in a nuclear family, be educated by his or her biological parents, learn in state-organised schools, and be outside of the labour sector, is at the heart of the current global travelling model of proper childhood, which is sent around the globe via UN-conventions, international policy making and development programs.[2] For Africa, this model fits in well with older sociological ideas on the subject of family change inspired by modernization theory.[3] This was based around an assumption of a unidirectional development of African family structures towards the Western model of the nuclear family, comprised of a monogamous couple living with a small number of biological children. Successful school careers should, following this model, be one of the priorities in parents' education and care for their children.

It is only during the last decade, that a key element necessary to implement such a modernisation model has been introduced in northern Benin, the area of my field research, with the relatively wide-spread introduction of a public school system. It is only since the 1990s[4] that small primary schools have been founded and equipped in nearly every village in the region[5] due to international agencies fulfilling international development policy goals. This transformation has finally made it possible for the majority of children in northern Benin to attend school, if their families wished them

---

[2] For the travelling model of a global childhood see Thelen and Haukanes 2010, for the concept of travelling models see Rottenburg 2009: 64.

[3] For West Africa, see, among others, Goode 1967, Seibel 1967 and 1969, Caldwell 1969, 1977, Oppong 1981. For a summary see Alber and Bochow 2006.

[4] Up to the 1980s, only a minority of children had this choice—due to the fact that schools were not available everywhere.

[5] Concerning the history and development of schooling in West Africa and the new schooling policy in Benin, see Bierschenk 2007 and Fichtner 2009

to do so. Consequently, this is also the first time that parents could take the decision to send their children to school and so fulfil the pre-condition of the modernization model implied in the travelling model of a proper childhood.

Nevertheless, the story of Abaz shows that this is not the only option available to parents in northern Benin. Despite all state and private efforts to cover the social and geographical landscape of Benin with a working school system, parents (and children) can still decide against integrating their children in the school system. In doing so, they opt for the model of a 'working childhood' which leads to other pathways into adulthood. As the example of Abaz has shown, they can even take children out of school and re-integrate them into a working childhood. As a result, their agency comprises the possible decision against state-introduced officially obligatory schooling system, a possibility that European parents normally no longer have. Furthermore, Abaz's example also shows that there are even parents who are fully aware of the chances schooling offers to their children, and who nevertheless still opt for this alternative.

Cases like the one of Abaz could therefore be seen as examples of a voluntarily change 'back' from schooling to work, against offi-cial law, the empirical tendency of increasing schooling rates and the massive schooling campaigns in the region. However, I do not see this decision as moving 'backwards' to an old model of childhood that will be replaced in the future. Rather, I aim to outline that in the actual decision-making processes within families, both models of childhood, schooling and working, are seen as two alternatives which are both necessary for a good and balanced household structure in rural Benin.

Of course, this is neither a new nor particularly original argu-ment, since neo-marxists and other social scientists have long time argued that rural and poor households in Africa and other peripheral areas of global capitalism tend to split their personal resources between different spheres of income-generation (Hugo 1991; Meillassoux 1973 and 1976, Stolpe 2008). However, the difference between these accounts from 40 years ago and today are the massive campaigns organized by the state as well as by international and global operating agencies such as UNICEF to ensure schooling for children and thus to influence children's life courses. Therefore, when thinking about peasants and peasant children in northern Benin, it is no longer possible to conceptualize them as uncaptured peasants (Hyden 1980) who are able to make relatively autonomous decisions about their children's work in the agricultural household economy and other working spheres. A second difference is the grade of participation of parents and children in the decision making processes.

Therefore, my paper aims to show that the question of children's work in recent rural West Africa has necessarily to be discussed in the frame of a concept of childhood that includes the alternative of either going to school or to work in the fields, even if official state policy and massive campaigns aim to delete the second concept. I attempt to explain why the idea of an easy pathway to a 'modern' childhood including schooling, leaving behind the notion of a working childhood, despite all campaigns, is not perceived in the rural context of West Africa as the only model that guarantees a future for children and the rural peasant economy, but as one model among others.

When I speak about schooling and a working childhood, I am talking about two models that rural people in northern Benin have in mind and choose between when they make decisions about schooling for their children. I do not talk so much about the working reality itself. As Jeannett Martin outlines in her chapter, school children in rural northern Benin are often very involved in field and household work; they may even work as much in the fields or the households as children who do not attend school. Nevertheless, I would argue that parents in northern Benin have these two models in mind when making decisions about their children's careers. One model is linked to the idea of possible success in the city and the option for a career in the formal labour market; the other is linked with the idea of preparing a child for peasant life, staying in the rural area and providing for their parents when they are old. These are mainly decisions about the future roles and positions of the children within family and society, and less about their present occupations.

In northern Benin, decisions have to be taken for every child. Within these processes, parents not only re-negotiate how they see the future of their children within the given living conditions, this is also done in the way they try to ensure the reproduction of their family and their own old age. Therefore, the model of a working childhood should not be seen as something traditional that is only fitting for very poor or backwards-oriented families, but in combination with the other model, as being one important option within an entire strategy concerning the reproduction of the family.

A short history of schooling in northern Benin

In the travelling model of a proper childhood as expressed in the children's rights convention, schooling is seen as being *the* alternative to children's work. Children should, following the model, not learn work, and they should by no means be 'used' to create family income. Over the last few years in the Republic of Benin there have been massive schooling campaigns that try to convince families to send their children to school. A special emphasis is put on girls, as the picture demonstrates.

But there has been a long pathway up until this point. The first schools in Dahomey (the name of the colony that later became Benin) were introduced at the beginning of colonization, most of them in the south. In the north of the colony, schooling got under way very slowly. Here, the first schools were founded in the second decade of the 20th century, starting with the very first primary school that opened in 1909 in Parakou.[6] From the beginning of colonialism

---

[6]   Archives Nationales de Benin, 26, Rapport Mensuel Trimestriel, Borgou, May 1910.

to independence, no more than one hundred children from the Borgu region had attended school.[7]

Schooling campaign. Picture taken in the village of N'Dali, in 2008.

After independence, schooling rates increased dramatically. Despite this, Africa still has the lowest schooling rate of all five continents and the Republic of Benin is among the countries with the lowest schooling rates in the world. In 1960, only 90,000 children in Dahomey went to school, more than 80 per cent of whom came from the south of the country. In 1972, ten years after independence, 200,000 children attended school. The numbers increased to almost a million pupils in 2000 (Guinigo et al. 2001). Yet these general

---

[7]   See Asiwaju 1975a and 1975b.

figures conceal remarkable differences. The Borgu, the region where the Baatombu live, has traditionally been the region with the lowest schooling rate. Therefore, the massive schooling campaigns at the end of the 20th century, and recently the campaign to send girls to school, has influenced and changed the practices in northern Benin even more than in southern Benin, where schooling rates have generally been higher.

Since colonialism, the hundreds of Baatombu who have attended school and made careers in the state administration not only serve as role models for the next generation, but they also run the first urban households in big cities like Cotonou and Parakou. These households had a pioneer character in many ways: the adults served as role models for young Baatombu from the north, they helped them to get into higher social positions, and, maybe most important, of all thousands of pupils from northern Benin were hosted and fostered so that they could attend secondary school.[8]

As in the villages there are mainly only primary schools, attending and continuing secondary school necessarily means that children have to leave their parents' homes in order to live and study in other households. In order to make that possible, new kinds of foster relations have been developed linking urban and rural households. They are unidirectional, because children are sent from rural to urban households, not vice-versa.[9]

Nevertheless, since the time of those education pioneers that attended colonial schools in the first half of the 20th century, it has become a shared experience for rural Baatombu that sending a child

---

[8] It might sound strange that a few hundred households could have housed thousands of pupils. But the majority of households belonging to this very first generation of Baatombu in Cotonou over time hosted more than 10 children and or young people. In the most extreme case I know of, one household hosted a total of more than 100 pupils. The grade of hospitality towards young Baatombu villagers has been incredibly intensive.

[9] I have mentioned elsewhere (Alber 2010) that it was the old institution of fosterage, albeit in a different transformed way, that enabled careers of Baatombu children to attend school.

to school signifies, if he or she is successful, his or her exodus from the village to town, and that nearly always they do not return or come back to live in the village. There are two reasons. First, children who have made their career in school will rarely find work in the villages.[10] Second, having once lived in a town and had the experience of being a pupil, nearly nobody wants to return to the village, apart from to visit or for short jobs. Living conditions and the rural way of life are seen as being part of a backwards-oriented world that the majority of pupils are happy to have left behind. They might send money and resources to their parents, they might visit the village for ceremonies or feasts, they might work as middlemen for all kinds of problems or administrative affairs villagers have in the city, and they might host rural guests and foster children in their urban households. But sharing everyday life in the village with peasants becomes unthinkable for them. Therefore, it might be reasonable for rural parents to keep some of their children at home.

Notions of work within the context of fosterage

In the peasant villages of northern Benin, children's work has been seen as a very important resource for the labour organisation of households, and it is mainly children's capacity to help their parents in the fields or in the household (in the case of girls) that provides children a special value. This is particularly true in a local setting in which the fostering of children is, and has been the norm for a proper childhood for at least the last 200 years. For many years, the majority of Baatombu children have been brought up by foster parents.

Today the elderly Baatombu confirm that almost all Baatombu children grew up as foster children at the end of the 19th and early 20th century. They were hosted by classificatory aunts and uncles, i.e. people considered as kin. The practices of fostering children were,

---

[10]   There are very few formal working possibilities available in the example villages except for teachers and a number of agricultural advisors.

among others, seen as an appropriate way of educating children, especially educating them to become good workers. Biological parents were not seen as suitable in this respect as they were said to spoil their biological children.

In short, the Baatombu had a strong belief in fosterage as being the 'proper' model of childhood. They shared the idea that children were better off raised by foster parents than biological parents. Foster parents were perceived as more objective and foster children as more self-contained, independent and better equipped to face the challenges of adult life.

The notion that children do not belong to their biological parents, but to others, who have the right to claim them, was crucial. These others were classificatory aunts and uncles, as well as grandparents, who as a rule came to claim 'their' child between the age of three and six. A vital aspect that facilitated child fosterage in precolonial times—and later challenged in colonial times—concerned the future life chances of the child: it was of little or no consequence where a child grew up. Since land was available to everyone and private land tenure did not exist, the question of heritage was irrelevant for the child's future wealth. Economic success depended on other factors, in particular the capacity to work hard and to be surrounded by numerous biological or foster children to assist with work.[11] This changed profoundly when schooling began to offer new life opportunities to children, increasing the importance of decisions on children's education.

The direct connection between notions of (children's) work and fosterage is, among others, proved by synonyms for fosterage in the everyday language. A common expression for the act of fostering a child is: *'na bii neni na wi gorimo'*—in English: 'I foster a child to have somebody to send around'. This has to be understood in terms of the fact that a very important task of children in the villages is to

---

[11] See Jack Goody's argument that wealth in West Africa was not wealth in land but in people (1969).

be sent to other households to pass on messages, bring things, to send food or to fulfil other little everyday tasks. Another expression is: 'Na bii neni u ka ne somburo ko'—'I take a child so that he/she can work for me'.

Among all factors that led to fundamental transformations in foster practices and norms, the introduction of schooling in the first decade of the 20th century, and in particular the creation of access to schools for a majority of the peasant children during the 1990s, has been crucial. Today, schooling is seen as being *the* alternative to the integration of a child into the peasant labour sphere.

This is seen as such not only because children who attend school do not have the same time to go to the fields as their brothers and sisters who do not attend school. Moreover, schooling is seen as being a central decision presiding over the child's future. Children who go to school could find jobs in town in the future, and they will have the possibility to continue their education in the cities and be part of a completely different world. This differentiation of future life chances has led to the fact that many parents prefer to send their biological children to school, whereas foster children are much more frequently kept at home.

This is proved by some statistical data I collected in three villages in northern Benin in 2002 and 2003. In each of these villages, I asked 60 people who were at least 50 years old about the schooling of their children. I got solid data about 980 children. As the figures show, 49 per cent of the boys who grew up with their biological parents were sent to school, whereas only 36 per cent of the foster boys attended school. Among the girls, the tendency to keep them at home is much more pronounced: Only 21 per cent of the non-fostered girls attended school. The lowest schooling rate is among the foster girls. Only 9 per cent of them went to primary school.

	Sent to school	Not sent to school	Total
Boys growing up with biological parents	198 **(49 %)**	207 (51 %)	405 (100 %)
Boys growing up in fosterage	33 **(36 %)**	59 (64 %)	92 (100 %)
Girls growing up with biological parents	59 **(21 %)**	220 (79 %)	279 (100 %)
Girls growing up in fosterage	19 **(9 %)**	185 (91 %)	204 (100 %)
Total	**309 (32 %)**	**671 (69 %)**	**980 (100 %)**

Source: Standardized interviews and questionnaires, 2002 and 2003.

These data on schooling and fosterage indicate that it has become general practice for families to primarily send their biological children to school, whereas foster children are schooled only to a lower degree. But the data also show that at the time of my data collection, there were a number of children, especially boys, who were growing up as foster children *and* attending school, and on the other hand, boys without foster experience who nevertheless were not going to school. This new differentiation within rural households, which arose with the practice of sending some children to school, continues today.

In the light of all of these factors, I will now come back to my case study presented at the beginning of my paper, and to some conclusions.

Back to the case study

Looking at my case study of Abaz taken out of school, the first point I would like to make is that it seems that it was not primarily Abaz himself who decided to drop out, but instead it was due to a decision made by his father. Later on, other people in the village confirmed Saka's version of the story in so far as they said that the boy had been taken out by Mora to make sure that he had at least one biological child who could go to the fields with him. It is possible that Mora's decision was made easier because Abaz really did not like going to school. Up until now, I have had no chance to speak in a quiet and confidential way with Abaz, which would be necessary to really get to know his own viewpoint. In the small conversations we have had, which were more or less in the presence of other people, he confirmed that he no longer wanted to go to school; but I am quite sure that he would have said that anyway so as not to go against his father.

I do not know if there has been more gossip and rumours[12] about Mora sending his biological children to school and keeping his foster sons as agricultural workers, but this is quite possible. One initial point of possible gossip can be identified in the person of Taairou, Mora's eldest foster son. Taairou himself quite often told me that he really would have liked to go to school, but it had been decided that he would have to go to the fields, whereas only Saka would be sent to school. I sometimes overheard him in conversations with his friends, young men from the village, saying that he would have liked to go to school. Saka and Taairou are the same age. They were close during their childhood in Tebo, but ever since Saka began successfully attending secondary school, their good relations ended, and Taairou often expressed regret about staying in the village.

If we assume that even Abaz really did not like going to school, and that it was mainly his father's decision that led him to be taken out of school, we can form a general rule about Baatombu children: relatively young children have little influence over the decision as to whether they attend school. It is first and foremost the parents, whether biological or foster parents, who decide if children are sent

---

[12] In the village context rumours are an excellent way of performing social control and making people behave following according to norms.

to school. Children may have some limited influence on the decision itself, but only if they really do not like going to school and their parents try to make them attend. In these cases, children can run away from school or not take the demands of school seriously. In most cases, this is quite a successful strategy for younger children who no longer want to go to school, and may lead them to drop out. The opposite is much more difficult. Many adults told me that they would have liked to go to school and regret that they were not sent, but that they did not have the possibility to oppose their (foster or biological) parents' decision at the time.

The fact they were not able to decide for themselves whether they could attend school, but instead had to respect their parents' or grand-parents' decisions was also the case for Taairou and Saka. Both are the same age and they and their whole family have confirmed that it was Mora's father who decided that Taairou should stay with him in the fields and that Saka would be sent to school.[13] But Taairou also fought against becoming a peasant. He had had a dream since being a young child, but due to a decision made by his (foster) parents, this dream could only be realized for Saka. As his foster parents did not send him to school, Taairou started a quite successful small business playing music cassettes at public events and repairing old radios. Later on, he expanded his business by selling alcoholic drinks at feasts. Today, he is running a small store selling alcohol, playing music as a local disc jockey and cutting men's hair. This enabled him to finally free himself from his father's household and fields and he now acts more as a bar-keeper and disc jockey than as a peasant. Taairou is one good example of how young men can and do exert influence over the decisions that their parents make about their children's lives. With the small possibilities he had, he tried to build up his life as an adult man without resorting to

---

[13] Mora's father himself confirmed that when the children were small, Taairou was more intelligent and open minded, so that he preferred him to stay with him, whereas Saka was to be sent to school. Taairou told me this too.

becoming a peasant. Once he explained to me that he did everything he could to 'make something of his life', and not just to do what had been expected of him by his (foster) father.

The example of Mora's sons shows, that in the decision-making process about a schooling childhood or a working childhood, it is not always the (biological or foster) parents alone who are involved but also other family members. In the case of Saka and Taairou, beside their father, Mora's father (the boys' grandfather) played a central role in the decision.[14] At that time, he had been head of the compound and had to be consulted on important decisions made on behalf of the household. Maybe Mora influenced the decision, but it was his father who argued that one of the boys should be sent to school and the other should be kept in the household. As at that time there were only these two boys in the household, it seemed plausible that one boy would stay at home, especially because at that time schooling was not as regular as it is today. Quite often it is the elderly people in the compound, or other relatives who have an influence. This can also be seen in the case of Dado's younger sisters whom she took as foster girls. In doing so, she took on the responsibility for her sisters which meant her parents were obliged to leave the girls with her and accept her plan to send them to school. If some relatives take on the responsibility for children and argue that they would send them to school and pay for it, Baatombu parents nowadays normally do not resist but let them do so.

The case of Abaz shows that even if Mora and Dado decided to take Abaz out of school, they did not openly stand behind their decision when speaking with me. They tried to give the impression that the child had decided not to go to school; a point of view that even if not being completely in accordance with the image of a modern schooling childhood, at least strengthens the impression that it is not parents who impose their decision over the child but the child who decides through his or her comportment. Mora and Dado know that

---

[14]   Taairou is the son of Mora's sister.

Europeans like me follow the idea that children should always have a
'schooling childhood'. As they did not want to me to think they are
so backward thinking that they would not let him go to school, they
tried to hide their responsibility for the decision. In my conversations
on schooling and childhood in general, I observed that many
Baatombu peasants try to demonstrate that they are aware of the
importance of schooling, even if they do not allow all of their children to go to school. When I asked Mora, for example, why his
second foster boy Mam Mam was not sent to school, he said that
when he took Mam Mam into fosterage he was already too old to go
to school. I met Mam Mam when he first became part of Mora's
household as a circa 5-year-old boy, and so I know that this is not the
truth.

The ways of communicating about schooling such as those used
by Mora and Dado demonstrate that the schooling campaigns in the
media and the public space in Benin influence the way arguments are
structured in the decision-making processes as well as in the way
how people talk about them. I am sure that Mora had no problem
justifying the decision not to send Abaz to school when talking with
his old father who never went to school himself. But speaking with
younger people or with people who went to school, Mora avoided
mentioning that he would leave some children at home and only send
some to school. This tendency can also be generalized. The
campaigns of the state and international organisations at least
strongly influence the positions people take in discussions in the
public sphere. Again, this is an argument which goes against the
picture of uncaptured peasants deciding freely and without state
influence or the influence of other institutions over the future of their
children.

The decision to take Abaz out of school was primarily a decision over one of the two childhood models—a schooling or working
childhood—and only secondly a decision about how they wanted
Abaz to live at the moment they removed him from school. As I have
argued, other 8-year-old village children (the same age as Abaz) do

work in the fields; those who attend school contribute probably less, and those who go every day to the fields work more compared to the amount of work that is necessary to maintain the family fields. When I asked at which age children's work starts providing a substantial contribution to the household and peasant work, the Baatombu often told me that this is a process and that children contribute more with time. But they always confirm that in order to be successful, besides the household head (in this case Mora), a household also needs at least one young man who already has a deep voice and is nearly reaching an age in which he can think about marriage. Abaz could have been left at school and taken out at that age.

But at the age of reaching adulthood, parents no longer have sufficient power of decision over their sons. Thirteen-year-old boys have the possibility of running away for work in Nigeria or in the city; and with those possibilities in mind they could resist the decision to take them out of school. Boys attending school at that age are normally already in secondary school, and thus, far away from their parents. If parents want to make the definitive decision against their child's school career, they must take them out of school at a relatively young age, as was the case with Abaz. Therefore, I argue that the decision for one of the two models of childhood for a specific child is above all a decision over his or her future: it opens up or excludes the possibility for the child to make a career in the formal sector.

As many children drop out during their school career, a majority of those village children who have started schooling do become peasants. Today there are many adults in the villages who speak French, who attended school for some few years and learned to read and write, but did not go on any further. As a result, there are also families who send all of their children to school and then decide which of them should stay on and continue. Mora's neighbour and best friend, a man who is the head of a household in which actually more than 20 children live, has always followed the strategy of sending everybody in his household to school, including two sons with impairments. Until now, all of his children have left before finishing secondary school, so he is still waiting for at least one really successful son or daughter. As many of his children have returned to his household and were not successful in the town, he continues to send all of his younger children and grandchildren to school.

In contrast, Mora's strategy was to ensure that Abaz would stay with him whatever the outcome of his schooling. In general such a decision is also influenced by the fact that household heads in the villages want to have at least one of their children in the village to provide for them in old age. Once again, fosterage comes into play in my case study: today, it is much easier for foster children to leave a household than for biological ones. For instance, they may return to their biological parents or go to some other place. Therefore, if they want to make sure they have a son close by when they grow old, parents have to ensure they hold on to a biological child when he or she reaches adulthood.

This is also clear from the case study of Mora and his sons: two years later in 2010, Mam Mam, who by this time was already married to a wife Mora had paid the bride price for, left the house and moved to his maternal village. In 2008, Taairou decided to split the reproductive unit (defined as people who eat and work together) and thus to separate his own household from that of his (foster) father. That was possible due to his economic success with the activities he practised besides working as a peasant in his father's fields. In a way, this demonstrated that Mora had been right to take Abaz out of school. Interestingly, in 2009 Mora and Dado allowed 5-year-old Saare, their youngest son and Abaz's little brother, to attend primary school.

Conclusion

In contemporary northern Benin, and I would like to extend this to other parts of rural West Africa, I have shown that two models of childhood not only exist side by side but that this is also necessary as well. The 'luxury' of sending children to school and risking losing them forever as household members, as they generally remain in town and only return from time to time as visitors, is in the understanding of people such as Mora and Dado, only possible if other sons are kept for a working childhood in the village. They might leave for Nigeria, or they could try to go to the cities to work in informal jobs, but the chance that some of them would return to the village is higher than in the case of school children. Villagers need children to take over the fields and become the next generation of working adults that are also able to care for their elders.

Despite all campaigns promoting schooling, the model of a working childhood remains a second possible option that many peasants choose for some of their children. This model will only disappear if parents can either be sure that sufficient numbers of children will return to the village, or if they would give up living in the village when they grow old and start living with their sons or daughters in the town. However, the opposite is still true: many first-generation migrants to the cities return to the village when they grow old.

If the state really wants to ensure that all children attend school, this is unlikely to be achieved by introducing more schooling campaigns. Rather, a social insurance covering the costs of old age for all peasants would have to be introduced. That would allow parents to think about the future of their children without making decisions based on their need for care in old age. As long as there is no efficient social security system, people will need sons and daughters who care for them. Until this changes the model of a working childhood, as was chosen for Abaz by his parents, will not disappear in rural Benin.

Archival material

Archives Nationales du Benin: Series, 26, Rapport Mensuel Trimestriel, Borgou, May 1910.

References

Alber, Erdmute (2003): Denying Biological Parenthood. Child Fosterage in Northern Benin. In: *Ethnos* 68 (4), 487–506.

Alber, Erdmute (2004): Meidung als Modus des Umgangs mit Konflikten. In: Julia Eckert (ed.): *Anthropologie der Konflikte. Georg Elwerts konflikttheoretische Thesen in der Diskussion.* Bielefeld: Transkript Verlag, 169–185.

Alber, Erdmute (2010): No School without Foster Families in Northern Benin. A Social Historical Approach. In: Haldis Haukanes, Tatjana Thelen (eds.): *Parenting After the Century of the Child. Travelling Ideals, Institutional Negotiations and Individual responses.* Aldershot: Ashgate Publisher, 57–78.

Alber, Erdmute and Astrid Bochow (2006): Familienwandel in Afrika. Ein Forschungsüberblick. In: *Paideuma 52,* 227–250.

Asiwaju, A.I. (1975a): Formal Education in Western Yorubalad, 1889–1960: A Comparison of the French and British Colonial System. In: *Comparative Education Society* 19, 434–50.

Asiwaju, A.I. (1975b): The Colonial Education Heritage and the Problem of Nation-Building in Dahomey. *Bulleitin de l'I.F.A.N* 37, 340–57.

Bierschenk, Thomas (2007): L'éducation de base en Afrique de l'Ouest francophone. Bien privé, bien public, bien global. In: T. Bierschenk, G. Blundo, Y. Jaffré, and M. Tidjani Alou (eds.): *Une anthropologie entre rigueur et engagement. Essais autour de l'œuvre de Jean-Pierre Olivier de Sardan.* Paris: APAD-Karthala, 235–257.

Caldwell, J.C. (1969) : *African Rural-Urban Migration. The Movement to Ghana's Towns.* New York: Columbia University Press.

Caldwell, J.C. (1977). *Population Growth and Family Change in Africa. The New Urban Elite.* London: C. Hurst and Co.

Fichtner, Sarah (2009): A Playground for Educational Reform or a Battlefield of Donor Intervention? Local Debates on Primary Education and the New Study Programmes in Benin (revised version). In: *Arbeitspapiere des Instituts für Ethnologie und Afrikastudien der Johannes Gutenberg-Universität Mainz.* Nr. 95 (http://www.ifeas.uni-mainz.de/workingpapers/AP95.pdf).

Goode, J.W. (1967): *Soziologie der Familie.* München: Juventa Verlag.

Goody, Jack (1969): Adoption in Cross-Cultural Perspective. *Comparative Studies in Society and History* 11 (1), 55–78.

Guinigo, J. et al. (2001) : Le Bénin. In: M. Pilon and Y. Yaro (eds.). *La Demande d'Education en Afrique. Etat des Connaissances et Perspectives de Recherche.* Senegal: Union for African Population Studies, 83–99.

Hugo, G. (1991): Changing Famine Coping Strategies under the Impact of Population Pressure and Urbanization: the Case of Population Mobility. In: H.G.Bohle et al. (eds.): *Famine and Food Security in Africa and Asia. Indigenous Response and External Intervention to Avoid Hunger. Bayreuther Geowiss. Arb.*, Vol. 15.

Hyden, Goran (1980): *Beyond Ujamaa in Tanzania. Underdevelopment and an Uncaptured Peasantry* Berkeley and Los Angeles: University of California Press.

Meillassoux, Claude (1973): The Social Organisation of Peasantry. The Economic Basis of Kinship. In: *The Journal of Peasant Studies* 1(1), 81–90.

Meillassoux, Claude (1976): *Die wilden Früchte der Frau. Über häusliche Produktion und kapitalistische Wirtschaft.* Frankfurt/ Main, Suhrkamp.

Oppong, C. (1981): *Middle Class African Marriage. A Family Study of Ghanaian Senior Civil Servants.* London: George Allen and Unwin.

Rottenburg, R. (2009): *Far-fetched Facts. A Parable of Development Aid*. Cambridge, MA: MIT Press.

Seibel, H.D. (1967): Struktureller und funktionaler Wandel der Familie in Afrika. In: *Afrika heute* 5(67), 1–8.

Seibel, H.R. (1969): *Die Afrikanerin in Beruf und Familie. Eine Untersuchung bei nigerianischen Industriearbeiterinnen*. Freiburg: Arnold-Bergstraesser-Institut.

Stolpe, Ines (2008): *Schule versus Nomadismus? Interdependenzen von Bildung und Migration in der modernen Mongolei*. Frankfurt am Main: Peter Lang.

Thelen, Tatjana and Haldis Haukanes (2010): Parenthood and Childhood. Debates within the Social Sciences. In: Tatjana Thelen and Haldis Haukanes (eds.): *Parenting After the Century of the Child. Travelling Ideals, Institutional Negotiations and Individual Responses*. Aldershot: Ashgate, 11–32.

Children's Work, Child Fostering and the Spread of Formal Schooling in Northern Benin

Jeannett Martin

Children's work and the practice of child fostering are two important facets of Fée culture, an ethnic group mainly consisting of peasants in Northern Benin. Work, mainly centred on peasant and household work, is seen as an integral part of children's lives, of their education and their way to adulthood. Fostering is regarded as an important feature of Fée kinship life and as a means of educating children in an appropriate manner.

In this chapter, I address the question of how children's work and the practice of child fostering are interrelated in this peasant society against the background of the massive spread of schooling which has taken place in Northern Benin since the beginning of the 1990s. In using quantitative and qualitative data from my research on child fostering in the rural settlement area of the Fée, my contribution aims to show the complex and ambiguous ways in which these aspects of children's lives—work, fostering and schooling—are interwoven. I will argue that schooling and the idea of a 'schooling childhood' gave rise to growing negotiations around children's work within rural households and that those negotiations today go along with frequent tensions and conflicts between those children who bear the bulk of the work.[1]

---

[1] My descriptions are based on empirical data which I collected in 2005, 2006 and 2010 (altogether 7 months) in the context of two DFG-financed research projects: 'Social parenthood on West Africa' directed by Professor Erdmute Alber and 'Child fosterage in the context of ethnic heterogeneity, Borgu (Republic of Benin)'. I am grateful to the *Deutsche Forschungsgemeinschaft* (DFG) and to Bayreuth University for their financial support for these projects and to Erdmute Alber who has awakened my interest in the research theme of child fostering, and for the numerous discussions with her.

When I talk about 'children', I am referring to local conceptions of childhood in Fée society where marriage and having children are seen as important steps on the way to adulthood, especially in the case of girls.[2] Thus, I designate unmarried girls and boys who do not yet have their own children, even if they are older than 18 years of age, also as children. 'Child fostering', as used in this article, refers to the social practice where children grow up with non-biological ('social') parents such as aunts, uncles, grand-parents or non-kin. This practice is widespread and particularly well documented for West African societies (see e.g. Bledsoe and Isingo-Abanike 1989; Goody 1982; Lallemand 1994; Meier 1993; Alber 2003, 2004).

In the following section I examine how social scientists have so far tackled the question of the interrelation between children's work, child fostering and modern schooling using examples mostly from African societies.

An ambiguous case: the interrelations between children's work, child fosterage and schooling

The outcomes of research into the interrelations of these three aspects of life in different contexts are neither consistent nor unequivocal. Esther Goody, in her influential 'Kpembe study' (Northern Ghana), systematically compares fostered children to children growing up with biological parents in terms of what is demanded of them and how they behave in regard to those demands. In a region and in a historical period where school attendance only played a role for a small minority of children, Goody came to the conclusion that no differences exist between the groups (Goody 1982: 55, 61ff.). Likewise, Mary Moran in her study on women in Liberia emphasizes the obligation of all children to work in the household. She denies differences in the workload and treatment of

---

[2]   The death of one's father, especially in the case of boys, is seen as a further step on the way to adulthood.

children living with foster parents and those living with biological parents (Moran 1990: 66; Moran 1992: 107). However, these results have been contested by other studies. Albert Schrauwers, using a neo-Marxist approach, points to the 'slavelike exploitation' of kin related children as cheap labour in households of related peasants in Central Sulawesi (Schrauwers 1999: 314). He sees the phenomenon as being rooted in the larger capitalist economy and related to economic and social changes within the region. In contrast, Erdmute Alber in her socio-historical study on kinship fostering in Northern Benin underlines the flexible character of this practice providing numerous village children access to education in urban centres (Alber 2010). Concerning the treatment of biological and fostered children Alber remains ambiguous: on the one hand she sees 'a tendency to send foster children to the fields and biological children to school'. On the other hand she points to the Baatombu's 'inclination to act conform with village norms... whereby parents are obliged to treat their children equally...' (ibd.: 72).

Against the background of a general shift towards more child oriented research in social sciences and the growing influence of debates on children's rights since the 1990s, the children's perspective and their well-being has become more prominent as a research focus in social science work. Thus, Ursula Atto, in her study on pupils living with foster parents in Abidjan, asks for the children's experience and their attitudes with regard to their work (Atto 1996a, 1996b). Her research shows that foster children have a high degree of awareness of their living and working situations. Here, the children themselves identified several different factors shaping their lives as foster children: the importance of the reasons for the foster arrangement and of the type of kin relations with the foster parent; the composition of the household and the notions of a gender-specific work division. Thus, where further (foster) children or a domestic aid lived in the foster parent's household, children were found to work less than where this was not the case. Some children found that biological daughters are more engaged with household chores than fostered boys living in the same household (1996a: 238f.).

Within the last decade, several studies have been undertaken in different African countries and settings, using different research methods in order to examine the impact of child fostering on children's workload and schooling. The results of these studies are often inconsistent. Certain studies suggest e.g. that fostered children are less likely to attend school (e.g. Ainsworth 1992). Others did not find any significant impact of fostering on school attendance (Gage 2005, with the exception of girls of secondary school age, Zimmermann 2003, Hampshire et al. forthcoming), while others found that fostered children are more likely to attend school than non-fostered children (Akresh 2004). Sometimes then, the results even appear to be contradictory. In a study on child fostering in Northern Ghana, where foster children as well as their foster carers were asked by staff of a local NGO, most children expressed satisfaction with their living situation in foster care despite experiences of intimidation, physical and emotional abuse (Kuyini et al. 2009: 440). The results of a large-scale comparative study in three African countries (Ghana, Malawi and South Africa) where quantitative (a questionnaire) as well as qualitative methods (personal interviews) were used, led to partly opposing results: while the survey clearly suggests that the status of children as fostered has no significant impact on schooling and on children's workloads, the interviews with fostered children gave a broadly different picture. From their perspective, fosterage appears to be a condition that often has a negative impact on their work loads and also on schooling (Hampshire et al. forthcoming).

With a focus on women as care-givers, Heidi Verhoef and Gilda Morelli (2007) suggest that the time budgets that foster children in an urban context in Northern Cameroon use for work, learning and playing depend on the lived relationship between foster mother and biological mother. Thus, if the relationship between these women is close, cooperative and warm, fostered children and biological children are likely to spend about the same time working, studying and playing. In contrast, if this relationship is shaped by distance and conflicts, foster children are likely to spend more time with work than the biological children of the foster mother (2007: 52f).

In my contribution I apply two different approaches and data sets. Firstly, I present qualitative and quantitative data with the aim of describing some general patterns in Fée society with regard to children's work, child fostering and schooling and to their interrelations.[3] Secondly, I apply an action oriented approach, focussing more on social actors' strategies and negotiations in everyday life. In using a case study of a female-headed household in a Fée village, I illustrate how children's work is negotiated in everyday life between the eldest girls in this household.[4] Finally, I discuss these results and draw some conclusions.

Children's work, child fostering and schooling in rural Fée society

The vast majority of children in the settlement area of the Fée, which is situated in the north eastern part of the Republic of Benin and comprises about 30 villages, grow up in peasant households which are built on social relations of agnatic kinship and alliance. Economically, these households depend—exclusively or principally—on *ice iko* (Feri; *ice* meaning 'work', *iko* means 'field').[5] As do other peasant societies, the Fée have a pronounced work ethic, whereby

[3] The quantitative data result from 3 surveys which I have conducted in Fée villages in 2006. They comprise of (1) a survey of 180 Fée households in the villages Fouet, Tui and Tia (henceforth referred to as 'household survey'), (2) a survey of 183 standardized interviews with men and women older than 50 years living in these three villages (henceforth referred to as the 'individual survey') and (3) data from a survey on 287 pupils of the primary and first cycle secondary school in the village Angaradebou ('school children survey').

[4] These descriptions are mainly based on data from participant observation, semi-structured interviews and everyday conversations with household members in 2006 and 2010.

[5] Peasants cultivate mostly corn, sorghum and millet for subsistence, supplemented by groundnuts, beans and vegetables. Cotton is the most important cash crop.

much importance is attached to the education of children. Obedience (*ide kuje* or *kudasi*), patience (*suuru*) and endurance (*adidi*) are values that are seen as important for further success in life and are taught to children from an early age onwards.

From an age of about 3 or 4, children are progressively given tasks according to their age and individual capacity that increasingly correspond to the local notions of a gender specific work division. As women are mainly engaged in household work (*ice icu awuu*) and in petty trading (*sia*), girls' work mainly centres on these chores. Since the 1970s when Fée women started cultivating their own fields, girls have also been given field chores. However, boys usually start working with their (biological or foster) fathers and/or elder 'brothers' on their fields and assist them with other tasks like menial jobs in house construction or manufacturing fences. As presently many peasants own plough oxen, the task of cattle herding is assigned mostly to boys and sometimes to girls. They usually start accompanying an elder 'brother', but over the years they gradually take over the responsibility for this task, later they also often initiate younger boys. From the age of about twelve years, boys are usually given their own small field where they start cultivating on their own responsibility and account. At least until they are married, they spend most of their labour on the fields and under the authority of their (biological or foster) father.

As a result of the introduction of state and communal institutions such as schools and health stations, there is also some waged labour (*ice batue*) in the villages.[6] Presently, the majority of men and most women in the villages adhere to Islam, while syncretistic forms of Islamic and pre-Islamic world views are widespread. Thus, many women and some men regularly worship fetishes or spirits (Feri: *inò iko*) and are partly initiated in the art of calling on and communi-

---

[6] Due to the late implementation of area-wide primary schooling in the region, the Fée are only gradually entering waged labour. In the communal health centres, some of the personal are locals. However, most civil servant school teachers are not from the region, and often originate from the southern part of the country.

cating with them (Halene 1999: 64, 71ff.). Although in some Fée villages, there are considerable numbers of Christians due to the activities of missionaries.

Child fostering is seen as a characteristic of Fée kinship life and is frequently practised. According to my 'individual survey', 59.6 per cent of the interviewed persons aged over 50 (n=182) assumed they were brought up as children by people other than their biological parents. The 'household survey' confirmed that child fostering is frequently practised until the present day: in 30.0 per cent of the households (n=180) at least one child was fostered.

However, the practice and its underlying norms are changing. New foster arrangements appear and the number of children being fostered in the 'traditional' sense is declining in Northern Benin (Alber 2010; Martin 2007; Alber et al. 2010: 46–52). In the Fée villages, this decline is gender specific: it is less pronounced in the case of girls than in the case of boys. Thus, women in the different stages of their reproductive lives continue to show interest in fostering children from their brothers, daughters or other relatives. This continuing or even rising interest among Fée women can also be seen in relation with a rising need for labour (Martin 2007: 227).

As among the neighbouring Baatombu (Alber 2003, 2004), the practice of kinship fostering in Fée villages is based upon local norms of a 'proper' childhood and 'proper' relations between children and parents, as well as upon ideas of 'proper' relations between kin related adults. One element of these norms in Fée society is the idea that siblings of the biological parents have rights regarding their younger brother's or to their sister's children. In the same way it is said that women and men have rights to the children of the children they have raised. Biological parents, however, and in particular biological mothers, are said to share comparatively few rights over the child they gave birth to. This points to the importance of age and gender related power relations in Fée kinship relations. It is also part of these notions that a relative's request for a child should not be refused and that giving a child to a foster parent would not harm the child or its development. On the contrary, growing up with other than the biological parents is usually seen as conducive to, possibly even necessary for, the successful education of a child (Alber et al. 2010: 46). However, from the perspective of children, fostering appears to be an ambiguous experience, which is—among other factors—related to kinship structures. Thus, Fée children who grew or grow up with a parent from the father's side and father's generation (that is, with a paternal uncle) more often describe foster experiences shaped by conflicts, frustration and attempts to run away from the foster parent's household than children who grew or grow up with a maternal aunt or uncle (Martin accepted 2011a). Although many children are fostered at an age where they have no say in the decision, later on they may develop a considerable amount of agency and they use kinship relations strategically in order to realise their personal aims (Martin accepted 2011b).

Schooling

For a long time, only very few Fée children were associated with formal schooling. The first school within the settlement area of the Fée opened in 1910 in Kandi, a small town which since 1899 had been *chef-lieu* of the colonial administrative department *Cercle du Moyen-Niger* (Colonie du Dahomey et Dépendances 1910: 10; Colonie du Dahomey et Cercle du Moyen Niger: 13). The small number of school children in this region for the most part of the 20th century is reflected in the results of the 'individual survey': out of the interviewed persons aged over 50 years (n=183), 90 per cent of them, (95 per cent of the 89 women and 85 per cent of the 94 men), had no formal school education. Nevertheless, against the background of different educational policies of different governments and international actors, school enrolment rates have changed profoundly in Benin (see Asiwaju 1975; Künzler 2007; Bierschenk 2007; Fichtner 2009). This is also true for the northern part of the country, including the settlement area of the Fée. Today, there are primary schools in almost all Fée villages and school attendance has become a reality for more children than ever before, although by far not for all. The household survey shows that 32 per cent of the children aged between 6 and 18 in these households (n=514) attended 'French' school. The household survey as well as the school children survey confirms a general pattern in Benin according to which girls are more rarely sent to school than boys, and girls often drop out earlier from school than boys. This tendency also proves to be true for gender specific school enrolment rates in Angaradebou, the village where the ethnographic case study was undertaken. Angaradebou has a primary school (founded in 1958) which was split up in 2004 into 'Group A' and 'Group B', due to the growing number of pupils. In 2006, the school comprised 548 pupils, 55 per cent of whom were boys and 45 per cent girls. The village also has a first stage secondary school (*Collège d'enseignement général* [CEG], founded in 2002) and a Koran school which I do not further regard here. The CEG had 383 pupils in 2006 (63 per cent boys to 37 per cent girls) who were taught in 3 classes of grade '*Sixième*', two classes of grade '*Cinquième*', one class of grade '*Quatrième*' and one class of grade '*Troisième*'.[7] The gender ratio in the classes of the lowest grade (grade 6 with 192 pupils) was 58 per cent boys to 42 per cent girls. In classes of the highest grade (grade 3 with 29 pupils) it was 17 per cent girls to 83 per cent boys.[8]

---

[7] In the French educational system the *Collège* comprises the first four years of secondary education. This is followed by the *Lycée* (high school) which comprises three grades: '*Seconde*', '*Première*' and '*Terminale*'. The successful completion of secondary studies leads to the *baccalauréat*.

[8] These figures were given to me by Ali Yarou Mohammed, school director of the primary school group B, on February 15, 2006 and by the director of the CEG Angaradebou in March 2006. However, in the northern department of Alibori there may be considerable differences between villages and school districts which are sometimes opposed to the image of the Muslim north with low enrolment rates, especially for girls (Künzler 2007: 165).

Schooling and child fostering

While in Angaradebou the relation between gender and schooling is quite obvious, at least for secondary school, the relation between fostering and schooling appears to be less clear. The household survey shows that out of all recorded children aged between 6 and 18 (n=514), 15 per cent lived with foster parents, while 85 per cent were staying with one or both biological parents. 29 per cent out of the 79 fostered children attended school. This figure is slightly less than the 33 per cent of those who lived with their biological parents. Nevertheless, among the foster children who attended school, there may also have been cases where schooling was the main purpose for fostering. This can be concluded from the results of the survey which I conducted among school children in Angaradebou.[9] 31 per cent of the interviewed pupils lived with a kin related or non-kin foster parent during the school year. Among them, 52 stayed with the foster parent during holidays as well. Thus, we can conclude that it is likely that 13 per cent of all children were fostered for educational reasons, while 18 per cent were fostered for other reasons, although they are nevertheless sent to school (appendix, table 2 and 3). These figures suggest that educational fostering does also exist in villages and they point to the flexible character of child fostering in view of modern needs (Alber 2010: 76).

Schooling and work

My survey data further suggest that working besides school is a general pattern among school children in Angaradebou. The vast majority of pupils (94 per cent) combine schooling with work in the

---

[9] I distributed a questionnaire in the primary school (class of *CM2*) and in the secondary school (classes of *6ième, 5ième, 4ième, 3ième*). Thus, 287 school children aged between 10 to 23 were asked e.g., with whom they stay during the school year and during holidays, whether, when and with whom they work on the fields or in the households they live, which chores they do on a regular basis and the time they usually get up in the morning.

fields. Most pupils help on their parents' or other relatives' fields with ploughing, sowing, weeding, harvesting; many with clearing the fields, and other farm related work. Besides, almost all pupils stated they conduct household chores on a regular basis before or/and after class times such as sweeping, preparing meals, doing the dishes, carrying water, collecting firewood, doing the laundry, running errands, selling goods and other chores such as taking care of toddlers and babies (appendix: table 5, 6, 7).[10]

The cultural notions of a gender specific distribution of work also apply in the case of school children. Much higher percentages of girls than of boys indicated that they do 'women's work' such as carrying water, doing laundry, doing dishes, cleaning bowls, preparing meals and collecting firewood. In contrast, higher percentages of boys than of girls indicated that they do field work such as ploughing, cattle herding, and cleaning the fields. Nevertheless, some field chores are taken on by comparable percentages of girls and boys: sowing, weeding and harvesting (appendix: table 4).[11]

I did not gather further statistical data, e.g. on when or to what extent the interviewed pupils carried out their work. Their answers to the question 'When do you usually get up in the morning?' at least provide a hint: almost 40 per cent stated they usually get up between 2 and 5 am, almost half of them between 5 am and 6 am and only about one-tenth usually gets up after 6 am (appendix: table 8). Here

---

[10] Work tasks in the fields have to be accomplished during the respective season. Many household chores have to be done on a daily basis while others, such as collecting firewood or doing the laundry, are done periodically. When I asked the children, which of the mentioned work they do 'on a regular basis', this formulation refers to the respective work and periods, in which they have to be done.

[11] As my research focus was more on the question of child fostering and not on children's work, I did not systematically follow the question, which out of these different actions are regarded by whom as ice (work). In the context of this article, I regard all of these human actions as meaningful and therefore as work.

again, gender specific patterns become apparent (see appendix: table 9).[12]

Does children's work have a negative impact on school performance? I did not make systematic enquiries in this direction. Therefore my assertions on this may only be tentative. My data confirm the results of other studies (Atto 1996a, b; Verhoef and Morelli 2007: 53) that children do not view working *per se* as something negative. Many Fée children are quite conscious about their work and they often do it without resentment and more or less enthusiastically. I have scattered references on children, also school children, who felt overwhelmed by the work load which had been assigned to them. I met a boy who left his foster parent because he felt that the workload was too much and was affecting his school performance negatively. Some of the school teachers with whom I spoke declared their conviction that some children's school performance is negatively influenced by the work assigned to them. This becomes obvious especially at the height of the growing season, in May and in September, when all available labour is needed. Then, many children arrive late to school or do not go at all for weeks; this has led some children to drop out of school because they were unable to catch up on the syllabus. Besides, girls' school performances are more likely to be negatively affected by their workloads than the school performance of boys.

I now come to a case study which shows how work is negotiated in everyday life by children who live together in one household. The protagonists of this case study are Samsia, Mujiba, Halimatou and Umhailu, the eldest girls in Djobiti's household.

---

[12] When I conducted the survey in 2006, watches were hardly used in the villages. Therefore, such information is rather difficult to confirm.

Djobiti's daughters negotiating work

Djobiti's compound is situated on the fringe of Angaradebou. In 2006, Djobiti was 56 years old. She had built her compound some years before, with the support of her younger brother Baye. The relationship between Djobiti and Baye is close and supportive: years ago, Djobiti, with the consent of her husband, had left two of her sons to Baye, who at this point had no sons of his own to work with him. Baye provides reciprocal support to Djobiti when she needs help. Djobiti's husband, with whom she had eleven children, lived until his death in 2007 in his paternal compound with two other wives and their children. When I lived in Djobiti's compound in 2006, it comprised of twelve persons, ten of them related by kinship ties: besides herself, five foster children (four girls and one boy between 3 and 18 years) and four of her biological children (three girls and one boy between 8 and 15 years) worked, slept and ate here together. Additionally, a school teacher together with his 12-year-old son lived in a separate building on the compound. From at least the time that her husband fell sick in 2005, Djobiti has been solely responsible for her own and her children's needs. In 2005, with the support of her children, she cultivated 3 ha of cotton, 2 ha of maize, 1 ha of millet and 1.5 ha of groundnuts.

Samsia (17) was fostered by Djobiti from her parents when she was 4 years old. Djobiti had already fostered Samsia's father when he was a child, and he did not hesitate to leave her his first daughter, when Djobiti asked him for Samsia. Mujiba (15), however, is one of Djobiti's biological daughters. Of the four eldest girls in the household, she was the only one who went to school. The third girl, Halimatou (18), is the daughter of Djobiti's younger brother Baye. When Halimatou's biological mother separated from Baye, her paternal grandmother took her. After her grandmother died, it was Djobiti, her paternal aunt, who took care of her. Although Halimatou was the eldest of the four, she was the quietest and most reserved girl among Djobiti's daughters. The youngest of the four girls was Umhailu (14). She was fostered at the age of three by Djobiti, after Djobiti asked Umhailu's father, her cousin, if she could take her. After Umhailu's mother delivered the next child, Djobiti went to her cousin's compound and took the girl with her.

In 2006, the main burden of household chores fell on the shoulders of the four eldest daughters. They were responsible for all the physically heavy chores, notably drawing and carrying water from the well several times a day, and processing and preparing crops. The girls had to do the laundry; they washed the dishes for everyone and took care of the small children in the morning. They were sometimes supported by the younger children in chores such as sweeping the compound and house twice a day, carrying the babies of visitors or bringing the corn to the mill. When I asked Samsia about the distribution of household chores among the four girls, she explained to me that each of them had to go to the well three times each morning. After carrying the water, they were responsible for preparing breakfast and for washing the small children. During the dry season, all the household members collected firewood on Saturdays, a task that took about half the day. Once in a while the eldest girls produced shea nut butter or peanut cakes and oil which they sold later in the market.

During the rainy season, usually occurring between the beginning of May and the end of October, the children generally worked in Djobiti's fields, which are half an hour's walk from the compound. This period of the rainy season, the most intensive work period when 'there is no rest', as Mujiba put it, is filled with farm-related work, from cleaning the fields, sowing and weeding to harvesting. Only if there is heavy rain or somebody is sick would Djobiti allow them to be absent. This is when Samsia, Umhailu and Halimatou go to the fields every day, together with the other children who do not attend school. During this period Djobiti usually gets up at 6 am and prepares lunch, mostly Akassa, a maize porridge that the girls would carry in huge bowls to the fields, together with a sauce in smaller bowls. The four eldest girls are expected to be the first to get up in the morning after Djobiti, in order to carry water from the wells so that breakfast can be prepared and so that all the household members can have a shower. During the rainy season, the girls usually leave the compound at 9 am and return around 6 pm. The other schoolchildren in the compound, accompany their mother and the others to the fields on Wednesday afternoons, when there is no school, as well as on weekends and during holidays, as Mujiba explained to me. After returning from the fields, one of the four girls was always responsible for the preparation and distribution of the porridge for two days, whereas Djobiti prepared the sauce. After the meal, the same girl was also responsible for washing the dishes and bowls.

On one such day, Mujiba came home late from school, at 7 pm. It was her turn to prepare the meal and she first had to go to the mill to get the corn ground. After her return she started making the fire and then prepared the porridge for all. The other girls did not assist her in any way, although at this time they had nothing to do. After the meal, Mujiba washed all the dishes and the huge bowls, again alone. This day, as on many other days, Mujiba only had time to do her homework and study for school after the meal, after dark at around 9 pm. She did her homework by the light of a gas lamp, trying to solve geometrical and arithmetical problems, trying to imagine life in a subpolar climatic zone, or writing an essay about the discovery of America. During my stay I observed that Mujiba often worked alone, while Samsia, Halimatou and Umhailu usually worked together and helped each other. This was even manifested symbolically in the location of the water casks: while Samsia's, Halimatou's and Umhailu's casks stood together in a central place in the compound and they always filled them together, Mujiba's cask stood somewhere apart and she only fetched water from her own cask, which she always filled alone. When I told her later about my observations, Mujiba answered that the other three girls 'never' helped her with anything.

In Djobiti's compound. Samsia (on the far right), Mujiba (third from right), Umhailu (on the far left) and some of Djobiti's other biological and fostered daughters preparing Akassa (Photo: J. Martin, 2006)

During my stay in the compound the girls quarrelled several times. One recurrent point of discussion was about drawing water from the well in the morning. There were days when Mujiba got up later than the other girls and then did not have enough time to draw water before leaving for school. When this was the case, Djobiti obliged her to catch up on her task during the lunch-break. But sometimes she only went twice instead of three times, and on a few days did not even go at all, as she had obligations at school. This regularly raised Samsia's ire. She complained to the others about the 'lazy' schoolgirl and on those days there was a deafening silence between the two. Samsia, Halimatou and Umhailu also quarrelled with Mujiba about her contribution to the work in the fields. Sometimes Mujiba had lessons between 8 and 10 am and in the late afternoon between 5 and 9 pm. Samsia asked Mujiba to join them in the fields after morning classes. The latter refused to do this, arguing that this was the only time she had to study for school. Djobiti supported her daughter and released her from work that day, but on other days she obliged her to join the others on the farm.

On a few occasions I realised that the role of a schoolgirl gave Mujiba not only a cause for quarrel and tension, but sometimes also a pretext in order to avoid unpleasant work. One day she told me in secret that she had successfully avoided grinding shea nuts, a job she does not like because it blisters the skin. She had told Samsia and the other girls that she had classes although this was not true. Sometimes she thus profited from the other girls' lack of knowledge about her class schedule.

In spite of such disputes amongst them, Samsia, Umhailu and Halimatou by and large felt well in Djobiti's household, according to their own appraisals. They saw Djobiti as the mother they felt most attached to, and saw no reason to seek contact with their biological mothers. None of the girls doubted that one day Djobiti would fulfil her obligation as a mother and release each girl into marriage with an appropriate dowry. Although Umhailu would also have loved to go to school, she did not feel unlucky in Djobiti's house—because Djobiti did not beat her very often and she did not suffer from hunger. The schoolgirl Mujiba, in contrast, complained about her nutritional situation. She explained to me that she was so thin because she attended school, where she often had nothing to eat between 7 am and midday, and in the afternoons. In the 2006/07 school year, four people contributed in order to enable Mujiba to attend school. Her father paid the school fees. Her elder married sister Zaratou paid for her schoolbooks. She received the money for exercise books and pens from her maternal uncle Baye, and the school uniform from her mother. She usually received 50 FCFA from her father each morning for breakfast at school. Since he had fallen sick, she had avoided asking him for money. Since then she had only occasionally received the money for breakfast from her mother. According to Mujiba's perception, Samsia, Umhailu und Halimatou had more regular access to food and they would eat 'up to eight times a day'. She also let me know that she looked forward to Samsia's marriage. When Samsia left the household for her husband's home, Mujiba would take over the household's cash supply during the periods of Djobiti's absence and then there would be 'enough food for everybody. Samsia is always so penny-pinching'.

The head of the household, Djobiti, was vigilant about avoiding giving the impression that she favoured her biological children. Therefore she had given a small field to all the four eldest girls where they had the right to work on their own account each Friday. In some cases she even seemed to privilege the foster girls. Thus, the three foster girls were usually the first to get their present on the Islamic holiday of Ramadan. Samsia had some additional income opportunities when Djobiti left her some of the peanut cakes which they had produced together. And it was also to Samsia, not to Mujiba, that she handed over important responsibilities, such as managing the financial resources she left for the children, and preparing the sauce, in periods when she was absent. Those acts can be interpreted as a sign of Djobiti's appreciation of Samsia and her work, but also as a strategy to avoid conflicts between her fostered and biological daughters.

At the end of my stay in 2006 Mujiba was preparing for the *Brevet d'études du premier cycle* (BEPC), an exam that if she passed, would permit her to continue to the second stage of secondary school. She dreamt of leaving Angaradebou and living in a city. 'Always the same village, always the same work. Even Kandi would be better!'

In May 2010, I lived again in Djobiti's compound and met Mujiba the day that Halimatou married. Mujiba, now 19, was then living in Kandi as a foster girl in a relative's household. Four years before she had failed the BEPC, but passed the following year. In her foster father's household, who is her paternal uncle as well as a maternal cousin, she worked under his wife's authority and shared the household chores with two other school foster girls. From Monday to Friday she attended the first year of high school ('*Seconde*') and during weekends she often helped her foster father's wife to manufacture cheese or groundnut cakes for sale.

Although living in Kandi, Mujiba continued to contribute to her biological mother's household economy. During her last holidays she spent three months in Angaradebou where she worked on the fields of a state agency and gained some money which entered her mother's household economy.

> M: My mother invested my salary for the first and second month in her fields. During the third month I gained 26,000 FCFA [about €40]. When our cotton became infested by caterpillars, I bought insecticides for 11,000 FCFA and treated the plants. From the remaining 15,000 my mother took 10,000 FCFA for my school fees. With the remaining 5,000 I spent 2,000 FCFA on transport to and from Kandi, when I had to go to pay the school fees and for coming here for Halimatou's marriage. I bought a pair of new shoes for 700 FCFA and soap for 300. With the remaining 2,000 I have lived three weeks now and I still have 100 FCFA with me.

As Mujiba did not have time this year to cultivate her own field in Angaradebou she was depending on the support of her relatives. Intermittently, she got some additional money from her elder sisters, her maternal uncle Baye and from her mother.

But how were Djobiti's three other daughters living in 2010? Samsia, together with her first child, a two-year-old boy, lived in her husband's compound elsewhere in the village. According to her own appraisal she felt happy there, although the workload with a baby and no co-wife or foster girl was heavy. Therefore, she was thinking about asking one of her brothers for a girl. Umhailu still lived with Djobiti, with a three-month-old baby. A few days after my arrival she married the father of her child and she was preparing for the move into his parents' compound. Only a few weeks later, Halimatou also married. After the ceremonies, where she received a large trousseau in compensation for her work, she was brought to her husband's compound and from then on worked for him and his relatives.

Since the eldest of Djobiti's daughters had left or were about to leave, Djobiti had to redistribute the household chores. From then on, the main burden fell on the shoulders of Djobiti's now 15-year-old twin girls Assana and Kusseina. They got up at 5 am and carried four lots of water from the water pump (which had been constructed in the meantime) together with Umhailu. After this, they prepared breakfast together with Djobiti, before going to school at 7 am. Also, during lunch break and after classes, the twins were now the ones responsible for the bulk of the work. Despite the heavy workload I never heard them complaining. They were well aware of the new household situation and seemed to accept their obligations. In order to get her fields tilled this year, Djobiti asked her brother Baye and her eldest married daughters, some of whom had also left children with Djobiti, for help. Baye, together with his foster sons (two of whom were born to Djobiti) helped her more than usual this year in ploughing the fields and other field work.

During my stays I became aware that tensions and conflicts around children's work between elder children who attend school and those who do not are quite common within households. Apart from the quarrels which I witnessed in Djobiti's household, there was another conflict which had rumbled on in the compound of Djobiti's brother Baye and which Djobiti's daughters discussed intensely. Djobiti's elder sister had lived in this compound with four fostered girls aged between 15 and 18 years, two of whom had come from a neighbouring village in order to attend secondary school in Angaradebou. Some weeks earlier the sister had died and since then the girls had lived alone. That evening I wrote the following summary of the discussions in my research diary:

Since Djobiti's sister died, the girls... are alone responsible for all household chores... Together they have to prepare [food], they have to carry water and to run the household. The problem is now that the only girl that does not attend school fetches the water for all four, she prepares *la bouille* [a soup eaten as breakfast] in the morning, she prepares lunch and after this she accompanies one of the married women in Baye's compound to help in her fields. After working in the fields she prepares dinner for all the girls in the evening. Today, this girl complained bitterly that the other three do not support her adequately. Even during lunch breaks and if they are free of school obligations they do not help her. [...] The four girls quarrelled until the married woman for whom the girl works in the fields intervened. This woman did not agree with the three schoolgirls. She argued that she herself had fostered a girl who was attending school. However, that girl would do her household chores; she would get up at 5 am every morning in order to carry water and to prepare *la bouille* before going to school (Research diary, Angaradebou, 25.2.2006).

Discussion and conclusion

What can be drawn from this material on the relation between child fostering, children's work and schooling in Fée society?

In the first part of this chapter I mentioned studies on the impact of fostering on children's schooling and work load in different African settings and their partly inconsistent results. Some studies suggest that there is a negative correlation between fostering on schooling, others see a positive correlation and yet others see no correlation at all.

My data suggest a more complicated situation. Firstly, working and schooling in the Fée villages are not exclusive, but related to each other. Virtually all children, whether fostered or not, are integrated into the household economy over long periods and often to a considerable amount. At the same time, today, more village children than ever before attend school. Therefore, a sheer schooling childhood with children's lives commuting between learning and playing does not exist in this peasant society.

Secondly, there are differences in children's workloads. These appear according to gender, age and the respective household composition, but they may also appear according to the question of whether a child is sent to school or not and whether a child is fostered or not. Thus, children who are not enrolled, of course, accomplish more work than pupils who work after classes, on weekends and during holidays.

Thirdly, fostering can promote working as it can promote schooling. Some children are given to relatives, sometimes to contribute to the foster parent's household economy. Others are sent to relatives for the main purpose of schooling, while they also contribute to the household economy of the foster parent. Therefore, it might be misleading or even inappropriate to search for correlations between fostering and schooling or children's workloads without taking the reasons and circumstances behind foster arrangements into consideration.

Child fostering, children's work, and the question of whether a child is sent to school are deeply embedded in kinship dynamics and long-term kinship politics. Djobiti took care of her brother's daughter Halimatou, after the child's mother had left, and profits from Halimatou's work in her household. She furthermore left two of her own sons to her brother when he needed labour. Reciprocally, the brother helped Djobiti to construct her own compound and he contributes financially to allow several of Djobiti's younger children to attend school. Such reciprocal exchange relations, which are based on trust between kin related adults and which may also include the exchange of children, remain of pre-eminence for Fée peasants up to the present day. Therefore, children's living situations in terms of work and schooling are also affected by the relationship between biological and foster parent. In Fée society, the relationship between adult siblings in their social roles as biological parent and foster parent of a child (e.g., father and father's brother, mother and mother's brother) often plays a central role.

The case study exemplifies that the combination of children's schooling and work may lead to tensions and quarrels between children living together in one household. Samsia, Halimatou and Umhailu basically accepted the roles assigned to them and also seem to have equally accepted the imbalances in workloads due to the school attendance of Djobiti's younger biological children. Nevertheless, the recurrent quarrels and tensions between the girls point to the fact that this acceptance has its limits and that children also actively negotiate their workloads among themselves.

One does not necessarily need to apply Jens Qvortrup's notion of children's learning at school as a form of work (Qvortrup 2001) in order to recognize that in rural contexts as the one described above, school children, especially elder girls, have a hard task in order to combine work and successful schooling. Elder girls usually spend the bulk of their time with household chores and this is especially the case for school girls attending secondary school, a phase during which much time is needed for preparations and exercises. These girls often find themselves in the situation of competing demands, especially in households, where no or few other girls of a respective age live. My case study and figures of school attendance rates according to class and gender in one Fée village allude to this.

My results confirm those of most studies according to which fostering does not *per se* have a negative impact on foster children's workload and schooling. But a foster child's living situation and his or her representation of their situation may be influenced by a multitude of factors. In rural Fée society it is likely to make a difference for a boy's living situation in terms of work and schooling whether he was *claimed* by an father's elder brother who did not dispose of his own children of working age and so needed somebody to pasture his cattle and work with him on his fields; or whether the child was *sent* by his mother to stay with a maternal uncle with whom the mother shares a warm relationship and where the mother pays the child's school fees and sends a sack of corn once in a while. While these children share the fact that they are living under the authority of non-biological parents, their living situations might be very different. Here, as Verhoef and Morelli (2007: 52ff.) state, the reasons behind the fostering and their specific circumstances, the relationship between biological and foster parent, but also the child's will and aspirations may all play an important role.

Finally, I would like to come back to the inconsistencies in the results of studies which focus on the relation between fostering, children's work and schooling and reflect on my methodological conclusions. It could be argued that these inconsistencies may be induced by local differences, but to me they seem most often caused by the choice of research methods.

Some of these studies rely exclusively on statistical data on singular variables (foster status, school enrolment, age, wealth, household size etc.), and the authors search for correlations between these variables. They do this without looking into the circumstances and reasons behind people's decisions about fostering or decisions about schooling. Purely statistical analyses also hardly take into consideration cultural notions and norms, such as those concerning the belonging and raising of children.

Other studies apply purely qualitative research methods. They may better elucidate people's ways of acting and the reasons behind the way they act in a particular way. And they may identify factors that influence children's living situations in terms of work, schooling and fostering. But these studies often fail to offer information on the prevalence of certain phenomena and may thus sometimes appear somewhat arbitrary.

I argue the case for useful combinations and methodological triangulation in order to deepen our understanding of the relationship between fostering, children's work and schooling. Such combinations may help us to understand better, for example, parental decisions on children's work or schooling (see the contribution of Erdmute Alber in this volume), children's representations of their living situations or how they negotiate fostering arrangements, work and schooling, as well as the prevalence of certain phenomena.

The example of Djobiti's daughters elucidates that the practice of child fostering as such does not cause the conflicts around children's work. Conflicts arise against the background of the implementation and the massive spread of western schooling with its time consuming compulsory attendance, which is partly in opposition to parents' labour needs. Thus, school children—whether fostered or not—have to juggle between these competing needs and allegiances. In the context of an international and national educational policy that aims to send *all* children to school, more research is needed on the views of children in rural contexts and how they make these decisions, and so how they succeed or fail to juggle their lives between work and school.

Appendix

Table 1: Household survey (n=180)
Schooling of children living in the household (aged 6–18)

	Schooling		Overall
Children	**yes**	**no**	
aged 6 – 18	167	347	514

Table 2: Survey of Schoolchildren
Children's place of residence during school year

Living with	Absolute frequency	Percentage
biological parent(s)	198	69
other parent(s)	80	28
other person	9	3
Overall	**287**	**100**

Table 3: Survey of Schoolchildren
Children's place of residence during holidays

Living with	Absolute frequency	Percentage
biological parent(s)	235	82
other parent(s)	47	16
other person	5	2
Overall	**287**	**100**

Table 4: Survey of Schoolchildren
'Which of these field chores do you do on a regular basis?'

Field Chores	Boys (Percentage of boys)	Girls (Percentage of girls)	Overall (Percentage of all children)
Ploughing	157 (*89*)	23 (*21*)	180 (63)
Sowing	160 (*91*)	102 (*92*)	262 (91)
Weeding	159 (*90*)	95 (*86*)	254 (88)
Harvesting	158 (*90*)	85 (*77*)	243 (85)
Cattle herding	93 (*53*)	12 (*11*)	105 (37)
Cleaning fields	94 (*53*)	29 (*26*)	123 (43)
Other field work	63 (*36*)	23 (*21*)	86 (30)
Overall	**176**	**111**	**287**

Table 5: Survey of School children
'Do you do household chores on a regular basis?'

Household chores	Absolute frequency	Percentage
Yes	270	94
No	17	6
Overall	**287**	**100**

Table 6: Survey on School children
'Do you do household chores on a regular basis?' * Gender

Household chores	Boys (Percentage of boys)	Girls (Percentage of girls)	Overall
Yes	160 (*91*)	110 (*99*)	270
No	16 (*9*)	1 (*1*)	17
Overall	**176**	**111**	**287**

Table 7: Survey of School children
'Which of these household chores to you do on a regular basis?'
* Gender

Household chores	Boys (Percentage of boys)	Girls (Percentage of girls)	Overall (Percentage of all children)
Sweeping	100 (*57*)	104 (*94*)	204 (71)
Preparing morning meal	20 (*11*)	57 (*51*)	77 (27)
Preparing midday meal	50 (*28*)	82 (*74*)	132 (46)
Preparing evening meal	24 (*14*)	91 (*82*)	115 (40)
Doing dishes	62 (*35*)	101 (*91*)	163 (43)
Carrying water	116 (*66*)	109 (*98*)	225 (78)
Collecting firewood	65 (*37*)	95 (*86*)	160 (55)
Doing laundry	144 (*82*)	106 (*95*)	250 (87)
Running errands	68 (*39*)	92 (*83*)	160 (56)
Selling goods	57 (*32*)	77 (*69*)	134 (47)
Other chores	10 (*6*)	19 (*17*)	29 (10)
Overall	**176**	**111**	**287**

Table 8: Survey of School children
'When do you usually get up in the morning?'

Time	Absolute frequency (Percentage of all children)
until 5 am	112 (*40*)
until 6 am	138 (*49*)
until 7 am	33 (*11*)
Overall	283

Table 9: Survey of School children
'When do you usually get up in the morning?' * Gender

Gender	Time			
	until 5 am	until 6 am	until 7 am	Overall
Male	49	102	24	175
Female	63	36	9	108
Overall	112	138	33	283

References

Ainsworth, Martha (1992): *Economic Aspects of Child Fostering in Côte d'Ivoire*. World Bank: Washington, DC.

Akresh, Richard (2004): *Adjusting Household Structure. School Enrollment Impacts of Child Fostering in Burkina Faso.*, New Haven: Yale Economic Growth Center. Discussion Paper No. 897

Alber, Erdmute (2003): Großeltern als Pflegeeltern. Veränderungen der Pflegschaftsbeziehungen zwischen Großeltern und Enkeln bei den Baatombu in Nordbenin. In: *Anthropos* 98, 445–460.

Alber, Erdmute (2004): Denying Biological Parenthood. Fosterage in Northern Benin. In: *Ethnos* 68 (4), 487–506.

Alber, Erdmute (2010): No School without Foster Families in Northern Benin. A Social Historical Approach. In: H. Haukanes, and T. Thelen (eds.): *Parenting After the Century of the Child.*

Travelling Ideals, Institutional Negotiations and Individual Responses. Aldershot: Ashgate Publisher, 57–78

Alber, E., T. Häberlein, and J. Martin (2010): Changing Webs of Kinship. Spotlights on West Africa. In: *Africa Spectrum* 45 (3), 43–67.

Asiwaju, A.I (1975): The Colonial Education Heritage and the Problem of Nation-Building in Dahomey. In: *Bulletin de l'I.F.A.N* 37 (2), 340–357.

Atto, Ursula (1996a): Verpflichtung, Belastung, Freude. Pflegekinder und ihr Verständnis der Hausarbeit. In: K. Beck, and G. Spittler (eds.): *Arbeit in Afrika*. Berlin: Lit Verlag, 225–242.

Atto, Ursula (1996b): '*...et tout le reste pour les filles*'. *Zur Hausarbeit von Kindern in Abidjan, Côte d'Ivoire*. Bayreuth : Bayreuth African Studies Breitinger.

Bierschenk, Thomas (2007) : L'éducation de base en Afrique de l'Ouest francophone. Bien privé, bien public, bien global. In: T. Bierschenk, G. Blundo, Y. Jaffré and M.T. Alou (eds.): *Une anthropologie entre rigueur et engagement. Essais autour de l'oeuvre de Jean-Pierre Olivier de Sardan*, Paris : APAD-Karthala, 235–257.

Bledsoe, C. & Isiugo-Abanike, U. (1989): Strategies of Child-Fosterage among Mende Grannies in Sierra Leone. In: R.J. Lesthaeghe (ed.): *Reproduction and Social Organisation in Sub-Saharan Africa*. Berkeley: University of California Press, 442–474.

Colonie du Dahomey et Dépendances (1910): Cercle du Moyen-Niger, rapport mensuel, mois de Novembre. Poste de Kandy. Archives nationales du Bénin, Série 1 E 13/4 (3).

Colonie du Dahomey and Cercle du Moyen Niger (without date): Note pour servir de contribution à la monographie du cercle du Moyen-Niger et d'introduction aux notices sur les chefs. Archives Nationales du Bénin, Série 1E 13 (5).

Fichtner, Sarah (2009): A Playground for Education Reform or a Battlefield of Donor Intervention? Local Debates on Primary

Education and the New Study Programmes in Benin (revised version). In: *Working Papers of the Department of Anthropology and African Studies Johannes Gutenberg University Mainz* 95, 1–35.

Gage, Anastasia (2005): The Interrelationship between Fosterage, Schooling and Children's Labor Force Participation in Ghana. In: *Population Research and Policy Review* 24 (5), 431–466.

Goody, Esther, N. (1982): *Parenthood and Social Reproduction. Fostering and Occupational Roles in West Africa.* Cambridge: Cambridge University Press.

Halene, Inge (1999): *Heilkunde in Fouè. Begrenzt systematisierbares Wissen der Fee (Mokolle) im Borgou (Nordbénin).* Unpublished MA thesis, Fachbereich Philosophie und Sozialwissenschaften II der Freien Universität Berlin.

Hampshire, Kate et al. (forthcoming): Significant Lives? Understanding the Impacts of Fostering on Education and Children's Workloads in Ghana, Malawi and South Africa.

Künzler, Daniel (2007): *L'éducation pour quelques-uns? Enseignement et mobilité sociale en Afrique au temps de la privatisation, le cas du Bénin.* Paris: L'Harmattan.

Kuyini, A.B., A. Alhassan, I. Tollerud, H. Weld, and I. Haruna (2009): Traditional Kinship Foster Care in Northern Ghana. The Experiences and View of Children, Carers and Adults in Tamale. In: *Child & Family Social Work* 14 (2), 440–449.

Lallemand, Suzanne (1994). *Adoption et Marriage. Les Kotokoli du centre du Togo.* Paris: L'Harmattan.

Martin, Jeannett (2007): *Yakubas neues Leben. Zum Wandel der Kindspflegschaftspraxis bei den ländlichen Fée (Mokollé) in Nordbenin.* In: Afrika Spectrum 42 (2), 219–249.

Martin, Jeannett (accepted 2012a): Experiencing Father's Kin and Mother's Kin. Kinship Relations and Norms in the Lives of Foster Children in Northern Benin. In: E. Alber, J. Martin, and C. Notermans (eds.): *Child Fosterage in West Africa. New Perspectives on Theories and Practices.* Leiden: Brill.

Martin, Jeannett (accepted 2012b): Handlungsstrategien und Hand-
lungsmacht (agency) von Pflegekindern in Nord-Benin,
submitted to: *Sociologus. Zeitschrift für empirische Ethno-
soziologie und Ethnopsychologie.*

Meier, Barbara (1993): *Doglientiri. Frauengemeinschaften in westaf-
rikanischen Verwandtschaftssystemen, dargestellt am Beispiel
der Bulsa in Nordghana.* Berlin: Lit Verlag.

Moran, Mary H. (1990): *Civilized Women. Gender and Prestige in
Southeastern Liberia.* Ithaca, N.Y.: Cornell University Press.

Moran, Mary H. (1992): Civilized Servants. Child Fosterage and
Training for Status among the Glebo of Liberia. In: K.T.
Hansen (ed.): *African Encounters with Domesticity.* New
Brunswick: Rutgers University Press, 98–115.

Qvortrup, Jens (2001): School-Work, Paid-Work and the Changing
Obligations of Childhood. In: P. Mizen, C. Pole, and A. Bolton
(eds.): *Hidden Hands. International Perspectives on Children's
Work and Labour.* London: Routledge Falmer (Future of Childhood Series), 91–107.

Schrauwers, Albert (1999): Negotiating Parentage. The Political
Economy of 'Kinship' in Central Sulawesi, Indonesia. In:
American Ethnologist 26 (2), 310–323.

Verhoef, Heidi and Gina Morelli (2007): 'A Child Is a Child'.
Fostering Experiences in Northwestern Cameroon. In: *Ethos* 35
(1), 33–64.

Zimmerman, Frederick J. (2003): Cinderella Goes to School. The
Effects of Child Fostering on School Enrollment in South
Africa. In: *The Journal of Human Resources* 38 (3), 557–590.

Work and Play:
Economic restructuring and children's everyday learning in rural Sudan

Cindi Katz

'Development'—political-economic as much as child—is uneven, and situated in shifting social relations of production, reproduction, power, and privilege; in history and geography. In the political-economic sense, development is neither a staged teleology nor a process that can be simply imposed or encouraged by one part of the world or one sector of a social formation upon another. It is better conceptualized as the uneven motion of capital finding, producing, and reproducing places and people in particular and differentiated relation to specific strategies of accumulation. Development occurs at various scales, simultaneously making and unmaking places and modes of production and restructuring social relations of production and reproduction. The characteristic form of development in the second half of the twentieth century was between the 'first' and 'third worlds' or what has more recently been reframed as the global north and south. Rather than situating development solely in this particular frame and period, I think of it more generally as a form of economic restructuring, implying a broad shift from one production regime to another. Economic restructuring encompasses such processes as industrialization, deindustrialization, 'post-fordism', and neo-liberalization in addition to economic development and its various entailments.

As a social, cultural, and political-economic process, development is always an encounter. It and its purveyors—whether representatives of NGOs; political actors such as government representatives, missionaries, and bankers; or parents and other care providers—are met, engaged, and countered by historically situated social actors, whose own biographies, social histories, and geographies enable and call forth broad and differentiated material social practices which may embrace, rework, or be disrupted by the encounter (sometimes all three). In the course of these engagements new social relations and possibilities are created. Western economic development's signature form for the past few centuries has been capitalist. Its aspirations have been global even as it takes place at and through all scales from the body, household, and local through the regional, national, and transnational. All of the relations and processes that come into play in children's development and with regard to children's everyday practices of work, play, and learning are situated in this material social context, and are affected by it. This chapter focuses on one period of economic restructuring in a single place—a village in central eastern Sudan where I did research intermittently over 15 years between 1980 and 1995—to tease out some of its implications for children, households, and the village economy (Katz 2004). In this way I hope to understand better the place of children in development, and examine how development as such alters children's activities of work, play and learning along with their meaning and significance in time and space.

Agricultural development and children's everyday lives

The state-sponsored, multilaterally funded Suki Agricultural Development Project was established in 1971 in a 1600-square-kilometer area between the Blue Nile and Dinder Rivers in central eastern, Arabic speaking Sudan, enlisting 7 500 tenants to cultivate cotton and groundnuts in 100 per cent rotation on small (4.2 hectare) allotments. This project and what it represented in terms of the national and global economy were the driving forces of change in the long established riverside village of Howa[1] during the time of my research. Until it was incorporated in the project, Howa was charac-

---

[1] The name of the village and its residents has been changed to protect their privacy.

terized by a largely subsistence economy rooted in the rain-fed cultivation of sorghum and sesame, small-scale animal husbandry, and
forestry in open woodlands interspersed with the fields and grazing
areas around the village. The project made sweeping changes in the
local environment as over 1 000 hectares were cleared and graded to
enable the irrigated cultivation of cash crops for the world market on
250 farm tenancies adjacent to the village. It also altered land tenure
arrangements as a fixed number of tenancies were secured by most
but not all village households, while the number of households
continued to grow, putting newly formed households in an often
precarious position. The labour requirements of cultivating cotton
and groundnuts were higher than, and different from, those of
sorghum and sesame, and changed the gendered division of labour in
many village households while at the same time intensifying local
reliance on children's work.

The practical, environmental, and economic effects of the agricultural project singly and in concert led to increases in children's
labour time. From as early as seven years of age, boys and girls in
Howa worked in their families' fields, collected firewood, fetched
water, tended livestock, cared for younger siblings, ran errands, and
occasionally hawked items for sale in the village (see Table 1). This
assortment of tasks had long been characteristic of children's work in
the village, but as noted above, the requirements of irrigated cultivation in the project demanded significantly more labour than had
previous agricultural regimes. While project planners had assumed
that much of the work would be accomplished mechanically or with
hired help, the reality was that the available machinery was
frequently out of order, spare parts were unavailable, fuel was in
short supply, and in any event the costs of using machinery or hiring
outside help were outside the means of most tenants. The majority
relied on the participation of household members, most commonly
children, and during the cotton harvest women as well. At the same
time, inclusion in the agricultural project incorporated the village
more firmly and intricately in the cash economy, which also affected

the work children did and how much time they spent on it as families relied on their contributions—however small—to bolster household income. To earn money children and teens in Howa sold water, worked as agricultural labourers, and helped produce charcoal and other forms of fuel wood for sale, among other activities. Finally, the environmental shifts associated with the project, most notably the clearance of 1 050 hectares adjacent to the village from mixed land use to graded irrigated fields, put pressure on the remaining grazing and wooded areas nearby, and eventually increased the time and effort required to feed animals and procure a decent supply of fuel wood. These increases fell largely to children or young men.

Focusing on children's environmentally oriented work reveals these dynamics quite clearly. In agriculture, for instance, the work of children as young as nine or ten was critical in the time-consuming tasks of planting, and was called upon frequently during the four rounds of weeding required by the project administration, and during the labour-intensive harvest. Most children in the village—even those quite young—participated in seed preparation. Children and young teens roved among the tenant households in their extended families, shelling groundnuts as the planting season neared. In a cacophony of talking, shelling, munching, and minding younger siblings, groups of children sometimes worked for hours at a time, earning a few piasters for their efforts. In those households with more than a handful of small animals (about 30 per cent of all village households in the initial years of my research), the tasks of herding were largely the province of their sons, who commonly began shepherding by nine or ten years of age. Shepherds worked pretty much from sunrise to sunset day after day the whole year round, although in April and May, the hottest, driest parts of the year when pasturage was at its worst, many were relieved by brothers or other male relatives at some point in the day to protect them from excessive exposure to the harsh conditions when temperatures routinely exceeded 40°C. While conditions became more difficult in the wake of the agricultural project's absorption and transformation of so much nearby grazing land for farm tenancies, stressing the pastures that remained, the project also had unanticipated positive effects on herd boys' work time. With the encouragement of their fathers, many boys would let their flocks graze in their families' cotton fields just as the cotton was ripening. Since the income from cotton went largely to the project, these escapades were minor acts of resistance, at once denying income to the project and providing high quality fodder with minimal effort. A third key environmental task for which girls and boys in Howa were commonly responsible was the collection of firewood for household cooking. Some older children and many teens also cut larger pieces of wood for fuel and construction. Jaunts to the savannah woodlands around the village and to the wooded windbreaks within the agricultural project were routine, with some children and teens going out as much as three or four times a week, while others—as young as eight years old—collected wood only occasionally. As was the case with grazing, the deforestation brought about by the altered land use patterns associated with the agricultural project increased the time it took children to accomplish these chores. They were forced to go further afield only to get poorer quality wood, and as they increasingly filled their households' needs from younger and smaller trees, their efforts exacerbated the process of devegetation in the area. These examples suggest an ecology of children's work, and reveal some of the ways environmental degradation was intricately entwined with prolonging and intensifying children's work, rendering its intergenerational costs all the more profound.

Children's work is connected with school attendance and play. While it was not possible to have accurate measures of school attendance before and after the project, local teachers estimated that relatively fewer children of school age (7–12 years old) were able to attend the village school consistently after the project because of household demands for their labour time. Many children left school prior to completion or never enrolled at all even though the three-month school holiday fell during the rainy season, a period of peak labour demand in the fields.[2] Children's work and school attendance were both subject to an amalgam of factors including gender, birth order position, and household resources. Among other things, there was an aversion to girls studying with boys much past the first or second grade, older children—especially girls—tended to have more household responsibility than their younger siblings, which did not get passed on as the younger children got older, and households with either many or very few resources had greater need for their children's labour. All of these factors, among others—demographic, cultural, and economic—affected school enrolment and attendance, which then had its own repercussive effects in discouraging girls' enrolment and continued schooling. It is not surprising, then, that enrolment declined throughout the course of primary school, and dropped significantly afterward. Only a handful of children from Howa went on to the regional secondary schools, as these would have required their absence from home during term time. In addition to the expenses of school fees, uniforms, transportation and boarding, most households could not afford to lose the labour of their teenage children, (in this case their sons as at that time girls did not leave Howa to attend secondary school), for months at a time. Indeed, my 1981 household survey of the village revealed that fewer than 2 per cent of those children ever enrolled in school completed higher secondary school.

---

[2] School was in session during the harvest, which was a period of quite intense labour accomplished largely by girls and women from Howa as well as hired migrant workers.

TABLE 1[3]
Children's labour contribution
to the environmental work of the village by task

Activity/Duration	Per cent Accomplished by Children	Nature of Children's Contribution	Importance of Task in Village Economy &/or Household Maintenance
Agriculture (May-February)			
Shelling groundnuts (seed preparation)	90	Independent	Central
Clearing/Hoeing/Ploughing	10	Auxiliary	Central
Planting	60	Auxiliary	Central
Irrigating	10	Auxiliary	Central
Weeding	30	Auxiliary	Central
Harvesting	40	Auxiliary	Central
Bird scaring	100	Independent	Important
Animal Husbandry (Year-round)			
Feeding/Watering	20	Auxiliary	Important
Animal care	20	Auxiliary	Important
Milking	5	Auxiliary	Important
Herding (<50% of households	90	Independent	Important
Water Provision (Year-round; Daily)			
Household	70	Independent	Central
Commercial	100	Independent	Central
Fuel Provision (Year-round)			
Collection fuel wood (regular, not daily)	60	Independent	Central
Cut fuel wood (weekly)	20	Auxiliary	Central
Charcoal manufacture (seasonal, regular)	10	Auxiliary	Important
Scavenge charcoal/Flotsam (seasonal, occasional)	70	Independent	Marginal
Wild Food Procurement			
Trap birds (seasonal, occasional)	20	Assistand/ Independent	Marginal
Pick/Gather fruit (seasonal, occasional)	90	Independent	Marginal

---

[3] Adapted from Katz 2004: 261-64

School attendance notwithstanding, children's learning was obvious and almost riotous everywhere in Howa. From their earliest years children learned a great deal in the course of their routine activities, which prepared them well for an agricultural life. Work, play, and learning were intricately intertwined in time-space and meaning in children's daily rounds, and while children worked hard, their lives were anything but bleak and oppressive (cf., e.g., Liebel 2004). They played while they worked, engaged in work playfully, and play 'workfully'; played at tasks they themselves undertook at other times; and played at things they might do as they came of age. Across the board they learned the vocational knowledge and work skills of their community, and these practical ways of knowing were, of course, interwoven dialectically with its theoretical formulations and categories. The connections here were much more organic than those I saw in the rote learning common in the classrooms of the local school.

Work and play were commonly spliced and simultaneous. For example, children at work in the fields would run off to set bird traps or fool around with their friends and siblings; herd boys played all manner of games, went swimming, and gathered and cooked wild foods for themselves as their animals grazed and sometimes wandered away; and girls collected firewood and fruit in the course of playful and adventurous excursions, often singing as they walked or spontaneously dancing in the riverbed or clearings along the way. At the same time but in a different register, children played in miniature at many of the work practices of their community, including their own. While their participation in many tasks was piecemeal and/or guided by an adult, playing at them in miniature gave the children a chance to master the sequencing and overall relationships among tasks. Children were commonly absorbed, for instance, in miniature dramatic games of 'fields'—tellingly distinguishing subsistence fields from tenancies in their rounds of play. They also played elaborate games of 'store' and 'house', using all manner of found objects and waste as their props and handmade toys. One boy, who toiled each day helping his father to cut wood and build earthen charcoal kilns, built miniature charcoal mounds, from which he produced small amounts of usable charcoal that he gave to his mother, who otherwise had none. As these examples suggest, separating work from play was not straightforward. Many routine tasks, such as herding and fuel wood collection, were carried out playfully among peers, while occasional activities like bird trapping or gathering wild foods were treated like adventures, even as they resulted in items of use to their households. In most of these activities the children learned by doing, through apprenticeship and the direct instruction or guided assistance of elders, or through copying what they saw more experienced people around them doing. In the course of these engagements they moved fluidly in and out of numerous overlapping communities of practice and acquired the knowledge and skills necessary to keep these communities going. Their material social practices of work, play, and learning in settings that brought them together with people of different ages sharing different kinds of knowledge exemplified what Jean Lave and Etienne Wenger (1991) call 'legitimate peripheral participation', a means of situated learning.

Ten years into the agricultural project, the easy unity of work, play, and learning was threatened by the intensification of children's work and extended labour time, and the looming question of what their rich environmental knowledge might be good for as the very resources they were learning to use and manage so effectively were limited or disappearing. Setting aside how the intensification and expansion of children's work were apt to drain away some of its playfulness in time-space and meaning, thereby altering children's everyday experience and acquisition of knowledge, there are a number of socioeconomic consequences of the separation of work, play, and learning to consider. Primary among them, children in Howa were learning how to be farmers; yet the land tenure arrangements associated with the agricultural project with its fixed number of tenancies coupled with typical household demographics (early marriage and childbearing with an average of five children per household) ensured that most of them would not have access to a farm tenancy as they came of age. At the same time, the deterioration of agricultural, grazing, and wooded areas outside of the project's irrigated fields made alternative agrarian livelihoods in the vicinity unpromising to say the least, the children's detailed environmental knowledge notwithstanding. Yet just as the promises of schooling might seem more attractive, the demands for children's labour were intensified and compromised children's ability to attend school.

These sorts of disjuncture are perhaps typical of 'development', yet their consequences bear some attention, not least because some of them might be easily avoided, but also because they are often eclipsed in the assumptions of development planning and its typically synchronic benchmarks. As noted earlier, one challenge of the project was that the increases in children's labour were realized to some extent at the expense of schooling. Such trade-offs may be almost tautological but, as the social and economic context shifts, their significance for young people and their communities changes. It was a sore contradiction that just at the moment when greater literacy and numeracy might have been called upon by a growing number of people coming of age in Howa, the wherewithal to acquire these skills and knowledge was harder to manage for most households. Yet the school schedule might easily have been more accommodating of children's responsibilities. The long break for the rainy season, for instance, was timed to allow teachers from other (usually more urban) areas to be home during the rains, which made many rural areas, including Howa, inaccessible for days on end. Perhaps a more pressing priority should be to accommodate local households' labour demands, which might mean scheduling a long break during the harvest rather than at the start of the rains. This accommodation could also be accomplished by having a later start to the school day so that children could work in the fields during the cooler early morning hours whatever the season and then go to school in late morning. Villagers were well aware of such equations. About a dozen years into the project, when the Village Council wanted to encourage girls' school attendance, they built standpipes throughout the settlement using self-help funds. While their intent was to facilitate easier access to water from the two local artesian wells, their gesture encompassed a recognition that unless girls were freed from the most time-consuming aspects of fetching water several times a day, there was no way they could attend school[4] (cf., Mascarenhas 1977).

Playing Fields

---

[4] In this part of Islamic Sudan women of childbearing age remained in their extended families' compounds to the greatest extent possible. Thus much of the work done by women in other parts of the world fell to children in Howa.

In a different vein, development projects might be more systematically sensitive to their intergenerational effects. Displacement was virtually built into the project as planned, and this is the norm. Yet this situation could be avoided by understanding the time-space of 'development' less narrowly, away from the project scale with its temporal horizon of five years or so, to the village or regional scale with a time frame that might extend to a decade if not a generation. Indeed, a childhood might be the most appropriate timeframe for assessing a development intervention. With an expanded frame, or explicitly social temporality such as the duration of a childhood, development planners might be compelled to consider a staged distribution of land for tenancies or other purposes such as market gardens or orchards so that young people growing up within an agricultural project might find ways to be part of the process and find new forms of employment in it, rather than be essentially cast out of its promises. Similarly, planners might work against the mono-logics of most development projects, which, like the Suki Project, tend to focus on a singular (albeit large) concern like the irrigated cultivation of one or two cash crops. Rather, projects could encompass lateral diversification and/or vertical integration from the outset. These ideas are not new, but actualizing them remains unusual. Processing plants for cotton or seed oil might be established in the vicinity as a matter of course, while things like textile manufacturing would be understood as part of 'agricultural' development. This sort of integrated development, which could be done in stages with funding from different sources, might have a chance of absorbing at least some of the young people disenfranchised and displaced from viable local futures in the course of standard development projects. While my intent here is not to recommend specific policies or practices, I raise these issues to make the point that the time-space of development's arc is central to its effects on children, youth, and families. When this consideration is not part of the program—and it almost never is—the seeds of young people's deskilling and dislocation are sown alongside those of the introduced cash crops.

'Development' in time-space

If the effects of development and other modes of economic restructuring bear scrutiny across time and space, so too do the varied responses to them, which range from enthusiastic acceptance to organized resistance. Most situations produce fluid and differentiated responses that fall somewhere between the two, and I have found it useful to examine the registers through which individuals, households, and larger communities engage the multiple and varied effects of restructuring in order to temper the tendency to see any response short of unalloyed acceptance as 'resistance', and to see these everyday material social practices in all of their vibrant potential. I have categorized the responses I found as 'resilience', 'reworking', and 'resistance'. Individually and together, their associated practices have great consequences for children's lives and futures, with particular resonance for the kinds of work they may be called upon to do in the course of economic restructuring. 'Resilience' is seen in the everyday small acts of initiative that enable people to get by, manage the circumstances in which they find themselves, enter into and maintain reciprocal relations, recuperate the means of their everyday lives, and shore up material and social resources. 'Reworking' involves more conscious acts wherein people take on problematic conditions and devise focused and fairly pragmatic responses to them that either redirect and reconstitute available resources or that involve retooling themselves as social actors. 'Resistance' incorporates more conscious acts of opposition that confront and try to redress historically and geographically specific conditions of oppression and exploitation. While initially I sought resistance, what I found more commonly—and in many ways more impressively—were concatenating acts of resilience and reworking, many with extraordinary bearing on children and their everyday practices of work, play, and learning.

One of the most astonishing was the almost complete turn-around regarding schooling, particularly for girls, that took place in Howa over little more than a decade. This shift in attitude and prac-tice—a profound *reworking* of local conditions—is all the more remarkable given the increases in children's labour brought about by the changes associated with the project. As documented above, it seemed that for the first generation of children—born just before and during the initial years of the Suki Project—the economic, environ-mental, and practical changes associated with the project reduced their likelihood of attending school. But the next group of children— those born after the project's first decade—grew up in altered circumstances that, on the one hand, appeared to reduce their labour and, on the other, encouraged enrolment even when their labour might still be needed by their households. While I cannot pinpoint the exact cause of this rather profound shift, I think it was in part the result of changes and instability in the government of Sudan starting in the mid-1980s, which for several years resulted in the state's near absence from running the project. Without the state's close admin-istration, farmers in Howa reduced the area in cotton cultivation to almost nothing, largely stopped growing groundnuts, diverted irriga-tion canals in every direction, and resumed sorghum cultivation using project land. These shifts appeared to have reshaped the demands for children's agricultural labour back to the ways they were prior to the project. Also, and importantly, an international aid organisation had installed hand pumps throughout the village in the intervening years, drastically reducing the labour time required to fetch water. Finally, villagers reported that many animals were lost in the drought of 1983–4, and many households did not restock after-ward. Those that did tended to graze their animals at some distance from the village during the dry season; all of which would have reduced children's labour time around grazing.

Beyond these practical changes, this formidable act of *rework-ing* was founded in a number of things, including proximity to the headquarters of the agricultural project where resident managers, technicians, and other staff uniformly sent their children to school, and the increased travel—and thus exposure to town life—of village residents. But at heart it seemed that as parents in Howa grasped the looming disconnections between what children learned during their youth and what they would need to know as they came of age in vastly changed circumstances, they quickly scrambled to make school enrolment and attendance a greater priority. Yet it is telling that this recognition did not spur them simply to build a school and assume its enrolment as development planners might, or to expect girls all of a sudden to attend the existing school as it seemed many of the local teachers and project administrators did. Rather, just as they had earlier tried to provide standpipes in part to free girls' labour time, the Village Council with the support of the local population focused its efforts on providing means to facilitate girls' school attendance. Using self-help funds, the village leadership hired women teachers and built separate classrooms for girls' matriculation, both of which were effective in boosting female enrolment tremendously. While only 4 per cent of the girls 7-12 years old attended school when I completed the first part of this study in 1981, 43 per cent were enrolled by 1995, an astonishing increase of 1000 per cent in less than a generation. During the same period there was a 75 per cent increase in boys' enrolment, from 42 per cent to 69 per cent of boys between 7 and 12 years of age. These shifts are remarkable for both their speed and their largely local impetus.

Howa's new culture of education was also reflected in secondary school enrolment rates, which increased as well, ultimately leading to the construction of a secondary school in Howa itself by 1995 so that the burgeoning number of secondary school students in the village would not have to board in regional towns. Secondary school enrolment and attendance were enhanced considerably once students didn't have to leave Howa to attend. Not only were the costs of education reduced, but also teens were then available to participate regularly in the work of their households, making their formal education less of a sacrifice. These dramatic shifts around schooling

make clear the dynamic nature of development and the responsive-
ness of local populations to the effects of economic restructuring.
They also underscore the lasting complicated relationship between
children's work and education in these settings and the ways in
which they are not necessarily incompatible (cf., Bass 2004: 99–
124).

Yet despite this dynamism, the hobbled and war-plagued economy of Sudan could not absorb the growing population of educated
young people. Deformations and stagnation in the national economy
had curtailed employment possibilities to the frustration of many of
the newly educated, particularly those who had managed to complete
their secondary school certificates. To make matters worse, the
already limited capacity of the university system was further
constrained by the strictures of structural adjustment, making a
coveted place in higher education even harder to secure. While these
things were frustrating and even infuriating to young people and their
families, they do not obviate the possibilities that inhere in the
expansion of formal education and a more educated population. They
do, however, caution against assuming that the work is done when
schooling is made more widely available. It may be that that is when
the difficult social work of 'development' is just beginning. In any
case, as these limits were faced on the heels of, and in tandem with,
the practices of reworking outlined here, it provoked acts of both
resilience and resistance.

Resilience was vividly expressed in the material social practices
of what I came to call 'time-space expansion'. David Harvey (1989)
suggests that 'time-space compression' is one of the hallmarks of
contemporary capitalism, noting that advances in communication
technologies bring far-flung places together and enable almost
instantaneous communication so that decision-making processes
accelerate while their effects reach further faster. This compression is
readily observed and palpably experienced in the global north and
amongst the middle and upper classes worldwide, but its effects play
out quite differently for others. For many poor and less privileged

people, sped up communication and its associated compression of space and time are experienced as extension; extension of the space required to accomplish the work of everyday life and of the time absorbed by the material social practices that ensure social reproduction. This recasting of everyday life is the local fallout of time-space compression at a higher scale. In other words, as people, capital, information, and things moved further faster at the global and national scale it often produced and required larger grounds of production and social reproduction. These shifts are witnessed in both the lengthening of daily commutes and the dispersed household forms that have become increasingly common in many parts of the world as members endure long periods of labour migration, for instance. They are also seen in the protracted working days of household members, including—and often centrally—children, scrambling to secure its reproduction under new conditions.

What I found in Howa over the fifteen years I intermittently worked there, was quite simple and yet startling in the resilience it afforded young people coping with the diminution of local environmental resources, a skill set and body of knowledge geared to drawing upon those resources, and the incapacity of the national economy to absorb them in the workforce even when they had appropriate skills. As the children with whom I worked came of age, many of them continued to work at the same mix of things as their parents had, but because of environmental degradation and land tenure issues, they had to go upwards of 50 kilometres to find agricultural work, 100 kilometres to graze their animals during the dry season, and more than 200 kilometres to cut wood for charcoal production. Their extended range often included a seasonal stint in provincial towns or more distant cities where they would find casual labour. Although through these means many young people were able to establish their own households in Howa and continue to follow the livelihoods common to their community—thus circumventing some of the effects of a national economy unable to employ them—it took an area *1 600 times larger* than what had been required just ten years earlier to carry out the same mix of tasks. Remarkable as this response was, all that was accomplished by these efforts was staying in place, in every sense of the term. Still, time-space expansion enabled young people to tap the knowledge and skills they had acquired in childhood and make good on their many years of practice in using and caring for the local environment rather than migrating to cities when they were poorly prepared for urban life and employment.

These acts of resilience and reworking demonstrate the vitality of local responses to the effects of economic restructuring, revealing how the global and the intimate are sieved through one another in routine and extraordinary ways (cf., Pratt and Rosner 2006). They also make clear how dynamic are social 'investments' in children and in the nature of children's usefulness. As Jens Qvortrup (1995) astutely notes, investments in children, and thus the nature of children's work, shift in the course of economic restructuring. Looking at European industrialization, he makes the point that as the need for children in the factory declined, their value was better realized with education. Schooling thus became the work of the child not some sort of 'freedom' from work, and 'scholarization' marks the shift from one kind of usefulness to another.

When people in Howa came to see that their children's value might come to fuller fruition with education, they made it increasingly possible for them to enrol in, attend, and stay in school rather than toil in the fields and woodlands. But these plans were routinely frustrated. The expected employment of newly educated young people was derailed by the structural problems associated with underdevelopment and neoliberal structural adjustment coupled with Sudan's decades of civil war—initially between north and south, and later in Darfur. Those who had managed to graduate from secondary school, including some who even had been accepted into university, were among the most frustrated and angry young people in the village. Having retooled themselves for a different future than their elders, these young people found the circumstances different and more hostile than they had imagined. It was difficult for many of them to deal with their aspirations for that future and the place they had expected in it. This situation is not unique to those striving to 'make it' in the global south. Elsa Davidson (2008), for example, insightfully examines aspiration management among people coming of age during an economic downturn in Silicon Valley, California. The comparisons are telling.

North and south, contemporary political-economic conditions have made it difficult for many young people to find employment, especially those who have been ill served by public education or otherwise lack called-for skills. As these young people come of age, they may find themselves excluded from the (above ground) economy. Many of the young people with whom I had worked in Howa found themselves precisely in this predicament as they came of age. Finding no viable place for themselves in the local or national economy, they may migrate in search of work, join or be drafted into the military or militias, or find work in the 'underground' economy, which may lead to prison, a key site for the containment of those who don't find viable legal means to secure the means of their existence and future.

The case of Ismail—a child with whom I worked in Howa—stands out here. Ismail was one of the gentlest, caring, and honest people I've ever known. He managed to complete secondary school and pass the national examination to receive his certificate or diploma, which has long been an important—and not easily attained—qualification in Sudan. After searching high and low for employment in a variety of places and sectors—in business, in the government, in retail—he finally secured a teaching position in a nearby village. Ismail was desperately trying to save money to get married, but his government salary—even with a 100 per cent subvention from the village where he worked—was woefully inadequate to establish his own household any time in the next several years. Angry, disappointed, and discouraged he was scheming to get a job with his cousin in the district tax department so he could skim from the money collected. That Ismail—so proud of his educational achievement and once so earnest in his desire to teach—was contemplating criminal activities was indicative of the desperate situation faced by him and so many of his contemporaries. Another young man from the village, Rashid, had managed to secure a place at Khartoum University, an extraordinary achievement given the competition for university places in Sudan. Yet after only one year he withdrew from the University because he was unable to afford the fees and expenses of living in the capital city, even with a job at the National Fund for Students, which was meant to subsidize his studies. During our last interview, Rashid was seething with bitterness and frustration, at once taunting me to say what education was good for and refusing to let go of his educational opportunity. These experiences, two among many, were typical. Although such outcomes are difficult to quantify, they must be counted as part of the toll on young people of economic restructuring whether in the form of 'development', structural adjustment, 'deindustrialization', or the neo-liberalization of the public sector.

Such examples should make planners, policymakers, and development professionals more aware of how tortured the line from one political-economic social formation to another can be, and more attentive to how the fallout of these shifts affects children and young people coming of age. It was precisely around that fallout and the sorts of frustrations it provoked that the government of Sudan perversely took an extra pound of flesh, spurring acts of *resistance*, which themselves had contradictory effects. Still embroiled in its decades long civil war when the young people with whom I worked were coming of age, the government was desperate for conscripts. As is all too often the case, the growing population of unemployed youth was particularly vulnerable. Among the government's cynical strategies for filling the ranks were to register young men when they sat for the secondary school certificate exam, and to require military service in order to receive a visa to work abroad. Thus two of the key paths toward a viable future for young men detoured through conscription. Mothers in Sudan occasionally protested against the former by keeping their sons from sitting the exam, a contradictory if not tragic form of resistance that protected their sons from military service but also disqualified them from many avenues of potential employment. The latter strategy forced would-be migrants into illegal transit, putting their families at risk, making them vulnerable to arrest upon return, and depriving the state of revenues that might come with more open channels of labour migration. In all kinds of ways and for all parties, these strategies undermined any notion of 'development' that would deserve the name. They reveal the vexed issues that can arise when an expanded culture of education meets hard limits on the expectations it raises. While an expanded culture of education is key to virtually all development agendas, the rippling effects of foundering expectations are rarely considered at all and must be. Sustainable development—of nations and children—hangs in the balance.

The examples I have traced here from my long-term ethnographic work in rural Sudan are meant to highlight some of the broader contextual issues of development and children's work in relation to education and their futures, but also in relation to play. It was largely the vitality of these children's work, in part made so vibrant by its playfulness and thick interweave with playing itself, that was at the heart of their and their community's security and wellbeing as adults. These relationships suggest the interlocking nature of development's multiple and unfolding effects, as much as the indeterminate but productive overlap in the events of economic development and child development. Taking these practices, processes, and outcomes seriously calls for an expanded time-space of development planning, less flat and synchronic measures for assessing its effects, and more fleshed out and dynamic means for understanding the social, cultural, and political-economic nature of economic restructuring and everyday life. At their heart is a call for understanding children's everyday lives in a dynamic political-economic and cultural context. Seeing their work, play, and learning as vividly and vitally connected can bring to the fore not only a more playful sense of children's work and its important interconnections with their knowledge, futures, and households' wellbeing, but also highlight the ways play is both a realm of self-creation and a reservoir of political imagination.

References

Bass, Loretta E. (2004): *Child Labour in Sub-Saharan Africa.* Boulder, CO and London: Lynne Rienner.

Davidson Elsa (2008): Marketing the Self. The Politics of Aspiration Among Middle-Class Silicon Valley Youth. In: *Environment and Planning A* 40(12), 2814–2830.

Harvey, David (1989): *The Condition of Postmodernity.* Oxford: Basil Blackwell.

Katz, Cindi (2004): *Growing Up Global. Economic Restructuring and Children's Everyday Lives.* Minneapolis: University of Minnesota Press.

Lave, Jean, and Etienne Wenger (1991): *Situated Learning. Legitimate Peripheral Participation.* Cambridge and New York: Cambridge University Press.

Liebel, Manfred (2004): *A Will of Their Own. Cross-Cultural Perspectives on Working Children.* London and New York: Zed Books.

Mascarenhas, Adolfo (1977): *The Participation of Children in Socio-Economic Activities. The Case of the Rukwa Region.* Dar es Salaam: University of Dar es Salaam, BRALUP. Research Report 20–I.

Pratt, Geraldine, and Victoria Rosner (eds.) (2006): The Global & the Intimate. In: *WSQ (Women's Studies Quarterly)* 34 (1 & 2).

Qvortrup, Jens (1995): From Useful to Useful. The Historical Continuity of Children's Constructive Participation. In: A-M. Ambert (ed.): *Sociological Studies of Children* 7, 49–76.

Children Learning Life Skills through Work: Evidence from the lives of unaccompanied migrant children in a South African border town

Stanford T. Mahati

Introduction

This study is about how Zimbabwean children who have migrated from their homes and are living in South Africa without accompanying adults are learning life skills through work. It explores whether these children learn something useful whilst working in a foreign country, an informal and child-unfriendly environment. The study also analyses humanitarian workers' responses to children's behaviour and the implications this has on their well-being and development.

The ethnographic study was conducted in South Africa's border town of Musina, a major frontline of migration into other parts of South Africa. As Zimbabwe's economy melted and its service delivery system collapsed at the start of this millennium (see Raftopoulos 2009), Musina's population grew rapidly with migrants, including children, desperately searching for a means of survival among the limited livelihood opportunities.

The majority of unaccompanied migrant children were in transit, many having left their country to look for work (Fritsch et al. 2010). They were predominantly boys and were living in temporary shelters for children run by a faith-based organisation, in private residences in the low-income suburbs, on the streets, and at the border post.

Parents and guardians often emphasize the importance of acquiring skills that will enable children to succeed in adulthood. Following Boyden's (2009) argument that children's work is potentially a source of skills development, I investigated whether the skills mobile children were acquiring were helping them to take control of their lives, settle and remain focused in a foreign country, and whether the children's strong work ethics helped them to survive in an exploitative, dangerous, and resource-poor area.

Thousands of unaccompanied minors from Zimbabwe have left their guardians and schools in a move from a poor country to a better economy. However, South Africa is also characterised by poverty and insecurity and there are few humanitarian workers assisting migrant children. Very few of these children attend school. Thus, children face many adversities that can potentially ruin their lives. Understanding the impact this has on the acquisition of life skills can contribute to averting and reducing problems (see Boyden 2009).

Since life skills are often taught in the domain of parenting, a key issue in this study is the conflict between the common policy idea that associates migration, especially migration for work, with family disruption, exploitation, and loss of schooling. Thus, analysing how working migrant children, under the direct and indirect care of humanitarian workers, are learning life-skills may bring to the fore issues like how migration both empowers and dis-empowers children. The dominant child care and support discourses tend to ignore the former.

Associated with this anti-child migration stance is the dominant idea that children are passive victims. This has recently been challenged in the literature (see Hashim and Thorsen 2011 on the experiences of mobile children without their parents within West Africa). There is also a perception that children do not have the competence to make calculated decisions that are in their best interests.

The chapter draws on the new social studies of childhood (see O'kane 2008) which sees children as social beings. Typical of other recent studies on African children in precarious situations, this study sought to take account of children's agency, which influences processes and events, rather than understanding children as passive. However, as I explore how unaccompanied minors are learning life skills, I pay attention to the fact that their actions are very much embedded in a wider context of relations and structures.

Thus, this chapter suggests that it is essential for humanitarian workers working with unaccompanied migrant children to dismiss the ubiquitous presumption that child migration is counter to the acquisition of life skills. The problem with this representation of child migration is that it does not recognise learning through working. This chapter also calls for humanitarian workers to have a clear understanding of child agency, the context in which child migrants are living, the life skills working children are acquiring and respond in ways that help children to thrive in childhood as well as during adulthood.

Research methods

The data presented in this chapter come from an ethnographic study that was conducted over a period of ten months during 2009 and 2010. The aim of this broad research was to provide an understanding of the constructions and meanings behind the humanitarian workers' predominant representations of Zimbabwean unaccompanied migrant children.

Data were collected through interviews and observation; in the case of children, focus group discussions were also used. Although I did not participate directly in all the working practices of either children or of humanitarian workers, I did profit by being partially embedded in the work of the selected service providers.

Interviews with children and some care workers were conducted in Shona, and for the purposes of this chapter their responses have been translated by the author. Critical thematic content analysis was used.

Participants

The research sample was selected by both snowballing techniques, which depended on children's social networks, and the purposive selection of the children. The selection of boys and girls for interviews stopped at 60 as it had reached a point of sample redundancy. Generalising the results to a large number of unaccompanied minors and humanitarian workers was not the aim of the study; rather the aim was to understand the constructions and meanings behind the humanitarian workers' predominant representations of these children. However, to ensure variation in social patterns, the study explored the experiences of unaccompanied migrant children in a wide variety of migratory circumstances by including those who were in transit, working, school going, not going to school, living in temporary places of safety, living on the streets, and living at the border.

The ages of children in this study ranged from 7 to 20 years. Contrary to the formal policies of their organisations, most of the workers in government and non-governmental organisations did not have a rigid understanding of a child as someone aged below 18 (see Skinner 2004). The definition of a child was continuously being constructed and negotiated.

Broadly, an unaccompanied migrant child has either crossed a border alone or has subsequently found himself or herself living in a foreign country without an adult caregiver (not being cared for by an adult who, by law or custom, has a responsibility to do so—Hillier 2007). However, the state of being unaccompanied is not static since some children migrate with parents or guardians but end up alone either for a short or long period of time.

The study focused on humanitarian workers in one international agency and one faith-based organization. The former's programmes were informed and guided by the United Nations Convention on the Rights of the Child (CRC) while the later was influenced by a combination of the CRC and local understandings of childhood.

Humanitarian workers were predominantly women but mixed in terms of nationality, ethnicity and levels of education. Other key informants were from non-governmental organisations and a few were from relevant government departments. Both enriched my understanding of the interface between unaccompanied migrant children and service providers.

Study results and discussion

Children's backgrounds, work and the environment

In contrast to Zimbabwe's economy, South Africa is understood as the 'land of milk and honey'. This myth about South Africa is popularised by returnees and migrant workers to Zimbabwe who are popularly known as *'injiva'* (Ndebele lingua franca for a rich person—Mahati et al. 2006). Being an *injiva* is a status symbol. *Injiva* leave an indelible impression on their compatriots, including children, and lure others to follow. These imagine living large within a very short period of time.

However, the mass migration of children to South Africa without having finished at least form four (the fourth grade of secondary school), the standard level of education in Zimbabwe, was a serious cause of concern amongst humanitarian workers who were acting *in loco parentis*, and always tried very hard to convince children to go back to school. Besides being worried that these children were exposed to abusive and exploitative conditions in South Africa, they also feared that they were not being prepared for adulthood.

Soon after arriving in Musina, the majority of children start looking for sources of livelihood. Every day, children walk door-to-door in residential areas looking for temporary jobs, popularly called 'piece jobs'. These jobs include working as vendors, car washers, firewood fetchers, domestic workers, workers in neighbouring farms, shop assistants, commercial sex workers, barbers, hair dressers, porters, and hunters in neighbouring farms. Other boys supported themselves through crime. The last category hunted wild and dangerous animals, like warthogs. A few boys harvested mopane worms (*Gonimbrasia belina*) to either supplement their food or for sale.

Children faced a plethora of challenges at their workplaces: poor remuneration, not being compensated after working, delays in receiving payment, long working hours, doing dangerous work (for example, working as security guards in a crime ridden area usually in return for accommodation which was very poor, smuggling illegal migrants, smuggling tobacco from Zimbabwe), doing strenuous work, language barriers, and verbal and physical abuse.

The ability to communicate with other people including employers is an asset in life but usually a challenge to foreigners. Zimbabwean children usually speak either Shona or Ndebele. Soon after arriving in South Africa children learned the importance of speaking local languages, particularly Venda and Sepedi, which are the common languages in Musina. Migrants who speak local languages usually have an edge over those who do not when competing for 'piece jobs'. Failure to speak a local language also frustrated children's access to justice. This is illustrated by the case of 15-year-old Mukundi who was beaten up by a *magumaguma*.[1] He speaks English but could not speak Venda, the language usually spoken by the police, and so was reluctant to report the attack. Touched by his plight, a migrant girl aged 15 who could speak Venda assisted him to report to the police.

Due to their undocumented migration status, children were often harassed by the South African police. Police often launched crackdowns against child work. Contrary to South Africa's laws, the police also often deported children without involving the social workers or the courts. Consequently, children feared reporting violations of their rights to the police.

South African law prohibits children below the age of 16 from taking on employment, and all children from undertaking dangerous and harmful work. However, a critical shortage of labour inspectors has made these rules difficult to enforce.

---

[1] Magumaguma are mostly male criminals who ply their trade in the bush areas on both sides of the Limpopo River as well as in the towns of Musina and Beit Bridge. Their main targets are irregular migrants whom they way-lay at illegal entry points; violently rob them of their belongings; cheat and sexually abuse women and girls; and sometimes force male migrants to rape fellow migrants, and very often kill them.

Setting goals

This section discusses the goals of working children in the context of their background in Zimbabwe, the type of work they were doing, and their working environment. Humanitarian workers either tended to assume that children did not have clear objectives in life or that their objectives bordered on fantasy. Working children were rarely regarded as workers: 'They claim that they are doing piece jobs. Theirs are not piece jobs. They are being exploited.' Attitudes like this resulted in lethargic responses to calls by children for protection at work.

This study shows that children's lived realities bear on how they assess and structure goals in life, which in this case were mainly shaped by the poor economic situation in Zimbabwe. Children's lives in South Africa were intertwined with what had happened and was happening in Zimbabwe. Although constrained by incessant hardships in their lives, children vowed to improve their socio-economic status through working. Many of them engaged in circular migration to support their families with basic necessities.

As they strived to realise their objectives, children often understood humanitarian workers as people who regard them as incompetent and having 'self-destructive agency' (see Gigengack 2008:216 on street children in Mexico who acquired and consumed glues and solvents but were conscious of their destructive effects). Children also thought the humanitarian workers were not really interested in their welfare. This feeling emanated from the fact that humanitarian workers did not know the workplaces of most of the children, the work they were doing, nor the informal contracts they had with their employers. Frustrated by what they regarded as the patronising attitudes of humanitarian workers, children at times openly accused the humanitarian workers of being motivated by personal interest to earn a living rather than assisting them.

During my fieldwork, the humanitarian workers helped very few children receive payments owed to them. Children accused humanitarian workers of not being supportive when they report problems they were experiencing with employers since they often responded by saying, 'We told you to stop assuming adult roles. You should be in school not looking for money.' Humanitarian workers often did not follow up on the reported cases of abuse and exploitation. Consequently, a number of cases of exploitation were not reported to law enforcement agencies. In any case, few reported cases to the police resulted in prosecution and convictions. Children attributed this situation to neglect by humanitarian workers, and their own powerlessness due to their status as children. Humanitarian workers echoed the point of children's powerlessness but also chided the children for trying to appropriate adulthood responsibilities.

Children either tactfully or openly rejected attempts by humanitarian workers to mould or remould their goals in life arguing that they had scant understandings of children's situations and goals in life. Some humanitarian workers' ignorance about life in Zimbabwe solidified these children's resolve to define their own goals. 'They think our lives have always been characterised by poverty. We used to have a good life... Actually we want to do very well... even much better than their imagination' said a 16 year old boy, who thought humanitarian workers were contemptuous of children's family backgrounds.

On the other hand, many humanitarian workers perceive children who embark on migration without their guardians as having lost focus in terms of setting goals in their lives, and see the future of these children as bleak. Though cognisant of the structural factors that caused children to leave their country on their own, they often sought to reset the children's goals, which they regarded as ambitious and poorly conceived.

Considering that they had been failed by Zimbabwe's social security system and that aid targeting migrants was too little, erratic, and problematic in its distribution, children were learning to be self-reliant. Some children often told their colleagues, 'These humanitarian workers don't like us... Let's do our own stuff.' They were learning not to leave their fate in other people's hands, and to be prepared to do all sorts of jobs. Children used the little money they earned to support themselves and their families in Zimbabwe. Some children also saved money for transport to go to other areas in South Africa or to visit their families.

Migration to South Africa is also considered as a 'rite of passage' from boyhood to adulthood (Maphosa 2007). Since this is a very old tradition in many areas, social pressure is also often applied, directly or indirectly, to young men to 'act like a man' by following other men to South Africa. This conception of migration as the domain of men is now being challenged by women and girls, who also want to succeed in life through migration. As they did their 'piece jobs' in Musina, they planned and saved money to improve their life situation in other areas. Several girls spurned the repatriation programme despite often being labelled as sexual deviants, which sometimes led to expulsion from a temporary shelter.

Despite facing a host of challenges, children remained steadfast in pursuing their objective to work. For example, due to limited work opportunities in Musina and few places of safety for children, a large population of children, with or without legal documentation, responded to these challenges by moving to other South African urban areas and farms.

They drew lessons from the experiences of others who had left Musina in search of a better life. 'I can also succeed in life if I make a plan,' said Cliff, aged 17, as he planned to emulate his friends who had come to renew their asylum permits in Musina. The friends were working as farm workers in Kimberly, nearly 1000 km away from Musina. Cliff had been doing odd jobs at the border post for two years. Frustrated by job insecurity, police harassment, quarrels with other migrant boys, the 'hopelessness of life at the border post' and living in unsafe places, he left Musina without telling most of his friends, and quickly got a job in Kimberly as a farm worker. These acts of courage and determination astounded many humanitarian workers, some of whom feared living in other areas.

However, a number of Cliff's friends remained behind pointing out, 'Cliff has his own plans. We have ours.' Considering South Africa's history of xenophobic attacks some children revealed that they were afraid to live in faraway places.

Taking control of their lives

South Africa's constitution and laws give protection to all children on its soil. However, in practice unaccompanied migrant children are not always well protected (see Fritsch et al. 2010; Palmary 2009). Abandoned and exposed to various forms of abuse, children learn how to protect themselves. Instead of reporting the people who were refusing to pay them to the authorities, some children teamed up and threatened to assault these people. This response is in conformity with the practice in this area of often solving conflicts using extra-judicial means. Noting their small physique, some children engaged the services of more powerful non-official people to help them get their money. Though the methods they employed were at times unlawful, these children were learning to take control of their lives and solve their problems.

Instead of trying to support such initiatives, some humanitarian workers labelled children who responded to violence with violence as criminals. Apart from being offensive, this response marginalised children from the workplace and indirectly endorsed the harsh treatment children often received from the police and members of the public, who sometimes treated them as dangerous criminals.

Children were not allowed to leave the shelter before 7:00 am and were expected to return before 7:00 pm. Noting that humanitarian agencies were failing to support them adequately, a significant number of children defied these rules, which limited their working time and consequently their incomes. Several boys working in neighbouring farms left the shelter to start work at 7:00 am or earlier. These boys and a few others, particularly those who assisted taxi operators, called *hwindi*, usually returned around midnight. Others

preferred not to live in shelters since they did not want their movements to be restricted as they looked for money.

The child *hwindi* also learned how to solve the problems they
encountered whilst competing with taxi drivers for potential passen-
gers. *Hwindis* often used violence against one another. Demonstrating their capacities to eke out a living in a difficult working environment, some boys avoided antagonising adult *hwindis*, and pre-
tended to be respectful towards these adults. Boys acknowledged that
their weakness meant they would be unable to engage in violent
contests. They also unquestioningly ran free errands for these adults,
like buying cigarettes for them. In return, adults tolerated them as
friendly competitors. The utility of this strategy was cemented when
one of the boys who was perceived as stubborn by the adult *hwindis*
was stopped from working at a rank in town. Other boys heavily
criticised their colleague for not using deception to solve the problem
of working with adults who demand respect.

Reports of unaccompanied migrant girls from Zimbabwe being
vulnerable to sexual harassment at the workplace were abundant.
Migrant girls, apart from new arrivals, were aware of this challenge
and the moments when they were at greatest risk. Desperation forced
them to continue working or to look for work in risky areas. However, as social beings these girls learned through sharing experiences
to employ a number of strategies to minimise risk. One was to regard
any man as a potential abuser and therefore not to be trusted. For
example, they refused to trust even those employers, men and
women, who had been referred to them by the humanitarian workers.
The experiences the girls had with such trusted men taught them to
be vigilant at all times. Girls also learned to minimise risk of sexual
abuse by avoiding situations or spaces where they would be powerless, for example, by refusing to negotiate the amount of payment
inside a house without another person, especially an adult woman,
around.

'One finger-nail cannot crush a louse' (Chimhundu 1980: 42).
This Shona proverb suggests that it is futile to solve some problems

alone. Although some new arrivals from Zimbabwe were reluctant to seek the help of others to deal with their work-related problems, with time a number of children learned this wisdom. They consulted others including humanitarian workers on how to negotiate for fair compensation before or after working, on how to deal with someone who was not willing to pay them for the services they rendered and many other problems they faced at the workplace. For example, children who worked as vendors were often accused of failing to account for all the money they received from selling goods. One of them was Brighton, aged 13, who had only attended school up to grade three. He had difficulties in accounting for the eggs he sold. Other boys often assisted him to do so and showed him how not to have short-falls. They also assisted him to claim his wages from an old lady who was refusing to pay him. Using the status of being minors as social capital, children threatened her that they would tell humanitarian workers to intervene. Fearing being accused of child abuse she grudgingly partially paid Brighton.

The 'incompetence' of childhood is an ideological construction. Evidence for this includes children also learning to take control of their lives by acknowledging their weaknesses and seeking help from others. After bitter experiences, some acknowledged their incompetence in handling money. They regretted wasting money on sex workers and 'buying useless things like expensive food and clothes'. Children learned to consult their colleagues or other adults (including humanitarian workers) on what to buy, the cheapest place to buy goods, and where to store goods. It was common to hear boys advising each other on how to live within their means and to stop spending money on women, through serious talk and teasing each other. 'Some people are there to use you... When you have money you just have to be careful,' said a 14-year-old boy as he urged other boys to remain focused on why they migrated. Children's ability to devise coping strategies to deal with challenges like exercising financial prudence and drawing lessons from their daily experiences shows that they were acting on, as well as being acted upon by, their social world (Christiansen et al. 2006).

Adaptability

Contrary to their expectation that life in South Africa would be rosy, migrant children were often shocked to find it characterised by poverty and unemployment. They found themselves struggling to find food, even a temporary job, and safe accommodation. Though prior to coming to South Africa, most of them had regarded it as a violent country, they were still surprised by the extent of this violence, which was even perpetrated by law enforcement agencies. They felt very insecure due to abuse and exploitation. This precarious situation forced children to learn life skills of adaptation through work.

Migrant children as social actors showed that they were not limited by adversities which exist in their environment like the scarcity of 'piece jobs' and the difficulties of having to look for work almost every day. They were learning to be multi-skilled and versatile in the work they could do. It was common for a boy, for example, to be very knowledgeable about the sexual behaviour of adults, as he worked as an informal pimp; heavy vehicles, as he washed many at the truck stop; running a business, as he worked as store keeper, bar man, or vendor. These diverse skills made it possible for children to survive. Children's competencies in doing various jobs and increased involvement in waged employment underline the relevance of work outside the home environment as one of the markers in children's transition processes from childhood to adulthood.

As children did all sorts of menial jobs, they were learning about the importance of adapting to the lives of working people. They learned to be punctual and smart at work, for example, those who were working as vendors and store keepers. Although most of them claimed that they had been inculcated by their parents and teachers with a culture of bathing every day and being smart, they also drew lessons from other children who had been dismissed from work for continuously being late for work or who failed to get piece jobs because they were dirty. Despite not having access to safe and clean bathing places, they strived to bath regularly and dress smartly. They often bathed in a disused swimming pool and some bathed in the Limpopo River (and consequently, a number periodically suffered from Bilharzia).

While acknowledging the high levels of risk they faced due to their exposure to men who demanded to have sex with them, particularly at night, some of the girls working in the streets and at the border post countered these threats every evening by approaching adult women who were either cross-border traders or vendors, and asking to share their sleeping place. Adult women noting that girls living in the street were at great risk of being raped at night also often invited the girls to come over to where they slept. Many humanitarian workers were not aware of these girls' efforts to adapt to the risky situation and protect themselves from sexual predators. Instead humanitarian workers portrayed girls as sexual delinquents or victims of sexual abuse. Some accused these girls of having survival sex, also referred to as transactional sex. Girls vehemently rejected the label of being sexual deviants.

As children battled to cope with economic exploitation and lack of protection, a number of those who had privileged backgrounds in Zimbabwe quickly realised that they would have to learn to work under these difficult conditions. Some of these children revealed that they had been hoodwinked to think that life in South Africa would be much better. The majority of the children had no history of working in Zimbabwe and found working life taxing.

Faced with enormous difficulties in South Africa, these children showed that they had the competency to respond to difficulties by lowering the standards of the type of work they would do and the amount of money they expected. 'Poverty forces us to accept being exploited. It's either you accept the little money or you die from hunger,' said a 14-year-old boy, who undertook odd jobs like carrying bags across the bridge which divides South Africa and

Zimbabwe. Maybe their behaviour was guided and informed by the Shona proverb 'A chief's son is a subject in another land,' (Chimhundu 1980:6) which is usually taught in primary school in Zimbabwe. Though he and his colleagues viewed sex workers and their clients as sexual perverts—'if I see my sister doing sex work I will beat her' said one boy aged 14—they still worked as informal pimps since they wanted to survive. By doing this kind of work humanitarian workers regarded them as delinquents in urgent need of rehabilitation.

Some of the children initially refused to lower their standards of life or the work they were prepared to do; but their suffering, such as having a rigid, poor diet forced them to do so. Children who spent their days idly were met with disapproval by both humanitarian workers and children (see Boyden 2009). Working children some-times managed to buy their own food, clothes, and goods to support their families in Zimbabwe—something which a number of children greatly wished to do. Within a few days these children's resolve not to do dirty work was eroded as they joined others in looking for any type of 'piece job'.

Children have different readings of their vulnerable situation and this leads them to devise different responses. Biggs and Matsaert in their paper on how to strengthen poverty reduction programmes using an actor-oriented approach urge us 'to realise that different actors may have different interpretations of reality' (2004:11–12). For example, some migrant children who were working in the streets quickly learned to survive through begging for food, sharing food, stealing from their workplaces, harvesting wild baobab fruit for sale, and scavenging for food in bins. However, children's responses were informed by different values: those who lived in the shelters roundly described the practice of eating from bins as poor as it was an unhealthy survival strategy, thus distinguishing themselves from street children.

Social actors usually attempt to create space for themselves when they face challenges. Realising that they would save a lot of

money if they did not continue to live in 'comfort' in temporary
shelters far away from their workplaces, a number of children opted
to live in unsafe places near their sources of livelihood. This can be
illustrated by the case of Molife, aged 17, who during the week lived
in the open, or under bridges at the border post where he worked as a
vendor, porter, gambler, and human smuggler. He minimised the
discomfort by spending the weekend in the shelter for boys. Due to
poor monitoring of the movements of boys in and out of the shelter,
Molife had dual 'homes' in Musina for over a year. Some children
acquired safe accommodation by guarding *spazas*[2] at night for no
pay.

Some boys worked in Musina but usually returned in the
evening to their parents' or guardians' houses in Beit Bridge, the
Zimbabwean town across the border. They walked every day to
Musina from Beit Bridge without any documentation to cross the
border. They either negotiated for border entry with agencies
manning the border on both sides or they crossed the crocodile- and
hippopotamus-infested Limpopo River when there is tight monitoring at the legal entry point.

The border officials of both countries usually allowed them to
pass without demanding payment as they were rooted in a discourse
which sees children as innocent. They trusted children to come back.
Zimbabwean soldiers often gave the children some money to buy
some groceries for them in Musina. In return, these children demonstrated cultural competence when they acted according to the expectation of these adults who 'want well behaved children' (as expressed
by Raymond, aged 16) by showing great respect to them as adults.
This tactic also inculcated in them pro-social skills as they were
learning to co-exist with adults.

However, the situation was different when they used the many
illegal entry points as the *magumaguma* sometimes demanded

---

[2]   A *spaza* is an informal shop, which is usually located in the South African
townships

money from them. To minimise being harassed by *magumaguma*, the children sometimes agreed to run errands for them like buying food, beer, and cigarettes. They were fully aware that *magumaguma* were fugitives from justice but said they had no option since they were desperate to survive.

Children's perspectives on *magumaguma* were at times contra-dictory, and there were many things they were doing as human smugglers that the children did not like. The recent arrivals often said *magumaguma* were imparting some anti-social values while the boys who had been working at the border for long periods tended to nor-malise their criminal survival strategies. Fearing the corrupting influ-ence of such people, Cliff expedited plans to escape from this life by going to work in Kimberly.

Working children were very vulnerable to *magumaguma*, who often harassed them and demanded money. For a long time *mag-umaguma* used to position themselves strategically at places where children were working. Soon after children were paid, *magumaguma* would forcibly take all the money. To eliminate this threat to their livelihood, children plotted with their employers to pay them later when criminals were not there. This often meant not receiving money at that time although they were in urgent need of it.

Contrary to the popular notion that children were powerless when they interact with *magumaguma,* children learned that they had considerable power over these thugs, who were feared even by state agencies like the police. They strategically used this to protect them-selves. Some children including girls at times tipped the police on the whereabouts of *magumaguma* who were terrorising them, and how to trap them. They worked and lived in the same environment as the *magumaguma*. 'We know where they operate, types of crimes each of them usually committed, socialise, sleep, live in Musina or Beit Bridge and the times when they are drunk,' said Mukundi. Chil-dren observed that *magumaguma* were aware of the power children held through knowledge about their movements and activities. This knowledge, amongst other factors, often deterred some *mag-umaguma* from harassing children.

Since they were living in a high risk environment, some children often made arrangements to keep their money and goods with respectable and apparently trustworthy adults at their workplaces, like elderly women who worked as vendors. This strategy was particularly used by those who had not lived in Musina for long enough to be in a position to protect their possessions, which included groceries they earmarked for their families in Zimbabwe. However, some of these adults (including humanitarian workers) abused this trust. To minimise this risk, children avoided dealing with adult migrants who were planning to visit their own families in Zimbabwe in the near future. According to children, these adults would be under pressure to go home with a lot of goods. Thus, children learned the importance of scrutinising people's behaviour and not simply trusting anyone, and to understand one's environment and how to derive a living within it.

Thus, whilst working in a foreign country is characterised by all sorts of risks, it exposed the children, many of whom were from rural areas, to the workings of an advanced economy, and they also learned how to manipulate it to make a living. For example, a refund of value added tax (VAT) can be claimed by non-resident travellers when they leave South Africa, and some of the boys learned to forge shopping receipts for sale to adults, such as Zimbabwean women who would claim a VAT refund.

In addition, children learned that in today's world, both working adults and businesses are usually supported by a credit system. Children with no experience of borrowing and lending money quickly learned how to negotiate such deals. Children lent as much as R2000 (approximately US$280) to adults and negotiated repayment terms. However, some adults, including some humanitarian workers, kept giving excuses for failing to repay the debt. This action shocked the children as one of them, a boy aged 15, dejectedly said, 'Humanitarian workers must quickly return the money they borrowed. They know we are children and do not have many options in life like adults.' By not quickly giving children their money, humanitarian workers blurred the difference between childhood and adulthood in terms of vulnerability. This resulted in children learning to put into place tight systems to minimise the risks of lending money to bad debtors, for example, by assessing the credit worthiness of a person.

Labour bargaining and social relationships

One of the challenges faced by migrants in South Africa is labour exploitation. Their ability to negotiate a fair wage is compromised if they do not have the proper documents to live and work in South Africa. None of the working migrant children in Musina had these documents. In addition, a lack of labour bargaining tactics often facilitated their exploitation.

Drawing from their personal experiences as well as those of other children, working children learned that employers seek to maximise their profits and reduce labour costs by any means available. For example, local people often refused to honour their under-takings to pay children fairly when they had finished doing the work. After children had finished working without having agreed on the amount of payment the employers who appeared friendly before the children had started work often turned cold and threatening, and would simply dictate the amount they were going to pay. Children often had no option but to accept the small payment. A number of children complained that on several occasions they had not been paid at all. Consequently, children developed some tactics to minimise exploitation. Some employers gave children working for them some food, usually very little; afterwards they would give the children very little money claiming that they had also spent it on the food. In response to such tactics, some children refused to work before final-ising with the employer how much they were going to earn. And some children, regardless of being very hungry, refused to eat any food offered by the employer in order not to weaken their bargaining power. The more confident children claimed that they would first ask whether food is part of the payment for their labour before they ate what they were being offered.

On the other hand, a number of children manipulated adults' expectation that children are passive and have an uncritical approach to life. Children said they acted like a 'normal child': not questioning the actions of employers and respecting them as they were adults. According to these children this approach was sometimes very rewarding when they had finished work as some employers responded by giving them more money than they had expected to receive. On top of the money they give the children, some of the satisfied employers would give these children things like clothes and food. They also improved the working conditions by giving them light work, break time, and flexible working times. Children often used this approach the first time they worked for any employer, and quickly abandoned this strategy if the employer did not respond appropriately. Children also noted that some of the new employers tested whether they were behaving like children and if they passed the test they would improve working conditions. Thus, children learned to examine their working terrain and to devise appropriate strategies of manipulating the situation to advance their goal of getting fair compensation.

In accordance with Foucault's (1980) point that power is everywhere, children also appropriated it by using threats of witch-craft and violence to instil fear into the minds of employers who refused to pay the amount they had agreed on. Children who smug-gled illegal migrants sometimes threatened to beat those who did not want to treat them with respect by later refusing to pay them. These threats usually worked as children were quick to briefly appropriate power from adults who were not familiar with border entry require-ments and the bush environment where terror reigned supreme. Fearing violence, arrest and deportation, the terrified adults grudg-ingly paid the children, some of whom were as young as 13 years. Thus, contrary to the common perception of unaccompanied migrant children as vulnerable, there were moments when these children exercised power over adults.

As stated earlier, the use of scare tactics by some boys resulted in some humanitarian workers labelling them as *magumaguma*. However, their view of these children was not static as on some occasions, for example, when they lived in temporary shelters for children, they were considered as having normal childhoods. These different representations of children support Prout and James' (1990) point that 'childhood is a social construction which varies with time and place' (Holloway and Valentine 2000:5).

At an early age, the children learn that in life one has to be self-reliant and self-employed. When they arrived in South Africa, many of them had high hopes of working and being fairly compensated. However, a number of children revised their thoughts on how to earn a living after experiencing exploitation at various workplaces. Some started their own businesses of buying eggs from commercial farmers, boiling and selling them. Some of these children employed other children as vendors. Through drawing lessons from their work experiences, they structured their price system to make profits. Humanitarian workers often showered praises on resilient children.

Effective decision making

Effective decision making is important in life but challenging to many people. Through engaging in various working practices children were exercising one of their widely promoted rights, the right to participate in decision making particularly on matters that concern them. For example, they often withdrew their labour when they were unhappy with working conditions and others often tactfully refused to do exploitative work. Though children were making decisions which sometimes proved very costly to them, not surprising for young people still growing up, like other actors they were often able to draw important lessons from these experiences.

Children have the ability to actively determine their lives (see Prout and James 1990). They learned that procrastination or hesitancy in making decisions can be costly. For example, hesitating to discuss the terms of the work contract with the employer undermined their negotiating power. Children were often required to make tough but strategic business decisions at their workplaces. This can be illustrated by a second boy called Brighton, this time aged 16, who was demoted from being a store keeper to a herd boy over false accusations. Despite pressure from other migrants to quit, he continued to work as he thought it was not strategic to quit before having secured another job.

Contrary to the common perception that children are prone to peer pressure and are immature, a number of children learned to make their own decisions. Some refused to be discouraged from doing work that is considered dirty and inconsistent with the popular image of South Africa as having 'honourable' and highly paid jobs. For example, some boys defied their friends by fetching firewood and herding goats.

Despite defying the advice of their colleagues at times, children showed pragmatism when making decisions. Children learned to appreciate the power of consulting others in order to make informed decisions. They particularly consulted those who were more experienced than themselves regardless of their age or sex. For example, some children rejected offers of work by certain employers who had a known history of exploiting children and migrants in general.

Despite struggling to make a living, children on their own sometimes rejected offers of work they considered to be dangerous. I mentioned that the majority spurned several advances by one game keeper who wanted to recruit them to hunt, despite the incentive of a lot of meat.

Values and work

Migration is often seen as having a corrupting influence on children's behaviour since they are generally regarded as immature. For example, Brockerhoff and Biddlecom observed that migrants are exposed 'to a new social environment which has different sexual norms' (1999:835). Endorsing this view, a 15-year-old girl commented, 'Some of us have really changed. They did not behave badly like this whilst in Zimbabwe.' However, there was also evidence that children were learning the importance of high social values while they were working.

Children learned that it is usually rewarding to be respectful, trustworthy, honest, disciplined, hard-working, accountable, and transparent when interacting with employers, clients, and adults in general. Some children indicated that they used to misbehave but have since realised the futility of this behaviour as people detest it. Children who lacked the above mentioned attributes were often abused and marginalised by potential employers. There were other reasons for socially acceptable behaviour: Mukundi, who alongside paid employment, used to earn a living through stealing (some boys perceive stealing as a job), but stopped this practice after he escaped death by a whisker. His leg was injured by a car in a hit and run accident. The day before the accident, he had stolen 30 eggs from a vendor who employed one of his friends. Mukundi and his friend attributed this misfortune to the act of stealing eggs. 'When you wrong someone and that person laments his or her misfortune, he or she will be making a powerful prayer to God against you. You will not get away with it,' explained Mukundi who vowed never to steal again. This reveals that some children realise that their agency has limits.

Although the majority of children had no history of working for money in Zimbabwe, they learned new norms and values, such as the values of hard work, diligence, and time management. Children always tried to be very busy at work or looking for work. When humanitarian workers organised activities for them like soccer games or meetings to discuss health issues, children insisted that the times for these activities should not interfere with their work. Learning the importance of asserting their autonomy in matters that impact negatively on their lives, children without any hesitation or fear, snubbed humanitarian workers who did not listen to their concerns about when activities should be organised. Working life accelerated the transition from childhood to adulthood.

Children also learned the importance of working hard in life if one wants to succeed. It was common to see self-motivated children working very early in the morning and late at night. What children who worked hard were doing for themselves and their families often inspired other children.

Through working, children learned that individualism in life can threaten one's well-being. Considering that getting a 'piece job' was not guaranteed every day, they learned to appreciate the value of social solidarity in life and they were supporting each other. For example, children often voluntarily assisted their colleagues at their workplace to finish a task; they also assisted their colleagues in negotiating fair payment for work done and ganged together against thieves. Noting the problems of dealing with exploiters who delayed paying children, children often shared food during these difficult times.

Though humanitarian workers usually criticise children for being too young to face many adversities, they acknowledged that working provided them with some competencies like saving, and made a difference to their lives (see Boyden 2009). 'These children can save money better than many of us adults,' said one female worker as she expressed great admiration towards unaccompanied minors. This went against the common view among humanitarian workers that the children were too immature to handle their earnings prudently. Humanitarian workers criticised children for buying 'childish stuff like radios, food, and sweet things'. This infantilisation of children's spending patterns resulted in children objecting to adults' efforts to blur the childhood and adulthood divide. Although they acknowledged their poor backgrounds, children still wanted to have the freedom to buy goods which other children living with their parents including humanitarian workers' children had. As a result many of them ignored the humanitarian workers' advice as inappropriate, paternalistic and condescending. Children also countered the humanitarian workers' argument by pointing out that they were saving the little money they earned from doing all sorts of odd jobs for long periods of time. They bought goods like television sets, radios, large supplies of groceries, blankets, and clothing.

Children's sense of obligation as well as agency to support their families echoes the point made by Boyden in her study of how Ethiopian children contributed to their household's livelihoods: 'coping with adversity is a collective rather than an individual responsibility' (2009:129). A number of children claimed that they shouldered the responsibility of supporting their poor families. Thus children were learning to tackle threats to their households.

Some children resisted temptation to use the little money they had to buy expensive goods or buy 'childish' goods like snacks and sweets. Through criticising one another for being wasteful, and praising their colleagues who were buying goods and keeping in constant touch with their families, children remained conscious about the importance of not wasting money. They learned to prioritise their needs. However, their priorities were often misunderstood and degraded by humanitarian workers. Children accused humanitarian workers of treating them as adults by wanting them to have adults' spending patterns yet they were still children.

Conclusion

Although child work may disrupt the ideal learning process of children in a home and school environment, this chapter has shown that unaccompanied migrant children learn valuable life skills through working, even in an informal and violent economy. While learning through work is challenging—and was breaking some children (see Honwana and De Boeck 2005)—work exposed children to certain vital life skills.

This study has exposed the difficulties of learning life skills through the experience of risky situations. However, children as social actors, depending on the context within which work takes place, exercised considerable agency and refused to be constrained by the exploitative employment regime, or the dominant gendered and anti-child migration discourses, and instead learned life skills.

Instead of condemning working children by criticising their efforts, maintaining and promoting a perception of childhood as a period characterised by incompetence and passivity, humanitarian workers should acknowledge children's own perspectives and competencies to learn from the numerous difficulties of working life. Then, if necessary, capacitate their competences in ways which do not infantilise or pathologise them.

Again instead of emphasising children's vulnerability, humanitarian workers also need to focus on their resilience and ingenuity in dealing with problematic situations. Effective intervention should build on an appreciation of what social actors are trying to do for themselves, and the lessons they are learning through these attempts.

Through contextualising life skills, listening to and respecting children, it becomes possible to remove intolerable or unnecessary risks without undermining the processes of learning to avoid or overcoming risks. For example, humanitarian workers tend to pathologise unaccompanied minors particularly girls who are trying to survive and are using skills they consider as repugnant. Humanitarian workers should be aware of 'cultural understandings' (Boyden 2009) and environmental factors which shape how children learn to deal with challenges. That way they will be in a better position to provide appropriate behavioural change programmes and avoid circulating views which criminalise, demean, or portray mobile children negatively. Consequently, children's everyday resilient efforts will no longer be negated.

The general failure of humanitarian workers to acknowledge children's competencies in acquiring life skills through work and their lack of support for the children is worrisome. As the case of boys who were working as human smugglers makes clear, there were many opportunities where humanitarian workers could have intervened and inculcated children with some effective as well as socially and legally acceptable life skills, which would have helped them improve their lives as well as those of their families who depend on them. As humanitarian workers and other adults develop interventions aimed at improving the lives of children, it is also important for them to know which life skills are significant for children within the context of migration and informal employment.

Acknowledgements and funding

This research was made possible through the support provided by the Zeit-Stiftung 'Settling into Motion' PhD scholarship programme, Atlantic Philanthropies and National Research Foundation (NRF). I acknowledge the guidance I received from my study supervisor Professor Ingrid Palmary. I also thank the unaccompanied migrant children and humanitarian workers who shared their experiences with me. The opinions expressed herein are mine and do not necessarily reflect the views of the above mentioned funders and people.

References

Biggs, Stephen, and Harriet Matsaert (2004): *Strengthening Poverty Reduction Programmes Using an Actor-oriented Approach. Examples from Natural Resources Innovation Systems.* Network Paper No.134. Agricultural Research and Extension Network. http://www.odi.org.uk/work/projects/agren/papers/agrenpaper_1 34.pdf (download date: 14 December 2011).

Boyden, Jo. (2009): Risk and Capability in the Context of Adversity. Children's Contributions to Household Livelihoods in Ethiopia. In: *Children, Youth and Environments* 19(2).

Brockerhoff, Martin, and E. Ann Biddlecom, (1999): Migration, Sexual Behaviour and the Risk of HIV in Kenya. In: *International Migration Review* 33 (4), 833–856.

Chimhundu, Herbert (1980): Shumo, Tsumo and Socialisation. In: *Zambezia* 3 (1), 37–51.

Christiansen, Catrine, Utas Mats, and Vigh E. Henrik (2006) *Navigating Youth, Generating Adulthood. Social Becoming in an African Context*. Uppsala: Nordiska Afrikainstitutet.

Foucault, Michael (1980): *Power/Knowledge: Selected Interviews and Other Writings 1972–1977*. ed. Colin Gordon. New York: Harvester Press.

Fritsch, Cerise, Elissa Johnson, and Aurelija Juska (2010): The Plight of Zimbabwean Unaccompanied Refugee Minors in South Africa. A Call for Comprehensive Legislative Action. In: *Denver Journal of International Law and Policy Denver Journal of International Law and Policy* 38 (4), 623-658.

Gigengack, Roy (2008): Critical Omissions. How Street Children Studies Can Address Self-destructive Agency. In: Pia Christensen and Allison James (eds.): *Research with Children*. Second Edition. New York: Routledge, 205–219.

Hashim, Iman and Dorte Thorsen (2011): *Child Migration in Africa*. London: Zed Books.

Hillier, Lucy (2007): *Children on the Move. Protecting Unaccompanied Migrant Children in South Africa and the Region*. Pretoria: Save the Children UK.

Honwana, Alcinda, and Filip De Boeck (2005): Children & Youth in Africa. Agency, Identity & Place. In: Alcinda Honwana and Filip De Boeck (eds.): *Makers and Breakers. Children and Youth in Postcolonial Africa*. Oxford: James Currey, 1–18.

Holloway, L. Sarah, and Gill Valentine (2000): Children's Geographies and the New Social Studies of Childhood. In: Holloway L. Sarah and Valentine Gill (eds.): *Children's Geographies. Playing, Living, Learning*. New York: Routledge, 1–26.

Maphosa, France (2007): Remittances and Development. The Impact of Migration to South Africa on Rural Livelihoods in Southern Zimbabwe. In: *Development Southern Africa* 24 (1), 123–136.

O'Kane, Claire (2008): The Development of Participatory Techniques. Facilitating Children's Views about Decisions Which

Affect Them. In: Pia Christensen and Allison James (eds.): *Research with Children*. Second Edition. New York: Routledge, pp.125–155.

Palmary, Ingrid (2009): *For Better Implementation of Migrant Children's Rights in South Africa*. Pretoria: UNICEF.

Prout, Alan and Allison James (1990): A New Paradigm for the Sociology of Childhood? Provenance, Promise and Problems. In: Allison and Alan Prout (eds.): *Constructing and Re-constructing Childhood*, London: Falmer Press. 7–33.

Raftopoulos, Brian (2009): The Crisis in Zimbabwe, 1998–2008. In: Brian Raftopoulos and Alois Mlambo (eds.): *Becoming Zimbabwe. A History from the Pre-colonial Period to 2008*. Harare: Weaver Press, 201–250.

Skinner, D., N. Tsheko, S. Munyati-Mtero, M. Segwabe, P. Chibatamoto, S. Mfecane, B. Chandiwana, N. Nkomo, S. Tlou, and G. Chitiyo (2004): *Defining Orphaned and Vulnerable Children*. Cape Town: Human Sciences Research Council.

No Longer Willing to be Dependent: Young people moving beyond learning

Yaw Ofosu-Kusi and Phil Mizen

Introduction

Our paper considers the migration of children to live and work on the streets of Accra, Ghana. As part of the 'paradigm shift' in thinking about street children, their presence on the streets and urban centres is no longer seen solely in terms of abandonment, orphaning or pathology. Rather, recent debate has stressed children's active decisions to leave home and kin as their response to the push factors of poverty, unemployment, family violence, and poor schooling systems alongside their appreciation of the pull factors of the perceived advantages of city living. The analysis here develops this child-centred account of children's (often independent) migration, but its emphasis is somewhat different. Drawing upon an emergent literature that focuses upon destitution (Devereux 2003), our contention is that children's decision to migrate to Accra must be seen as the culmination of a process involving their progressive and active exclusion from homes and communities, in conjunction with a schooling system that offers them little hope of future employment or assimilation into the formal economy. We also argue that children are not simply the passive recipients of these processes of exclusion, because migration offers them an opportunity to exercise their limited agency to recreate their lives through work and experiences from the streets.

The conception of childhood in Ghana, as in many other societies, puts great store by the fact that it is a period of innocence and limited abilities. Children in this social space are collectively raised by all responsible adults in ways that conform to society's moral codes and practices. They are routinely integrated into the social and economic activities of both immediate and extended families, and over time assume responsibilities that are consistent with their social and biological abilities. Early on in life, the upbringing of the male is usually placed in the domain of the father or male adults while the female child is principally socialised by the mother in her professional and household activities, sometimes beyond adolescence. The child therefore becomes essentially dependent on the very social and economic system that reproduces life in the family and community. In traditional Ghanaian communities this dependency could continue well into early adulthood and ceases only when the young man or woman assumes his or her place in the extended family. In the course of these transitions in childhood, however, children are assigned a subservient status in family relations, and are offered little scope in 'public discourse' (Mizen and Ofosu-Kusi 2011: 256). They are expected to surrender their agency and show utmost respect for adults under all circumstances. But that social contract also means that no child is left uncared for, especially in the rural setting where urban distractions and competing interests are less significant. The transition from one stage of childhood to another therefore centres more on what Hashim and Thorsen (2011: 8) describe as 'social personhood', than biological or chronological maturation.

The pivot of the child's 'bio-social' transition is the extended family system which provides material support for biological development and socio-cultural infrastructure for the necessary socialization. However, this arrangement has come under the influence of a number of factors. A notable one is the conjunction of urbanization and modernisation. In Ghana, the lop-sided distribution of resources between rural and urban communities promotes migration to the cities as people pursue dreams of wealth, education, adventure, and glamour. Once they settle in the cities, the combination of modern trends of living and economic difficulties compels many to regard the extended family system as a burden on their limited resources, rather than an asset for the reproduction of the family. People therefore incline towards the needs and aspirations of their immediate family members, such as their spouse and children, instead of their extended ones. Moreover draconian economic policies rooted in the structural adjustment programmes of the past two decades have over the years reduced employment opportunities in the formal sector and accentuated the level of economic insecurity for those lucky to have jobs. As Davis (2006: 155) argues, African cities like Accra became 'trapped in a vicious cycle of increasing [im]migration, decreasing formal employment, falling wages and collapsing revenues'. Labour shed from the public sector, joined the ranks of the informal sector. However since the sector is characterised by unstable employment, underemployment, and fierce competition, many of the operators are marginalised and impoverished (Verlet 2000: 68) and so lack the capacity to fend for even themselves.

These and other factors in concert have been diluting the extended family system, thus undermining the inherent redistribution of wealth and responsibility. The dilution has also in some cases eroded the special place of children in Ghanaian societies; consequently activities that were regulated under traditional socialisation to ease the child into responsible adulthood have in many urban environments assumed exploitative dimensions (Ampofo 1994: 22). In some cases, children have been abandoned to their own fate or burdened with tasks and responsibilities that place in doubt the caretaking responsibility of the extended family. As appropriately noted by the Ministry of Women and Children (MOWAC) and UNICEF (2009: xvii) in Ghana, the 'increasing numbers of children in some parts of the country suffering from hunger, deprivation and exploitation are in contradiction with traditional values...'

Buoyed, however, by the abundance of information and social infrastructure that supports child migration, many children are reluctant to remain passive in the face of neglect and deprivation by their families and the government, because schools which are central to their socialization operate largely in dilapidated structures, and are blighted by inadequate resources and uninspiring teachers. Others are equally unwilling to continue the dependency on adults when they believe they could chart a course in life right at the early stages for themselves. The consequence of this and other factors is an on-going migration of children from the rural areas to urban areas in search of work, opportunities, education and the glamour of those places (Beauchemin 1999; Ofosu-Kusi 2002; Hashim and Thorsen 2011).

We have known for some time the push and pull factors for children's migration to the cities of Africa (see for example Beuachemin 1999; Gough 2008; Lindell 2010). Until the late 1990s, most rural areas of Ghana were largely isolated from the cities. The influx of cheap mobile phones, liberalization of the airwaves, and the subsequent establishment of radio stations in virtually all district capitals as well as expansion of the spatial coverage of television stations exposed city life to rural dwellers. The rapid information flow inundated most people with stories and images of the 'good' city life. The barriers to migration were further dismantled through the rapid opening up of the rural areas through improvements in the transportation systems. These processes demystified migration and in fact democratised it to the extent that it is no longer the preserve of those with connections to the city. The destination for a number of people, including children, seeking a better life outside their towns and villages has been Accra. But life in the streets of Accra is replete with complex surprises that easily disorganise the plans children constructed before migrating. Nevertheless, they develop their survival strategies that are situated in friendships, cooperation, and sheer determination (Mizen and Ofosu-Kusi 2010), to the extent that many of them are quite resilient in the face of adversities.

What this chapter contributes to the discourse is children's progressive engagement with the forces that govern their lives and their unwillingness to succumb to the helplessness of their families and communities. We therefore argue that many children, especially those from deprived families and communities, are acting as reflexive agents in shaping their future by predicating it on migration to the city. They do not do this because of a naïve simplification of life and the hazards associated with living in the city. On the contrary, they are generally aware of the difficulties and consequences of life in those places, but migration and work offer relatively more prospects for the future than what the family and rural economy could offer. Therefore children's decisions to migrate must be seen as the outcome of a progressive failure to provide emotional and material support and/or the consequences of family disputes, violence, and neglect. At their destination, they may be destitute as migrant children, but they utilise their limited agency to look to life and work on the street as the basis for the construction and reconstruction of new social relations.

Researching with children on the street

The paper in part is based on a three-year study of 75 children, aged between 9 and 16 years, who had migrated from various parts of the country, but mostly from rural areas of the Ashanti, Central, Volta, Northern, Upper East, and Upper West regions to the streets and markets of Accra, Ghana. Even though the term 'street children' is applied to children in a diverse range of situations, our interest was those children often designated 'of the street', rather than children of the urban poor. That is, we were interested in the lives of those children who did not return home or to kin each evening but spent significant periods of time living and working on the streets.

The children were encountered at various times in and around Obtesbi Lamptey Circle, the Central Railway Station and its environs, Rawlings Park, CMB, Kaneshi Market, Kwame Nkrumah Circle, Neoplan Station, and the markets and slums of Agbobloshie. Collectively, these areas represent a large social and economic space where shop keepers, traders, hawkers, street vendors, shoppers, porters, lorry and taxi drivers, street children, and city officials engage in daily transactions. These spaces, upon which a good proportion of the ubiquitous informal economy of Accra is anchored, were the homes and work places of the participants of the study. Such areas provide considerable scope for the activities of the over 30,000 children in Accra (Ministry of Women and Children— MOWAC—and UNICEF 2009) since there is little or no official regulation. A good part of what all these children and others do in this informal environment is, as Harriss-White (2010: 170) puts it, 'outside the regulative ambit of the state'.

Methodologically, we engaged the participants in what we termed 'dialogue with a purpose' through spontaneous and arranged encounters. During these dialogues the children reminisced about their lives back home, reflected on their current situation, provided testimonies of their most harrowing experiences in the markets and on the streets as well as laughed and joked about good times, friendships and dreams. Many hours were also spent at important meeting places in the markets and the refuge run by Catholic Action for Street Children to observe the lives of specific participants and their social environments as a whole. In order to capture some graphic detail of the lives that were portrayed in the dialogues, 15 children were provided with disposable cameras to record a 24-hour experience of their lives in the streets and markets. Even though there were practical difficulties in using this technique in the unpredictable environment, it was nevertheless an exceptional opportunity for the children to concentrate on areas and behaviours that were of greatest concern and interest to them. In the subsequent individual and group interviews, the pictures provided considerable structure and detail to the dialogues. While the use of cameras to co-opt children and young people into research has been practised for many years in other parts of the world (see for example Clark 1999; Bolton et al. 2001; Luttrell 2010), it is rarely used in sub-Sahara Africa.

Escape from poverty and neglect

Two major factors arise in the attempt to discuss children's migration in relation to their agency. These are extreme poverty, often bordering on destitution, and the dysfunctional schooling system in rural areas of Ghana. The conventional interpretation of destitution is that of an extreme form of poverty under which people lack food, purchasing power and the necessities of life. This stark reality compels them to subsist on the goodwill and generosity of others. Devereux

(2003: iii) in the attempt to develop a conceptual framework for the analysis of destitution suggests three key markers: 'inability to meet subsistence needs, assetlessness, and dependence on transfers'. Writing about destitution in South Asia, Harriss-White (2005: 882) also argues that people are destitute because the interplay of social, economic and political processes culminates in 'power relationships' that dispossess them of the means necessary for a decent existence. The lack of assets or powerlessness in taking charge of assets, inability to access insurance schemes, and to earn income on one's labour potential represent a destitution that is steeped in economics. The social dimension of destitution as mediated by 'social norms', she argues, results in disenfranchisement and disentitlement. Instead of guaranteeing social security and existence, the malfunctioning social institutions and norms rather debars the destitute from even depending on social structures for support. They are therefore deprived of their rights and are 'socially expelled' (p. 883). To be desperately poor at the point of non-existence, she argues further, also implies a complete deprivation of political rights; that category of people 'is stripped of political rights such that none are left to be violated' (p. 884). In effect, not only are they helpless but the dynamics of the political and economic system obstruct the poor with structural and social rigidities that reduce their potential to almost nothing.

We draw parallels between the status of many rural dwellers—adults and children—in Ghana and the categorization of Devereux and Harriss-White. Many rural dwellers live on a day-by-day basis, lack assets as a result of dispossession arising from man-made and natural disasters or disentitlement arising from social and cultural practices or a complete lack of opportunity to acquire them. The lives of many are therefore contingent on the goodwill of others, even though incomes are generally low in the country. For example, the gross national income per capita in 2008 was a measly US$670 (UNICEF 2009). It is even lower in the rural areas. Between 2003 and 2007, 30 per cent of the population were living below the international poverty line of US$1.25 per day. Besides, the percentage share of household income between 2000 and 2007 for the lowest 40 per cent was only 15 per cent, while the highest 20 per cent had 48 per cent (UNICEF 2009). The huge disparity in incomes is especially glaring in people's lives and the general environment of crumbling infrastructure and an absence of modern conveniences in the rural areas. The Greater Accra region on the other hand is relatively wealthy; in fact 64 per cent of its population are in the top 20 per cent wealth quintile. However, regions like Brong Ahafo, Volta, Northern, Upper East and Upper West have less than 7 per cent of their population in the top wealth quintile (Ghana Statistical Service—GSS—et al. 2009).

Moreover, household sizes are relatively larger in rural areas, with a mean size of 4.0 persons compared to 3.4 persons in the urban areas (GSS et al. 2009). Large family size increases the dependency burden, as well as deepens and lengthens dependence on the already poor parents. Yet, even though the majority of families are headed by males, about one-third of families are headed by females, most of whom are resource-deficient (GSS/GHS/ICF Macro 2009). The lack of resources and employment opportunities, coupled with meagre financial resources to engage in self-employment, erodes their ability to create a worthwhile life for themselves. Such outcomes result in gradual and long-term processes that culminate in a dependence on family and kin, usually on relatively better-off extended family members in the urban areas. By association, the children of such parents experience 'derived destitution' (Sen 1991: 103, cited in Devereux 2003) since as long as they remain part of the household their lives cannot be any better than those of their impoverished parents. This endemic poverty impacts more on children than any other social group because of their lack of entitlement to resources in Ghanaian societies. Thus in the absence of functional social welfare programmes targeting families and children in particular, destitution is simply transferred from parents to children. If childhood is a period of dependence as conventionally thought then children's problems would be addressed by adults. This responsibility underpins the adult-child relationship in virtually every society. However, the extreme poverty dispossesses many rural parents of the ability and authority to exercise care-taking responsibility for their children thereby portraying them as socially incompetent (Ofosu-Kusi 2002: 218).

The extreme form of poverty manifested in absence of material resources, employment and wealth-creation opportunities reduces many people in those societies to the equivalent of Davis's (2006: 175) 'surplus humanity' in the cities of the developing world. A major characteristic is their virtual exclusion from the formal labour market, a development which is 'identified as a primary route to destitution' (Devereux 2003: 9). The vibrant informal economy that absorbs labour surplus to the needs of the formal sector is non-existent in the rural areas. Without any power of persuasion or tangible economic opportunities, parents are so impoverished that they are simply incapable of reproducing themselves and even depending on the state and its institutions. The major casualties in this are the children who often are a generational version of their parents.

The second crucial factor is the way schools operate in Ghana's rural communities. Education is a critical medium for the socialization and eventual development of children in every society, yet the local education system is fraught with diverse difficulties. Schools in the rural areas are crippled by structural inadequacies, insufficient reading and writing materials, poorly trained teachers or a complete lack of qualified teachers (Ofosu-Kusi 2007). Yet children are expected to make the most out of such sparse conditions, and pass highly competitive examinations to facilitate their ascension to the next level of the social ladder. However, while free primary schooling exists in principle in Ghana for children in poor households, the failure of parents and guardians to fully provide requirements like uniforms, footwear, writing materials and lunch money coupled with the other inadequacies accentuate the disconnect between government's intentions and children's expectations. Besides, many families treat completion of primary school as an end in itself since those who continue to secondary schools are unable to obtain employment after graduation.

The lack of faith in schooling is evident in the statistics on enrolment and attendance at primary and secondary schools in the table below. The gross enrolment ratios between 2003 and 2008 for primary school were 98 for boys and 97 for girls. On the other hand, the net school enrolment ratios for primary school were 73 and 71 for boys and girls respectively, indicating that a good proportion of children of school-going age for that period were not enrolled in primary school. It gets worse at the secondary school level where both the gross and net enrolment ratios drop to nearly half of the gross primary enrolment ratio. The net enrolment ratio for females is as low as 43, while the net attendance ratio for both males and females is 45.

Primary and Secondary School Enrolment and Attendance Ratios in Ghana, 2003 – 2008

Primary school enrolment ratio				Prim. Sch. attendance ratio		Secondary Sch. enrolment ratio				Sec. School attendance ratio	
Gross		Net		Net		Gross		Net		Net	
Male	Female	Male	Fem.	Male	Fem.	Male	Fem.	Male	Fem	Male	Fem.
98	97	73	71	75	75	52	46	47	43	45	45

Source: UNICEF (2009) Statistical Tables; Table 5: Education.

The differential begs the question of what happened to the graduates of the primary and junior secondary school system in that period. It is likely that some of them entered apprenticeships, but the most plausible explanation is that they simply terminated their formal education at that level. Clearly, this large pool of primary school graduates forms the bulk of children in the informal economies of Accra and Kumasi where they work all day or combine work with informal education to acquire skills such as driving, trading, and cooking.

The pervasive poverty which might be linked to the poor enrolment and attendance ratios in rural areas in Ghana and in the northern regions of the country in particular, provides some causal background to the migration of school-age children. By choosing to act in ways that promote their interest in relations to the constraining social and economic structures manifested in deprivation, poor school systems, and limited opportunities, the children clearly are exercising their agency, however limited it might be. The desire to acquire alternative competencies that their schools or communities cannot offer and the bold decision to travel underpins an unwillingness to place their future in the hands of their parents alone; migrating simply decapitates their dependence for the time they are away from home. It is therefore apparent that some children choose not to be dependent on their poverty-ridden parents and the virtually non-existent state institutions. With thoughts steeped in the belief that adults are unable to fully act as providers of opportunity and development, they strive to construct a life based on their potential. Somehow, the pervasive poverty and its associated social problems underlie the inability and neglect, while the poor quality of education in the rural areas undermines the very reason for staying at home.

Migration as a reaction to structural and social problems

Parents in the rural areas certainly have a desire to be fully responsible for their children; it is the lack of resources and opportunities that renders them incapable. That incapability triggers a series of events that lead to children's eventual disenfranchisement and disentitlement. The resulting exclusion is characterised by families' progressive failure to provide emotional and material support and/or children's susceptibility to the consequences of family disputes, violence and neglect. But what is significant in this development is children's unwillingness to be passive recipients of the processes of exclusion. On the contrary, migration becomes both a symbolic and real act of children's unwillingness to be dependent on adults whom they consider to be negligent in the performance of their responsibilities.

Dan, a boy of 15 years, migrated to Accra when he was only 11 years old. The motivation for his migration was clearly the paucity of economic opportunities for adults in his home town; a development he thought did not bode well for his future as a child.

> There is no job in my home town which can give you money. There is no money in the village. Even if you go to school and finish secondary school, there is nothing you can do with it. The only work in my village is farming and selling of coconut. I can't do any of them so I decided to come to Accra.

The lack of faith in schooling is evident in his denigration of secondary education as a waste of time since its completion would not guarantee his future advancement. For him the future lies neither with his parents nor with education in the village, but in the streets of Accra.

Emma's (a boy) actions and decision to migrate to Accra is reflective of the behaviour of many other children in the research. He was the eleventh of his mother's 11 children, and had abandoned his education at primary four. Asked why, 15-year-old Emma noted:

> I used to go to school but I didn't have anybody to look after me. My parents are poor and they couldn't look after me so I stopped. One day one of my brothers came from Tema [port city near Accra] and wanted to put me back in school but my mother said no because she wouldn't be able to support me. That is why I decided to come to Accra to earn money to continue my education.

Though Emma talks about his parents' financial inability, the cost of schooling in the countryside is not as high as it is in Accra. However, the deplorable economic status of many rural people renders many incapable of meeting responsibilities associated with children's education and upbringing, however minimal. As rightly noted by Aba who abandoned schooling and headed to Accra when she was 13 years old, schooling 'is not as expensive [in the village] as in Accra, but as a child I needed somebody to be responsible for me, to give me the things I needed for school. I didn't have anybody to do that.' Kofi reiterated the helplessness of parents by lamenting the inadequacies of his mother:

> What bothers me is not been able to go to school, especially having to stop after I have been in it for some time. At the moment, it is impossible for me to get anybody to pay my school fees. My mother has very little. She lost her toilet-cleaning job, so she is idle now and stays home, doing some small farming. That is life in the village really; there is little hope even for my mother let alone me [Male, 15 years].

For Josh, a 14-year-old seller of plastic bags at Kaneshi, the catalyst for the termination of his schooling at nine years of age was his parents' divorce: 'My parents are divorced so we [siblings] are all scattered and have to find ways to fend for ourselves.' A victim of his father's financial incapability and mother's palpable dislike of her ex-husband, his mother 'would not bear that responsibility' because she believed that if she educated him some of the benefits would trickle down to his father one day.

Precocious 9-year-old Bless had had two encounters with the local police by the time we interviewed her. She earned a living by fetching buckets of water for a hairdresser and begging for money at the plush Kotoka International Airport intersection. Like Kofi, she had to terminate her schooling because of her parents' incessant quarrels, often violent confrontations and eventual separation. In defence of her actions, she noted:

> No, I didn't stop going to school, it was my mother who didn't allow me to go further because she had a fight with my father... She didn't put me back to school when we left my father. Any time my father comes for me and puts me in school, she will also

come and take me away so I ended up not going to school even
though I begged her to allow me to...

An effective Social Welfare Department would quickly have
removed Bless from what apparently was a dysfunctional family
because her father 'smokes marijuana sometimes and drinks lots of
alcohol and when he is drunk, beats me up and throws me out of the
house...' [Bless, Female, 9 years]. However, the department is so
financially and logistically handicapped that it is unable to effectively monitor such activities or to readily find alternative solutions
for children even when their attention is drawn to clear cases of child
molestation and abuse. The combination of parental neglect due to a
variety of reasons and institutional ineptitude culminates in an exclusion that places the burden of responsibility not on the state as
expected by the United Nations Convention on the Rights of the
Child, but on victims like Bless.

Pamela, a 14-year-old girl also had to terminate schooling at
primary four because there was nobody to assume responsibility for
her education: 'When I came back [from Kumasi], it was difficult for
me, because I couldn't get anybody to pay my school fees and to
provide other things I needed for school.' What is discernible in
these cases and many others in the study is an initial driver of parental neglect often attributed to lack of economic capability that incen-
tivises some children to quit school. There were remote causes such
as a lack of interest in schooling or a willingness to experience the
attractions of cities like Kumasi and Accra. However, these were
often secondary causes that gained prominence because of the primary parental neglect. Parents' inability to fully assume responsibility for children's schooling in combination with other factors leads to
a national dropout rate of 4 per cent (GSS et al. 2009). But in Upper
West, one of the major sources of child migrants, the dropout rate is
as high as 17 per cent at primary six, where the average age is 12
years. According to the Ghana Statistical Service, school attendance
starts to gradually decline after age 13, the period when children are
expected to be in junior secondary school. Clearly, children from this

age onwards would have become relatively older and assertive, and so begin to make decisions about the future.

Children's actions are not usually performed on the spur of the moment; many children somehow plan and reflect upon the consequences once they sense a rational explanation. According to Dameon nobody prompted him to travel to Accra since he:

> decided to come because back there it was very difficult for my mother to get money for me to go to school. There are many coconut trees in the area so I plucked some, sold them and got ¢20,000[1] which I used to board a bus to Accra [Male, 16 years].

Constance, a 16-year-old girl, on the other hand had to 'work on somebody's farm to raise the money (¢55,000)...' for her transportation. Others were not so enterprising in their quest for fares to Accra, as candidly admitted by a 14-year-old boy, Asumah.

YK: Who gave you the idea to come here?

Asumah: No one did. My grandmother visited us one day and I took her money to travel to Accra.

YK: You stole your grandmother's money to come to Accra?

Asumah: Yes.

Dan (male, 15 years) simply absconded with money meant for someone else. 'I was sent to go and give money to somebody but I didn't, instead I used it as money for my transportation and came to Accra,' was his frank response when asked about how he got money to travel to Accra. It is depressing to hear children confess to thefts of money at home, but might make some sense when contextualised in family environments of extreme poverty, violence, abuse, and neglect. A good deal of such dysfunctional behaviour could be linked to the neglect and exclusion perpetuated by parents, unresponsive governments, and corrupt and ineffective public officials.

For some parents, it made no difference if their children left home; in some cases this appeared to be a welcome relief. For

---

[1] The currency has since been redenominated as GHC1.00 to ¢10,000

example, instead of Bless's father dissuading her from leaving home, he rather provided her with the means to do so:

> ... when I told him that I wanted to leave [home] he gave me money to leave and told me that I could go to wherever I liked because he didn't care about wherever I went to... [9 years].

According to Kofi, 'My mother told me that she will never look for me if I got missing or something happened to me so I just left; now I don't have any contact with her...' [Male, 14 years]. Lack of capability accentuates the helplessness of some parents in determining what their children should do. For instance, even though Emma's mother would not let him travel, he did so nonetheless: 'Yes. I told her that I was coming to Accra...She said she won't let me come but I left early in the morning.' It is atypical for Ghanaian children to disregard their parents' instructions, especially for a major event like migration from home to far-away Accra. To leave for the city without the blessings or consent of parents is a challenge to the orthodoxy in which children are expected to passively remain with parents and provide support in the form of labour and company where necessary. In this orthodoxy, the child is acknowledged as a powerful connection to the future, hence passively succumbing to socialization prepares him or her not just for the future but also ensures a reproduction of the family and the society concerned.

On the part of government, the neglect is characterised by the failure to provide a truly affordable and functional education system. For instance, while government-approved school fees at the basic education level are minimal, head teachers and parent-teacher associations devise all sorts of creative accounting and billing systems to raise money from parents. This racks up the cost, makes it difficult for some parents to meet their financial obligations, and so provides the rationale for some children to drop out of school and head to the cities. In any case there is minimum value for what appear to be the 'exorbitant' fees charged by schools. The 'best' schools in those environments are the ones that have a few of the needed teaching-learning materials as well as one or two qualified or trained teachers.

The majority, as noted by Ofosu-Kusi (2007), are severely under-resourced. Often, children are saddled with the responsibility of tending teachers' farms or doing manual work that the school has been contracted for. In such cases, the school becomes a replica of the domestic environments that many children wish to distance themselves from. According to Emma:

> The government school there is bad, the teachers don't teach us well and we are made to work all the time. Today, they will say go and carry this load from this place to another, the next day, they will ask us to fetch water for the brick maker or to weed some-body's farm. We work instead of studying... [Male, 15 years].

Many Ghanaian children are no longer socialised strictly according to local norms and the community's set of moral values because of several intervening factors. According to MOWAC and UNICEF (2009), mediating influences from religious organisations with Christian and Islamic backgrounds, radio and television, and for urban children, the ubiquitous worldwide web are instrumental in how children construct their identity. Some of the influences are so pervasive and overriding that the authority of parents and adults are seriously undermined, especially if children are not directly under their influence. For, as long as children remain in the family set-up, they have limited ability to shape their lives since they are con-strained by the family's expectations. Even then they rely on their innate and social resources to wrestle some control of their lives. As Gough (2008: 244) points out, children hope to gain 'independence, competence, and maturity, and sustain social relations with peers'. But it is a reaction that sees them utilising their potential in inde-pendent ways.

Reproduction of adversity in the streets

Children's reluctance to remain passive in the face of neglect and deprivation at home is a testimony to their courage and innovation. In assuming some degree of responsibility for their lives through migration and a life independent of their families, they demonstrate a major disregard for the consequences. Predictably, when children abandon school and set off for Accra, they assume that their lives will improve significantly. This is not surprising since all categories of migrants rationalise their actions in the firm belief that the grass will be greener at their destination. The reality however, can be vastly different from expectations, as child migrants in Accra are faced with months and years of privations. Even holding on to the few possessions they acquire on the street can be a daunting task since they lack storage spaces and are constantly at the mercy of opportunists. For example, Abena, a 16-year-old girl, lost everything she had to thieves, and without money even had challenges in maintaining her personal hygiene.

> Abena: I used to [have some dresses] but all have been stolen so now I don't have anything.
>
> YK: So all you have left is the dress you are wearing?
>
> Abena: This dress is not even mine, it belongs to my friend.
>
> YK: You don't have anything at all?
>
> Abena: No.
>
> YK: Do you have a towel and sponge for bathing?
>
> Abena: No.
>
> YK: So how do you bath?
>
> Abena: [Silence].

Theft is a major part of the insecurity that bedevils the lives of street children. Not only do the very young and new ones have their money taken away through force and intimidation, their clothes are sometimes shredded at night as the culprits search for valuables. To just survive, migrant street children have to work long and unpredictable hours, on some days go hungry or sick. According to Bless, sometimes when she is sick: 'I go hungry for the whole day until someone asks me what the problem is, then I tell him/her that my stomach aches, then he/she will get me some drugs and later buy me food.' Many street children depend on the generosity of their friends to contribute to hire a taxi to the small clinic operated by the Catholic Action for Street Children (CAS) when they are very sick, else they have to self-medicate by purchasing herbal concoctions or drugs from nearby drug stores. However, the efficacy of these herbal concoctions is not clearly known and so could worsen their situation and even prolong the time of recovery, sometimes with long-lasting consequences.

In spite of the realization that children are socially capable and active in the construction of their own lives, their search for alternatives in the form of migration and work is seen negatively by many people in Accra. There is an instinctive *pathologizing* of migrant children by city officials and the public, especially through sensational accounts of street children's lives in the popular press. Children are written off as 'vagrants pursuing the elusive attractions of the city...' (Korboe 1997: 3) and are generally thought of as recalcitrant and labelled as thieves, truants and misfits. Public empathy therefore appears to be minimal. Unfortunately in the desperate bid to survive and to meet social expectations, many of them engage in actions that confirm the public's perceptions. On one occasion, Dan, a 15-year-old boy, narrowly escaped the might of the law possibly out of sympathy and the fact that he was a minor.

> Dan: I carried someone's things to her house one day and when I got there I saw her money, which was ¢700,000. I took it and used it to buy things which I took to my home town and was away for about a month. So when I came back, the woman saw me and had me arrested. When we got to the police station and she made her statement and they realized that it happened some time ago, they told her that it could not be a case; all the same they detained me for four days before releasing me.

There are innumerable barriers to the realization of their dreams; they have virtually no resources at their disposal, in some cases they are even prevented from utilising their labour potential because of opposition from their peers and city authorities. At Kaneshi, they compete for loads by running after vehicles to claim particular loads when the vehicle stops, but the older ones would simply take away that opportunity. They could also lose their money in the process:

Yes, some of the boys take from us the loads we've been able to lay our hands on and rather carry them. At other times others will be picking your pockets as you run after the vehicle for loads [Dameon, male, 15 years].

The neglect, abuse, and violence experienced at home are relived on the streets. Survival depends on their resourcefulness, ingenuity and ability to translate insignificant opportunities into major ones. Those who exploit children's labour in the markets, privacy of homes, in the streets and on plantations are hardly ever criminalised. In instance upon instance, clients refuse to pay for services they have rendered and are sometimes physically abusive when children protest at the unfair treatment. She 'beat me up and even scratched my face with her finger nails' was Asumah's recollection of his experience when he demanded what he thought was due to him for the work he had done. This exploitation is possible because in the majority of cases the children are not able to negotiate for payment before the work is done largely because of the competition for work. Thus they depend on the goodwill of the clients to pay a wage that can sustain them on the street.

Even though work is the practical solution to their survival needs in Accra, their success in doing so depends on their abilities to manipulate the social relations to their benefit. The work and social environments in the streets, markets and road intersections are unforgiving in many respects so children have to develop appropriate survival strategies and resilience. The living conditions are sparse; there is no support from the government or protection from the police; the public is unsympathetic, competition for work is tough because of the increasing number of street children while the older children are very abusive. By reproducing the adversity of children through a lack of political will to enforce the laws and conventions on child labour and child exploitation, children are sucked further into conditions of destitution. In spite of this it is apparent that many of them consider their actions as worthwhile and necessary for their future aspirations. When Emma was asked to compare his eating habits on the streets to those of his home, he argued that even though it was better in the village, there was a good reason for him to endure what was available on the streets.

> Emma: I had better food to eat there than here, but I came here for a purpose so I can't spend all   my money on eating good food.
> YK: OK, what is this purpose you are talking about?
> Emma: I want to save about ¢100,000 so that can I go back home and continue my education.

To be reflexive agents, children must have an idea of the present, the past and the future. This certainly is manifested in Emma's behaviour. Though it would take a lot of effort to earn and save that amount of money since they earn relatively little per day, his determination to prepare for the future this way is instructive. The children in effect have to utilise their capabilities in ingenious ways since the adverse conditions of impoverishment experienced in their areas of origin are reproduced in the streets and markets.

Conclusion

In the traditional socialization discourse, children are considered as *becomings*; they are not yet competent 'reflexive agents' and therefore are incapable of acting in their interest (Redmond 2010: 476). For this reason they are not socially and legally recognised while on the street, a development that reproduces the harshness and adversities that characterise their lives in the city. Thus even though we argue that the very act of migration implies a limited utilization of agency to wrestle some degree of autonomy from adults who might have been negligent in their responsibilities or abusive, the outcome of the process does not necessarily invigorate that agency. Nevertheless, expectations of a better life moderate the children's assessment of the harsh realities of Accra, such that they speak in comparative terms. For many, the privations of the street are relatively better and preferable to their earlier lives even if migration deprives them of the network of support and care that the extended family at home could provide. Thus, even though migration represents a big gamble, children's actions are founded on the belief that anything in the city would be better than continuing to be dependent on parents who are immobilised by extreme poverty. Consequently, they develop ingenious strategies to cope with the adversities and privations that govern their lives in the streets. Children's courage in leaving home and their fortitude in the midst of the harsh realities of Accra is emblematic of the new ways of 'seeing' childhood, that children are no longer passive recipients of parental and institutional failures. While the majority of children continue to depend on their parents for sustenance and for the future direction of their lives, there is a growing wave that sees migration as the solution to their predicament regardless of the adversities of the streets. Following Harriss-White (2010), we conclude that child migrants are destitute in Accra because they are not willing to be dependent on their kin in the places of origin.

References

Ampofo, Kinsley (1994): The Economic Recovery Programme and the Rights of the Child. In: Henrieta Mensa-Bonsu and Christine Dawuona-Hammond (eds.): *The Rights of the Child in Ghana: Perspectives.* Accra: Woeli Publishing Services, 18–27.

Beauchemin, Eric (1999): *The Exodus. The Growing Migration of Children from Ghana's Rural Areas to the Urban Centres.* Accra: Catholic Action for Street Children and UNICEF.

Bolton, Alison, Chris Pole, and Phil Mizen (2001): Picture This. Researching Child Workers. In: *Sociology* 35 (2), 501–18.

Clark, Cindy Dell (1999): The Autodriven Interview. A Photographic Viewfinder into Children's Experiences. In: *Visual Sociology* 14, 39–50.

Davis, Mike (2006): *Planet of Slums.* London: Verso.

Devereux, Stephen (2003): *Conceptualising Destitution,* IDS Working Paper 216. Sussex: Institute for Development Studies, Brighton.

Ghana Statistical Service (GSS), Ghana Health Service (GHS), and ICF Macro (2009): *Ghana Demographic and Health Survey 2008*. Accra: Ghana Statistical Service.

Gough, Katherine (2008): 'Moving Around'. The Social and Spatial Mobility of Youth in Lusaka. In: *Geografiska Annaler* Series B, *Human Geography* 90 (3), 243–255.

Harriss-White, Barbara (2005): Destitution and the Poverty of its Politics. With Special Reference to South Asia. In: *World Development* 33 (6), 881–891.

Harriss-White, Barbara (2010): Work and Well-Being in Informal Economies. The Regulative Roles of Institutions of Identity and the State. In: *World Development* 38 (2), 170–183

Hashim, Iman, and Dorte Thorsen (2011): *Child Migration in Africa*. London: Zed Books.

Korboe, David (1997): *A Profile of Street Children in Kumasi*. Legon: Centre for Social Policy Studies, University of Ghana.

Lindell, Ilda (2010): Between Exit and Voice. Informality and the Spaces of Popular Agency'. In: *African Studies Quarterly* 11 (2 & 3), 1–11.

Luttrell, Wendy (2010): A Camera is a Big Responsibility'. A Lens for Analysing Children's Visual Voices. In: *Visual Studies* 25 (3), 224–237.

Ministry of Women and Children's Affairs (MOWAC) and UNICEF (2009): *Children in Ghana*. Accra: UNICEF.

Mizen, Phil, and Yaw Ofosu-Kusi (2010): Asking, Giving, Receiving. Friendship as a Survival Strategy amongst Accra's Street Children. In: *Childhood* 17 (4), 441–454.

Mizen, Phil, and Yaw Ofosu-Kusi (2011): Unofficial Truths and Everyday Insights. Understanding Voice in Visual Research with the Children of Accra's Urban Poor'. In: *Visual Studies* 25 (3), 225–267.

Ofosu-Kusi, Yaw (2002): *Migrant Street Children in Accra. A Case Study of the Making an Adjustment Generation*. PhD Thesis, University of Warwick, UK.

Ofosu-Kusi, Yaw (2007): Inequitable Opportunities, Same Standards. Why Some Children Perform Below Standard in Basic Education Examination. In: *Social Educator* 3 (1), 180–195.

Redmond, Gerry (2010): Children's Agency and the Welfare State. Policy Priorities and Contradictions in Australia and the UK. In: *Childhood* 17 (4), 470–484.

UNICEF (2009): *The State of the World's Children: Special Edition.* New York: UNICEF.

Verlet, Martin (2000): Growing Up in Ghana. Deregulation and the Employment of Children. In: B. Schlemmer (ed.): *The Exploited Child.* London: Zed Books.

Children's Work, Education and Agency: The African Movement of Working Children and Youth (AMWCY)

Manfred Liebel

Young working children of Africa,
let us rise up and salute a new kind of work
working children from every region,
let us reinvent this work
For it is through working that man becomes
free and independent
It is through working that we gain our dignity
It nourishes our survival, our future
What will become of us without work
and generate the hopes of future working children
Working children, let us persevere in the work we do,
for the future of our country, our environment,
our family and the people we are
Rise up working children, walk hand in hand
and together we will build our future and toil
for the development of all our countries.

The working children of Kayes (Mali), 1999.[1]

Introduction

For about two decades a growing number of working children and young people in Africa have been making their voices heard as part of the African Movement of Working Children and Youth

---

[1] From the AMWCY journal, 'A Letter from the Street'.

(AMWCY). In 2009 the movement claimed almost 200 associations —as the groups at the city and regional level are called. These associations were from 21 different countries with more than 80,000 members in a total of 1367 groups at the grassroots level (AMWCY 2009a). Around 72 per cent of the individuals belonging to these organisations were children and young people below the age of 18; 54 per cent were girls or young women (Terenzio 2009). These young people are demanding that they no longer be simply treated as the objects of 'measures against child labour', and that their own initiatives be taken seriously. This chapter provides an insight into this relatively new social phenomenon and contributes to its explanation and understanding. To do so, this chapter focuses on the concepts of work and education and the interconnections between them articulated by the African Movement of Working Children and Youth (AMWCY), as well as its initiatives and experiences.

Very little data are available for independent academic studies of the AMWCY. Nevertheless, this organisation representing a specific group of children and young people in Africa, presents views of work and learning which are interesting in themselves. They should be taken seriously in discussions of children's work in Africa, even if we have no clear answers as to whether their views are effective or representative. This chapter is a presentation of these views, supported by some case studies.

After providing a short overview of the most import aspects of the movement and the reasoning behind it, this chapter concentrates on how work and education is understood in the context of the children's claimed rights, and the ways in which the movement strives for improvements in the daily lives of working children. Finally, it discusses the impact, scope and limitations of the agency of organised working children.

Understanding the movement's rationale

The AMWCY first came into being in the early 1990s in a number of West African countries. It then spread to other parts of the continent, often with the support of children's rights groups and humanitarian organisations (Swift 1999; Liebel 2001; Terenzio 2001; Coly and Terenzio 2007). *ENDA Tiers Monde*, an NGO that has carried out street work programmes with children and adolescents in Senegal, Mali and other African countries since the mid-1980s, played a particularly important role in the organisation's development. The great majority of organised working children live and work in conditions that clearly violate their human rights. As is the case with adult self-help organisations, the AMWCY faces difficulties reaching children in particularly dire working conditions: a child's ability to engage with working children's organisations largely depends on their having spare time and a minimum level of control of working relations to attend meetings and other activities (Liebel 2004; Nimbona 2005; Nimbona and Lieten 2007). Yet, working children are increasingly using their organisations to reach out towards children working in different contexts and to create alternative livelihoods for children confronted with particularly exploitative or dangerous working conditions (AMWCY 2009b).

A further challenge for the movement is how to ensure equal participation for children of different ages and gender within the organisation. The majority of children and young people active in the movement are between 11 and 18 years of age, but some are older and these are the ones most likely to represent the movement at national and international meetings. This is increasingly seen as a problem. In an effort to redress the balance, an agreement was made ensuring that only children below the age of 18 may be elected as delegates. A meeting of the AMWCY's coordination commission in 2009 set the target of 70 per cent of each association's members being children, and at least 50 per cent of them girls (AMWCY 2009a). Local groups also undertake specific activities to ensure younger children and girls are able to play an active role, with a certain level of responsibility in the organisation. The participation of children in the AMWCY's national coordination was further enshrined in the final declaration of the 8th African meeting, held in Cotonou (Benin) in 2009 (AMWCY 2010).

Working children and young people in the African movement frame their demands and actions in a discourse based on existing human rights and children's rights. In particular, they focus on those set out in the UN Convention on the Rights of the Child (1989) and the African Charter on the Rights and Welfare of the Child (1990). This is similar to working children's movements on other continents, and demonstrates that they view themselves as holders of these rights, and that they are entitled to have their rights applied and upheld. The children place particular emphasis on the provisions outlining the right to participate in decisions that affect their lives. Additionally, they use their many declarations to set out their own particular understanding of children's rights, rephrased according to their own contexts. This also demonstrates that they consider themselves subjects entitled to interpret and specify the significance of these rights, and that they reject the image of children as mere passive recipients of the benevolence of adults. Instead they go further, and demand certain children's rights which have not been codified internationally.[2]

Far from considering themselves victims or the passive objects of adults' agency and social structures, organised working children share a conception of children as active and competent participants in their social worlds. They feel capable of analysing their surroundings and devising strategies through which they hope to contribute, not only to an improvement in their own living conditions, but also to a long-term amelioration of social relations in their communities and societies. Included in this concept of self as a social subject, is a specific understanding of the economic participation of children (Liebel 2003). In contrast to the dominant Western model of childhood, working children consider their work to be an important

---

[2] On the concepts of 'unwritten rights' and rights as 'works in progress', see Ennew, 2002; Liebel, 2012; Saadi, 2012.

element in the making and maintenance of social life, and they demand recognition of this. A closer look at how the children consider 'work' will provide a better understanding.

The movement's founding document is known as '12 Rights', and it was adopted at the first African meeting in Bouaké (Ivory Coast) in 1994 (see Voice of African Children 2001). It claims the 'right to light and limited work', and explains this in the following way: 'When we take up the work, we negotiate the type of work which is appropriate to our age, but this agreement is never respected. There are no fixed hours, we start early and finish late. We ask that we not be given hours of work and tasks that you would not ask your own children to do.' The right postulated here is closely related to other rights such as the 'right to security when working', which is explained in the following manner: 'To work without being harassed by the authorities and people in general (not to be man-mistreated, but be trusted).' Other rights stated in the document that are related to the right to work are: 'to respect', 'to rest when sick', 'to healthcare', 'to be taught a trade', 'to play', and 'to learn to read and write'. The African movement argues that these rights are inter-connected and related to one another.

This was emphasised in the final declaration of the 6th African meeting, which took place in Thiès (Senegal) in 2003 (archive Pro-NATs, Germany): 'For nine years now, we have been organised in order to build and implement our rights to education, vocational training, health care, respect, dignity, safety, organisation, equitable justice, return to our villages, leisure, light and limited work.'

Three years later, during the 7th African meeting in Ouagadou-gou (Burkina Faso), the relation between these rights was highlighted in the following statement (archive ProNATs, Germany): 'Where ever we are organised, our rights have progressed such as the right to learn to read and write, to cure ourselves in case of illness, to work less hard... The development of our Income Generating Activities (IGA) is enabling us to struggle against poverty and to fund our rights. We have begun struggling against exploitation, violence, early migration with good results, but we are training ourselves in order to develop this indispensable activity so that African children will never continue to be victims.'

Understanding children's work

In general the African movement's concept of children's work is both wider and narrower than conventional definitions of children's economic activities (Saadi 2012). It is wider in the sense that it tends to include 'reproductive' and other unpaid activities which are not part of the United Nations System of National Accounting (Levison 2007). Examples of this are helping out in and around the home, working in subsistence agriculture and sometimes even schooling.

On the other hand, the concept is narrower than that set out in Article 3 (a-c) of the ILO Convention No. 182, which is aimed at eliminating the worst forms of child labour, namely, all forms of slavery and practices similar to slavery; child prostitution and pornography; and illicit activities such as the use of children in drug trafficking. The African movement is clear in its belief that strong and immediate action must be taken against all of these activities. Yet whereas international child labour legislation treats them as forms of children's work (Hanson and Vandaele 2003), working children's organisations argue that this is an unjustified amalgamation. They believe that such activities should be considered and treated as *crimes against children*. These activities then are viewed as having no relation whatsoever to the concept of children's work that the organisation endorses.

The movements on each continent differ in their views on the specific value of economic participation of children, and the reasons behind it (see Liebel 2004 and Nieuwenhuys 2009 for more details). Working children's organisations in Latin America generally seem to interpret economic participation in terms of empowerment and understand it as a precondition for the autonomy and independence of social actors. In contrast, most working children's organisations in Africa and Asia relate it less to choice than to the economic necessity faced by children and adults. This distinction does not imply that these organisations isolate children's work from its wider social setting. Instead, concerns about poverty, social inequality, injustice, or neoliberal reforms are regularly voiced in their statements, but these are more often linked to specific working conditions than to the existence of children's work in general.

Despite their differences, all of the various movements demand acknowledgement, respect and social recognition for the activities they consider children's work. They argue that working to sustain themselves and to help their families does not render them less of a child than supposedly non-working children in wealthier social strata and countries. Their declarations also go further, and consistently demand explicit legal recognition for their work, something that is considered a basic human right for adults. The children explicitly claim *the right to work* (Liebel 2004; Hanson and Vandaele,2003), and during the Dakar meeting (1998) this was expressed in the following words: 'We want all the children in the world to have one day the right to choose to work or not to work...' (quoted in Liebel, et al. 2001: 354).

These organisations are well aware of the fact that children can be exploited in their work, and that they often are. It would be surprising if the children were not aware of this, since most working children organise precisely because of the dire working conditions they encounter in their daily lives. Yet in contrast to abolitionists, who mainly relate differences in qualities of children's work to the age of the child performing the work, working children's movements strongly reject the underlying idea that this exploitation stems from a supposedly innate vulnerability shared by children (Nieuwenhuys 2009). They also reject the idea that putting age limits in place would end exploitation (see Bourdillon et al. 2009 for a critical discussion of minimum age standards in children's work). This is stated in the Dakar declaration (1998) as follows: 'Work should be in accordance with the capacity and development of each and every child, and not depend on his/her age...' (quoted in Liebel et al. 2001: 354).

Additionally, while continually voicing and, as we will see, practically implementing their resolve to fight economic exploitation, they also share a view on how this challenge should *not* be approached. Many working children have been on the receiving end of the abolitionist agenda over the course of the last decades. This has led them to be very sceptical of the 'protection' provided by those whose approach to children's work comprises of prohibition, boycotts, and compulsory schooling. In their view—and this has been widely corroborated by research (Boyden et al. 1998; Hungerland et al. 2007; Bourdillon et al. 2010)—such measures generally not only fail to improve working children's lives, but actually regularly cause severe harm by excluding children from basic labour regulations, and pushing them underground and into worse working contexts, and thereby making them more vulnerable to exploitation. Working children's movements consider children's exploitation to be the result of specifiç working conditions, which include a lack of proper wages, long working hours that deprive them of educational opportunities and leisure time, and insufficiently regulated and enforced occupational safety (on concepts of children's economic exploitation, see Liebel 2004: 194–215).

This leads working children to infer a need for the legal regulation of their working conditions, thereby postulating their rights also *in* work. Such an approach to exploitation is not at all novel, since it coincides with the general approach taken by national and international labour laws regarding adult workplace exploitation and work-related hazards (Hanson and Vandaele 2003). The significance of this approach to young people is reflected in the persistence and regularity with which the declarations and other texts produced by their organisations repeat their hopes and ambitions to both a right *to* work and rights *in* work.

In declarations made by children's movements the right to work is not related to any specific kind of work. Instead they repeatedly emphasise that they are demanding 'work in dignity', 'light work', the right 'not to work hard', and work that 'reflects their abilities'. At

first glance this could be understood to mean the children were asking for a limited right to work in 'child specific jobs'. However, from
the context it is clear that age is not the criterion for adequacy, and
instead that it is safeguarding human dignity which is important here.
The right to work, as it is understood by working children's movements, is the right to a form of work which is 'as good as possible',
and seeks to actively confront any kind of exploitation and abuse at
work. It entails a 'utopian surplus' going beyond waged work, which
is the dominant form of work in societies ruled by capitalist
economics. In addition, children are claiming the right to decide for
themselves whether a type of work is acceptable, and this decision is
based on criteria which they set themselves.

Human dignity between universal rights and African cultures

If working children claim dignity for themselves and their work, they
do so in a manner which stresses their wish for individual self-
determination as subjects, and for cooperative and common relations.
In this way, working children's movements expressly advocate rights
which refer to children as individuals, as well as to children as members of a social group. The first aspect stresses the right of the person
to be treated with respect, while the second emphasises the collective
right to be recognised as a member of a social group (or organisation) of working children and have influence over their own lives and
working conditions. It also enables the children to develop understanding of cooperation and solidarity in terms of work and the
economy, which is often associated with necessary transformations
in social and economic structures.

The concept of individual human dignity which resulted from
the European Enlightenment is combined here with collectively oriented concepts of dignity from non-Western cultures. The influence
of the European concept of dignity is most prominent in the adoption
and internalisation of the discourse of human rights. The collective
concepts of human dignity are presumably influenced by pre-colonial
African cultures and their respective philosophies.

According to the African Charter on the Rights and Welfare of the Child, children should grow up in a spirit of common understanding and cooperation with others, and be able to take over vital duties quite early in their lives. Thus an African child is expected to learn to share and work together with others for the community, and achievements are interpreted as aims which have been accomplished together. The collective consciousness evident in African cultures 'does not mean that the African subject wallows in a formless, shapeless or rudimentary collectivity. It simply means that the African subjectivity develops and thrives in a relational setting provided by ongoing contact with others...' (Ndaba 1994: 14). '*Inter*dependence' is then favoured over '*in*dependence', and this means mutual relationships and mutual reliance (Ramokgopa 2001).

The presumption that the status of working children as social subjects and of their concepts of work are influenced by these and similar cultural perceptions has still not been verified by research. It rests on the fact that the majority of the children come from migrant families or have emigrated from the countryside. It also assumes that so-called typical sub-Saharan African traditions have been preserved and to a certain extent still influence the economic strategies of survival in the urban slums where the children grow up.

However, the children's concepts of *subject* and *work* should not be simply understood as a revival of these traditions. They are also the result of a completely new kind of experience. Although they refer to village life, African children's expectations of developing ways of providing for themselves would presumably not have been formulated in this way without the children's new urban experiences and their specific living conditions. The ways of thinking and the viewpoints represented by the children's organisations and their actions are then creative responses by the children to their miseries of life and their new experiences. On the one hand, this leads the children to begin their life anew, but on the other hand the societies in which they are growing up find themselves in a situation of radical social and cultural change. The children then try to solve their problems by referring to the cultural traditions of their communities and people, but also to the 'modern' international discourse of human rights, which has reached them through the media or humanitarian and educational projects. And it is from these often contradictory models that the children weave their own answers.

The African movement expresses a vision of a better society, and within its practices and understandings of self, there are two central concepts which connect two separate concepts of dignity. First, the high value placed on self-organised, cooperative modes of education and capacity building and its endorsement, and second, the promotion of non-exploitive, cooperative, and self-determined types of work and economy.

Alternative education

In the document entitled '12 Rights', the African movement places particular importance on the right *to learn to read and write* and the right *to be taught a trade*. From the beginning, parts of the movement organised literacy workshops and training courses to develop their skills in labour and communication, which are seen as indispensable prerequisites for more powerful social positions and better incomes.

As part of these initiatives the movement deals with a large number of working children who cannot attend formal school; either their particular living conditions and experiences are not taken seriously at school, or the curriculum is largely useless in solving their specific problems in their everyday lives and at work (see Brock-Utne 2000; Tomasevski 2003; Kielland and Tovo 2006: 19–20). The AMWCY stresses 'that education is different from schooling in the sense that it is a much broader term. It wants literacy courses that can be combined with children's work.' (Lieten 2009: 192). The literacy courses not only focus on learning to read and write, but they are also about learning the knowledge and skills that provide children with the self-confidence to enable them to assert themselves in society and in their working life.[3] This also strengthens cohesion among the children.

A basic educational principle implemented by the movement is that the curriculum should be based on proposals made by the learners themselves, and through 'negotiations' with the learning group. The movement tries to provide answers to the specific situations of the working children and their associated requirements. This is strengthened by the fact that the organisation of learning processes is oriented towards children's working hours, and the courses are located close to their places of work. At the same time learning is intended to enable the children to extend their ideas and abilities to work, beyond those which would otherwise be accessible to them, and in ways which they can manage either by themselves or collectively. It aims to ensure all decisions are taken together, and teachers are expected to listen to the children. This offsets the more usual hierarchical relationship between teacher and learner (see *Éducation: Alternatives Africaines* 2003; ENDA 2005). Learning is experience and action-oriented, and is embedded in the wider activities of groups and associations at the grassroots level. Animators (also known as facilitators, in the tradition of 'popular education'; see Kane 2001), who accompany the groups and generally also lead the courses, are an illustration of this, and will be described in more detail in a case study from Senegal.

After getting to know the group, the animator facilitates the selection of one or two priorities of action. These priorities are established in a process of 'participatory action research' in which the group examines the work of its members in the entire context of their lives. Each member is asked to state his/her own hopes and expectations, and after comparison and discussion within the group, they try to develop a consensus on the issues that the group should work on. 'So the starting point is not external aid but the group's

---

[3] There are offered other courses too, e.g. on income-generating activities, communication techniques or participatory research and action.

own efforts in understanding, and in finding appropriate ways of responding to the wider context within which they work...' (Touré 1998: 188).

For instance, if the group were to concentrate on the right to read and write, it would be the animator's task to work out a plan with the young people as to how this right might be implemented. First, the group's aims would be defined together, and then the availability of teachers in the area and a place to learn would need to be assessed. It is also important to clarify the terms and conditions of the work, together with the young people. Sometimes the young people have to find other opportunities for education or training, such as short courses in stitching footballs, embroidery, domestic science or health and hygiene.

If a group were to decide that it wanted to concentrate on the right to health, the animator would begin by helping the young people determine their goals and priorities. If the group decided to establish a health-care scheme, help would be given to draw up a plan. In this way animators provide contact between the group and other actors. This could mean accompanying young people to hospital, facilitating a discussion with doctors in order to receive special arrangements for health care, or helping the group set up a fund to support the children in emergencies.

An evaluation of this type of learning group by Touré (1998), which focussed on 'self-employed workers', and 'house assistants' or 'domestic workers', produced the following results.

The following activities were considered most important by the 'self-employed workers':

- buying shoe-polish in bulk so as to reduce costs;
- organising a health care scheme;
- discussing and negotiating with property owners and local authorities aimed at the social integration and the acceptance of young people by those around them;
- identifying working children by using badges and uniforms;

- facilities to help them obtain official documents such as consular cards for the non-Senegalese;
- English and French language lessons to help young people work in tourism and in the market;
- driving lessons;
- financing small projects.

The 'house assistants' or 'domestic workers' placed most importance on the following:

- functional literacy classes in Serere [or another local language] as well as in French [or another official language], which focused on practical knowledge related to their lives and work;
- classes in knitting, crocheting, embroidery, cooking and home economics;
- nutritional guides for their children, as well as instruction and increasing awareness of hygiene and environmental concerns;
- community development activities in the girls' villages of origin, including setting up a health centre, a water-purification pro-gramme, the installation of a tap, and the identification of eco-nomic projects and participative research-action projects. These projects were aimed at preventing the need for girls to migrate to the cities to find work and to enable domestic workers to return to their villages.

These local groups also organise public actions known as 'outings' to draw attention to unsatisfactory states of affairs and demand their rights be implemented. In addition to the activities mentioned above, the groups also placed importance on film shows, cultural weeks, expeditions, dancing and competitive sports.

As they had at previous meetings, the delegates present at the 8th African meeting in 2009 assessed the achievements and chal-lenges for educational and vocational initiatives (AMWCY 2010). They 'observed some innovations on our training workshops, for our workshops which have influenced both our organisational concerns and the capacity building of our members in the petty trades.' The following examples are mentioned: 'listening; IGAs; storing of market gardening products; cloth dyeing and animal husbandry; peer educators (female & male); setting up and management of projects; communication, radio, writing, drawing, internet; management and accompanying of grassroots groups; Participatory Action Research or thematic techniques; techniques for advocacy and lobbying...' The delegates came to the conclusion that many working children 'have been strengthened with tools which help them to better organise their grassroots groups and accelerate their role as actors of social transformation. Concrete results have been observed on the ground concerning the number of children who have been approached and listened to as well as the problems resolved through the Participatory Action Research, resource mobilisation for small projects and negotiation with authorities thanks to the methods employed by facilitators during sessions.' Some facilitators also indicated that the children are increasingly using local resources during their workshops.

The delegates identified 'weakness in transferring tools between the grassroots groups and trained participants [and] less follow-up/evaluation activities of our training workshops'. They argued that it would be necessary to make the following improvements: 'train WCYs [working children and youth] in using follow-up/evaluation tools in order to be able to measure the impact of our activities on ourselves, the other children and the communities; to train our members in identifying opportunities and needs of our communities in order to face the realities; to consult our grassroots and our members ahead of the training sessions with the view to identify the topics for capacity building that could take their concerns into consideration' (AMWCY 2010).

Alternative work

A further kind of project in which the African movement is becoming increasingly involved is the creation of self-organised cooperatives known as Income Generating Activities (IGAs). IGAs can be understood as an attempt by the movement to establish viable and empowering alternatives, for both members and non-members alike, to particularly hazardous or exploitative working conditions. For example, in rural areas AMWCY grassroots groups engage in animal breeding projects, as well as in mobile phone, computer or Internet services, which are run cooperatively by children and adolescents.[4] With the assistance of supporting adult organisations from European countries involved in fair trade,[5] some of these handicraft cooperatives have been able to access markets outside of Africa (ProNATs & CIR 2008, AMWCY 2009b).

The IGAs were evaluated by delegates at the 8th African meeting, held in 2009, and they identified the following achievements and developments (AMWCY 2010):

76.7% of WCYs [Working Children and Youth] meet their needs since they joined the AWCYs [Associations of Working Children and Youth]. They invest in individual or group initiatives for the AWCY in the following activities:

- sale of head ties with the AWCY logo printed on them
- organisation of entertainment and cultural activities
- renting of chairs, plates and cutlery
- manufacture and sale of raffia bags
- sale of traditional clothes
- production and sale of liquid soap
- sewing and sale of embroidered bed sheets
- manufacture and sale of leather shoes,
- sale of mobile phone cards...

---

[4] Similarly, movements in Latin America and India have established, for example, bakeries, handicraft and soap production and wood working on a cooperative basis. Some children's organisations have been supported by adults in founding children's banks and providing micro-credit to working children's cooperatives. Others organise vocational and organisational training specifically addressing the needs of self-help cooperatives (ProNATs & CIR, 2008).

[5] While most fair trade organisations maintain the general principle of banning products which use child labour, there are others which explicitly promote the trade with products made by children in dignified, non-exploitative conditions, for example products from children's self-regulated cooperatives (ProNATs & CIR, 2008).

- The setting up of credit facilities or the creation of small of tradetional clothes an occupation and to take care of our basic needs, to pay for our trainings, to contribute to our family, to pay school/apprenticeship fees for our brothers.

They state that the main difficulty they face is gaining 'access to micro credit opportunities offered by specialised institutions in our immediate neighbourhoods'. They argue that a future perspective would be to 'approach the micro credit institutions in order to be able to examine together, the conditions needed in order to benefit from their services [and] to guide and accompany working children and youths in search of viable activities which can make it easy to obtain financial support'.

This kind of intervention at the micro level will not be able to completely alter the working and living conditions of working children. Nor will it be able to change structural contexts such as poverty and inequality which are characteristic of many of their communities. Nevertheless, IGAs remain fundamental instruments for the protection and promotion of working children's rights, and in fact they are often the only means of doing so. IGAs make working children's lives easier and reduce the everyday risks and harm that children are exposed to.

Cooperative IGAs provide working children with the chance to directly increase the control they have over their working conditions and to obtain non-exploitative work that is more compatible with their rights to education and leisure. Furthermore, IGAs may also reach working children who would otherwise be far less able to take advantage of the movements' other activities due to the particularly restrictive working conditions they face.

Yet it could also be argued that concentrating on immediate solutions to the everyday problems of working children takes the focus away from wider contexts and restrictions on activities, such as those found in the international debate on social and solidarity economy (see Santos 2006 for more details). However, the children are convinced that they cannot simply wait for governments and other

adult organisations that support them to implement the necessary
measures. From time to time, organised children do stress the
responsibilities of powerful and wealthy institutions. For instance, in
a statement addressed to the United Nations Children's World
Summit (UNGASS) in May 2002, the African movement declared as
follows (AMWCY 2001):

> We also develop new income generation activities for our asso-
> ciations and our members. We encourage savings and credit... In
> Africa we can fight against poverty, but the funds cannot come
> from the poor who are toiling and moiling to meet their needs...
> Rich countries must give francs 7.00 for every Franc 1,000.00 to
> the poor countries to assist their development. If they do not
> wish to do so, then they will not be able to help the poor chil-
> dren and their families to develop economic activities. Indebt-
> edness has to be stopped. Our governments and organizations
> must make good use of the countries' wealth and assistance
> received from the rich countries. It must be used for what it was
> meant for originally. We all have to fight against poverty and
> corruption.

Aims and impacts

An evaluation of the movement's aims and impacts needs to differentiate between two levels of engagement. First, there are the more
localised activities, which are aimed at raising awareness of working
children's rights and the respect which is accorded to them. This first
level of engagement aims to produce fairly immediate improvements
in the children's working and living conditions. Second, there are the
movement's efforts which are aimed at influencing and changing the
wider context of children's work: this includes public policy and
labour legislation at national and international levels, but also the
global context of poverty and inequality. While the latter constitutes
an important long-term goal for the movement, its everyday activities
are more oriented towards pragmatic changes at the local level. It is
to these which we now turn (see also Saadi 2012).

By regularly interacting with working children and adolescents of a similar age in an environment of mutual respect, support, and trust, the movement's members move away from social isolation and start a process of reciprocal recognition. They also meet to share and collectively discuss problems and devise strategies to tackle them. This can lead to a strong feeling of empowerment, and many organised working children and adolescents have provided an account of this. Group membership is an aspect which is greatly valued by children living without direct family support, and it can sometimes fill in this gap, while at the same time offering relative protection from abuse by the authorities and a public which is generally unsympathetic towards them.

These impacts are closely linked to the movement's pedagogical and consciousness-raising activities. For instance, the AMWCY still considers raising awareness of the '12 rights' to be at the heart of all of its activities. The instrumental importance of educating individual working children about their rights lies in the fact that knowledge of their rights can raise their self-esteem and provide them with the confidence to stand up to abusive employers, customers, police and parents. Furthermore, it helps strengthen their resilience.

When addressing the awareness of adults and the general public, working children's groups are concerned with building a constituency of support, or at least with reducing the widespread negative perceptions concerning working children. Some immediate and tangible rights-related benefits for working children have also been derived from basic and non-formal education programmes such as literacy programmes and vocational training. In addition this has improved the implementation of the children's right to education. Other examples are the provision of health care and health-related education, and counselling on reproductive rights. Yet the majority of working children's organisations are engaged in contexts in which no such services are available. Where service provision does exist, it is either very limited or insufficiently adapted to the specific needs of working children. Clearly, increasing the standard of health service provision may then constitute a significant improvement in their members' and other children's living conditions. Furthermore, in some cases health services are not only provided to working children, but also to non-working children and adult members of the communities in which the children live, thereby raising the social standing of working children and their organisations (AMWCY 2009b; AMWCY 2010).

If organised working children's perceptions and strategies are to be consolidated and strengthened, the standing they have in relation to policies at the micro and macro level affecting them is of particular importance. Seen in the context of the activities they are engaged in, it is reasonable to argue that most working children's groups have won small victories, and have contributed to the implementation of a number of both written and unwritten rights which they deemed necessary to protect working children. Nevertheless, the influence of organised working children in institutions which influence policy and law, in both the national and international arena, is more heterogeneous and less easy to trace.

In some African countries, working children's groups have formed partnerships to provide education, enabling them to directly influence curricula and timetables and adapt them to the needs of working children. Similarly, through their role in the dissemination of services related to health and reproduction, they have gained acceptance and acknowledgement by health authorities at various levels (AMWCY 2009a, Coly and Terenzio 2007). Working children have sometimes even developed strong negotiating powers in relations with political institutions and other important political actors.

In some countries working children's associations are explicitly acknowledged as representatives of working children and as partners by governments, local administrations, and other socially important organisations. However, their powers usually remain limited to directly influencing political and economic actors during decision-making processes. It seems that the closer the working children's movements approach the realm of international policy and labour law, the less able they are to produce the preconditions conducive to the movement's perspectives. One reason for this may be that at the local and national level the associations' activities are more accepted, and decision-making processes in which children only figure as objects are increasingly being called into question. In contrast, the International Labour Organisation (ILO), for example, does not even officially recognise working children as active stakeholders in child labour legislation.

In contrast to Latin America, the African movement is recognised as a partner by some ILO local authorities, but this cooperation is limited to questions of child migration with regard to the so-called 'worst forms of child labour'. Even when working children's organisations and their perspectives do gain access to the international stage, as during the preparatory process to ILO Convention 182, they find themselves confronted by the claim that they are not the real representatives of working children (Invernizzi and Milne 2002; Liebel 2004).[6] This lack of recognition may be rooted in conflicting socio-cultural conceptions of childhood and in a generalised tendency to question the authenticity and legitimacy of uninvited political engagement by children and youth (Milne 2007; Eltshain 1996).

In order to gain a better understanding of organised working children's agency, it may be helpful to look at the specific relations between working children's initiatives and the adult organisations

---

[6] Publications by the IREWOC research group (e.g. IREWOC, 2005; Lieten, 2009) assume that working children's organisations only represent 'privileged' sectors of working children. It is a fact that working children—similar to social groups of adults—need a certain amount of resources, time and liberty to meet and organise, a condition which is not equally available to all children. However, the IREWOC studies do not take into account that the formation and composition of organised movements is to be understood as a process which has to be analysed in the contexts of the children's lives. Therefore these studies can easily be—and in fact often are—misused to negate the representative qualities of the children's organisations.

which support them (see Schibotto 2001; Terenzio 2001; Coly and Terenzio 2007 for more detail). The fact that the movement presents itself as being child-led does not mean that adults have no role to play. Participatory activities and the support provided by ENDA, as well as other adult organisations, have been decisive in the African movement's formation and still provide an important structure for support. This support helps ensure organisational continuity, and this is particularly important in a context of a constant loss of members due to age, something which occurs less in adult organisations. At the same time, support is also needed because of the marginal social and legal status of children in general, and that of most working children in particular. Without support the movements would generally have very limited access to the information, education, and financial and logistical resources which are indispensable for organising and effectively transforming hopes and ambitions into action.

Additionally, the children are severely constricted by the fact that in most countries it is not possible for children to create formal organisations, nor do they have the right to conclude the contracts necessary for the logistical support of such organisations. Adults therefore have been important and probably will continue to play an important role in the organisational side of working children's movements (Myers 2009).

Although there is always a risk of dominating or even manipulating the children, the role of adults within these movements is understood as supportive. Adults are known as 'facilitators', 'collaborators', or 'animators' by the children, and are usually valued for their experience, advice, criticism, and solidarity (Coly 2001). Adults should not play a leadership or decision-making role in working children's organisations. This situation certainly presents a balancing act for both children and adults, but adult's compliance with this division of roles and responsibilities is usually eagerly monitored by the children, even in the case of adults who have been working with working children's organisations for decades. On the occasions that adults do take part in decision-making processes, they usually do so by the invitation of the children. "What is important is that adults make a special effort to ensure that children represent themselves authentically and are able to dissent from adult views free of pressure. The major working children's organizations and movements go to considerable effort to prepare their adult workers to skilfully maintain a respectful non-exploitative relationship with the young people.' (Myers 2009: 156). Overall, the everyday workings of these organisations demonstrates that their *raison d'être* lies in the fact that they are run by the children themselves, and that they translate their own attitudes and ideas resulting from their living and working conditions into specific structures, demands, proceedings and forms of action (Coly and Terenzio 2007).

Still, whereas at the micro level and in international networking this division of roles seems to be well established and effective, at macro policy-making levels it poses a number of challenges. For instance, it is still not clear how compatible this division of roles can be with the increasingly high levels of professionalism and the intellectual and institutional sophistication necessary to effectively and continuously engage in international policy and law making. An additional difficulty is posed by the way that adult interests promoting an abolitionist approach to children's work are deeply entrenched at the institutional level.

Conclusion

Whether and how these obstacles can be overcome is not a question which can be easily answered. At present, there are signs which provide grounds for both hope and concern. There is hope in that it appears that over the course of the last decade, movements of working children and adolescents have at least been able to open up the debate a little on child labour and working children's rights. In addition, many of their views have been confirmed by academic research. Also, what was originally a form of 'self-invited' political involvement is now in part eased by the strengthening of participatory approaches motivated by intentions to implement the children's right to participate and increase program effectiveness (Myers 2009). However, the actors supporting the eradication of child labour have made note of these changes, and are actively resisting them: this then provides the grounds for concern. In May 2010, at the Global Child Labour Conference held by the ILO and the Dutch government in The Hague, working children were once more completely excluded and were not able to participate or be involved in the decision-making (Saadi 2012).[7] Although the UNCRC stipulates that all children have the right to be heard and to participate in all matters affecting them, the conference organisers did not take this right into account. Additionally, and in contrast to the past, working children and their organisations are not even being mentioned as potential partners for cooperation. Even more worrying is the enormity of the task of tackling the global political, economic, and ideological structures that are at the root of the lives of impoverished and marginalised children (Hart 2008)—the same conditions that also lead working children to organise.

In a matter of a few years, the African movement has reached a remarkable level of organisation. This has enabled working children to become a visible and often recognised collective actor. Its performance is pragmatic: it places importance on cooperation with

---

[7] See the video message by Awa Niang, a member of the African movement, addressed to the conference. She explained her situation as a working child. She started with the hard work of picking sea shells for construction materials, before meeting the AMWCY and becoming a member together with her co-workers. The movement helped her to learn to read and write, and speak French; but also to work lighter, and fewer hours, to train and get more money for herself and her family. 'We are together with ILO, governments, and other actors against the worst forms of child labour... because we are also engaged against exploitation of our work. But I ask you to not confuse the worst forms of child labour, with our work which can be a benefit for us.' For Awa, children are the most important protectors of other children thanks to their solidarity. They need adult support, but not adults who make unilateral decisions on matters concerning children's lives. In this sense she deeply regretted the lack of any invitation to working children's movements by the conference organisers (CALAO Express, n° 76, May 2010).

governments and international organisations, including the ILO, so as to achieve short-term improvements in working children's daily lives. On the other hand, by focussing on projects that offer immediate improvements (such as IGAs) and by failing to urge for structural changes, there is a danger that the movement will appear to being misused by dominant groups as a 'stopgap'.

Still, organisations of working children and young people have demonstrated their importance and the impact they have on working children's lives and beyond. They do not simply accept the role of passive objects of adult benevolence. Instead, they take action to implement lasting improvements, in the areas of work and education, in their own and other children's lives.

References

AMWCY (2001): *A World Fit for and by Children. Our Point of View as African Working Children*; http://www.crin.org/docs/resources/publications/AWC.pdf (accessed 7 June 2011).

AMWCY (2009a). *Report of the Meeting of the African Commission 9ᵗʰ–21ˢᵗ of March 2009 at the hotel l'Amité in Cotonou*, Republic of Benin; http://eja.enda.sn (accessed 7 June 2011).

AMWCY (2009b): *WCY Face the Challenge. Annual News Bulletin of the African Movement of Working Children and Youth*, No. 9. Dakar: Enda Tiers Monde; http://www.maejt.org/page%20anglais/English%20media%20ro om.htm (accessed 7 June 2011).

AMWCY (2010): *WCY Face the Challenge. Annual News Bulletin of the African Movement of Working Children and Youth*, No. 10. Dakar: Enda Tiers Monde.

Bourdillon, Michael, Deborah Levison, William Myers, and Ben White (2010): *Rights and Wrongs of Children's Work*. New Brunswick, NJ & London: Rutgers University Press.

Bourdillon, Michael, Ben White, and William Myers (2009): Reassessing Minimum-Age Standards for Children's Work. In:

International Journal of Sociology and Social Policy 29(3),
106–117.

Boyden, Jo, Birgitta Ling, and William E. Myers (1998): *What
Works for Working Children*. Stockholm: Rädda Barnen/Save
the Children.

Brock-Utne, Birgit (2000): *Whose Education for All? The Recoloni-
zation of the African Mind*. New York & London: Falmer Press.

CALAO Express. Monthly Internet Edition. Dakar: Enda Tiers
Monde; http://maejt.org/page%20anglais/indexanglais.htm (accessed 7 June 2011).

Coly, Hamidou (2001): An Animator's Experience. In: *Voice of
Working Children*. Dakar: Enda Jeunesse Action, 138–147.

Coly, Hamidou and Fabrizio Terenzio (2007). The Stakes of
Children's Participation in Africa. The African Movement of
Working Children and Youth. In: B. Hungerland, M. Liebel, B.
Milne, and A. Wihstutz (eds.): *Working to Be Someone. Child
Focused Research and Practice with Working Children* (pp.
179–185). London & Philadelphia: Jessica Kingsley.

Éducation: Alternatives Africaines (2003): Dakar: Enda Tiers
Monde, Études et recherches n° 222–223.

Eltshain, Jean Bethke (1996): Political Children. In: *Childhood* 3
(11), 11–28.

ENDA (2005): « Je suis moniteur, Je m'inspire des Droits et Devoirs
des EJT ». Guide pratique du moniteur d'alphabétisation.
Dakar: Enda TM Jeunesse Action (= JEUDA 113).

Ennew, Judith (2002): Outside Childhood. Street Children's Rights.
In: B. Franklin (ed.): *The New Handbook of Children's Rights*
(pp. 388–403). London & New York: Routledge.

Hanson, Karl and Arne Vandaele (2003): Working Children and
International Labour Law. A Critical Analysis. In: *International
Journal of Children's Rights* 11 (1), 73–146.

Hart, Jason (2008): Children's Participation and International Development. Attending to the Political. In: *International Journal of
Children's Rights* 16, 407–418.

Hungerland, Beatrice, Manfred Liebel, Brian Milne, and Anne Wihstutz (eds.) (2007): *Working to Be Someone. Child Focused Research and Practice with Working Children*. London & Philadelphia: Jessica Kingsley.

Invernizzi, Antonella and Brian Milne (2002): Are Children Entitled to Contribute to International Policy Making? A Critical View of Children's Participation in the International Campaign for the Elimination of Child Labour. In: *International Journal of Children's Rights* 10(4), 403–431.

IREWOC (2005): *Studying Child Labour. Policy Implications of Child-Centred Research*. Amsterdam: IREWOC (http://www.childlabour.net/documents/GIE/giePublicatie.pdf).

Kane, Liam (2001): *Popular Education and Social Change in Latin America*. London: Latin American Bureau.

Kielland, Anne and Maurizia Tovo (2006): *Children at Work. Child Labor Practices in Africa*. Boulder, CO & London: Lynne Rienner Publishers.

Levison, Deborah (2007): A Feminist Economist's Approach to Children's Work. In: B. Hungerland, M. Liebel, B. Milne, and A. Wihstutz (eds.): *Working to Be Someone. Child Focused Research and Practice with Working Children*. London & Philadelphia: Jessica Kingsley, 17–22.

Liebel, Manfred (2001): 12 Rights, and Making their Own Way: The Working Youth of Africa Organise Themselves. In: M. Liebel, B. Overwien, and A. Recknagel (eds.): *Working Children's Protagonism. Social Movements and Empowerment in Latin America, Africa and India*. Frankfurt M. & London: IKO, 197–217.

Liebel, Manfred (2003): Working Children as Social Subjects: The Contribution of Working Children's Organisations to Social Transformations. In: *Childhood* 10(3), 265–286.

Liebel, Manfred (2004): *A Will of Their Own. Cross-Cultural Perspectives on Working Children*. London & New York: Zed Books.

Liebel, Manfred (2012): *Children's Rights from Below: Cross-cultural perspectives*. In collaboration with Karl Hanson, Iven Saadi & Wouter Wandenhole. Basingstoke: Palgrave Macmillan.

Liebel, Manfred, Bernd Overwien, and Albert Recknagel (eds.) (2001): *Working Children's Protagonism: Social Movements and Empowerment in Latin America, Africa and India.* Frankfurt M. & London: IKO.

Lieten, G. K. (2009): Child Labor Unions in Africa. In: H. D. Hindman (ed.): *The World of Child Labor: An Historical and Regional Survey.* Armonk, NY & London: M. E. Sharpe, 191–193

Milne, Brian (2007): Do the Participation Articles in the Convention on the Rights of the Child Present Us With a Recipe for Children's Citizenship? In: B. Hungerland, M. Liebel, B. Milne and A. Wihstutz (eds.): *Working to Be Someone. Child Focused Research and Practice with Working Children.* London & Philadelphia: Jessica Kingsley, 205–209.

Myers, William E. (2009): Organization of Working Children. In: H. D. Hindman (ed.): *The World of Child Labor. An Historical and Regional Survey.* Armonk, NY & London: M. E. Sharpe, 153–157.

Ndaba, W.J. (1994): *Ubuntu in Comparison to Western Philosophies.* Pretoria: Ubuntu School of Philosophy.

Nieuwenhuys, Olga (2009): From Child Labour to Working Children's Movements. In: J. Qvortrup, W. A. Corsaro, and M.-S. Honig (eds.): *The Palgrave Handbook of Childhood Studies* (pp. 289–300). Basingstoke: Palgrave Macmillan.

Nimbona, Godefroid (2005): Child Labour Organisations in Eastern Africa Still in the Making. In: IREWOC (ed.): *Studying Child Labour. Policy Implications of Child-centred Research.* Amsterdam: IREWOC, 27–29.

Nimbona, Godefroid and Kristoffel Lieten (2007): *Child Labour Unions: AEJT Senegal.* Amsterdam: IREWOC.

ProNATs & CIR (2008): *'Wir sind nicht das Problem, sondern Teil der Lösung.' Arbeitende Kinder zwischen Ausbeutung und Selbstbestimmung.* Berlin: ProNATs e.V. & Münster: Christliche Initiative Romero e.V.

Ramokgopa, Isaak Mashakgene (2001): *Developmental Stages of an African Child and their Psychological Implication: A Comparative Study*; http://ujdigispace.uj.ac.za:8080/dspace/bitstream/10210/1614/1/ DevelopmentalStagesofanAfricanChild.pdf (accessed 7 June 2011).

Saadi, Iven (2012): Children's Rights as 'Work in Progress': The Conceptual and Practical Contributions of Working Children's Movements. In: M. Liebel (ed.): *Children's Rights from Below: Cross-cultural perspectives.* Basingstoke: Palgrave Macmillan.

Santos, Boaventura de Sousa (ed.) (2006): *Another Production is Possible: Beyond the Capitalist Canon.* London: Verso.

Schibotto, Giangi (2001): Social Action with Working Children and Adolescents: From Empirical Description to Theoretical Models. In: M. Liebel, B. Overwien, and A. Recknagel (eds.): *Working Children's Protagonism: Social Movements and Empowerment in Latin America, Africa and India.* Frankfurt M. & London: IKO, 271–288

Swift, Anthony (1999): *Working Children Get Organised.* London: International Save the Children Alliance.

Terenzio, Fabrizio (2001): From Projects for Children via Projects with Children to Children's Trade Unions. In: M. Liebel, B. Overwien, and A. Recknagel (eds.): *Working Children's Protagonism: Social Movements and Empowerment in Latin America, Africa and India.* Frankfurt M. & London: IKO, 289–294.

Terenzio, Fabrizio (2009): « Le MAEJT en quelques chiffres: *Statistiques* 2009 ». Unpublished presentation held on the occasion of the 8th Meeting of the African Movement of Working Children and Youth in Cotonou, Benin (mimeo).

Tomasevski, Katarina (2003): *Education Denied: Costs and Remedies*. London & New York: Zed Books.

Touré, Marema (1998): A Case Study of the Work of ENDA in Senegal in Supporting the Association of Child and Young Workers. In: D. Tolfree: *Old Enough to Work, Old Enough to Have a Say: Different Approaches to Supporting Working Children*. Stockholm: Rädda Barnen/Save the Children, 179–200.

Voice of African Children (2001): Dakar: Enda, Occasional Papers, n° 217.

Reflections: Values, rights, and research

Michael Bourdillon

Conflicting ideologies

Charity Chakarisa, a Zimbabwean who studied law at the University of Cape Town, had this to say in her doctoral thesis:

> I come from a family and a society which firmly believes that 'nothing is more favourable to morals than early habits of industry'. From about the age of 4 to the time we left home, my siblings and I cooked, cleaned, ran errands and did all the chores that my parents expected of us. Thus domestic work was an integral part of my childhood which I believe moulded me into the person I am today.
>
> Until I enrolled for postgraduate study in human rights law, I had considered myself to have received an upbringing which was normal and well worth emulating. But, as my studies progressed, I soon realised how child rights activists, the world media and child development experts had pathologised my parents' child rearing methods and those of the generations before them. The work which I had engaged in as a child, and which my parents believed had been in my best interests, was by international standards 'abusive', 'exploitative', 'harmful', 'dangerous' and generally satisfied most of institutionalised elements of child labour.
>
> I therefore became aware of the discord between cultural norms which had shaped my childhood and the Western-inspired universal children's rights principles which I was now being taught. (Nhenga 2008: 212.)

This discord motivated her to examine the efficacy and appropriateness of the universal standards in the context of Lesotho, Zimbabwe, and South Africa.

The discord between cultural values and international standards is not confined to indigenous African cultures. I was brought up in

Africa on a farm in a different, English-based cultural context. Like
many of our generation in a variety of contexts, my siblings and I
took for granted various tasks from a very young age. Our work[1] was
not directly related to the careers we followed, but it did not interfere
significantly with schooling: we all did well at school and acquired
university degrees and professional careers. I was surprised later to
discover that much of our work would now be classified by the
International Labour Organisation (ILO) as under-age economic
activity and therefore as 'child labour' to be abolished (see ILO
2008, 11–14).

The activists and experts of whom Chakarisa speaks are not all
outsiders to Africa. Many of the African elite, in government, in
social work, in non-governmental organisations, and among academics, uphold international ideals of a romantic childhood, largely
free from work and responsibility. Was the moulding of which
Chakarisa writes an important learning process? Or was her childhood work genuinely harmful to her or to society? Is there perhaps
something wrong with the standards that condemn it?

In the introduction to this volume, we mentioned the tension
that can arise between the concern of academics for the well-being of
children, and the task of social scientists to describe and analyse
rather than to judge. The chapters in this volume illustrate a variety
of childhoods, both in the values espoused by communities and in
the decisions that children make as they try to control and improve
their lives. These studies make clear the need for informed and

---

[1]   Our work fitted many of the patterns emerging in this volume. Much of it was
simply participating in family activities on my parents' farm, like putting
chickens away in the evening or cleaning eggs for sale. When help was needed,
not even guests were exempt. Some of the work, particularly of older children,
was urgently needed for the enterprise, like turning the hay after rain (fun), or
fighting a grass fire (fun, challenging, and occasionally hazardous), or preparing
chickens to meet a customer's demands (certainly economic). Some tasks were
undertaken for enjoyment or a sense of achievement (though doing a job
incorrectly could result in humiliation). Some tasks were demanded by my father
as a matter of discipline.

nuanced approaches to children's work. But how do such studies relate to intervention and policy? In this final chapter[2], I reflect on my experiences of academic study of children's work and of intervention on behalf of children.

Social science and human rights

First I take up a point raised in the introduction. One of the aims of social science research is to understand human behaviour through analysis of observations, putting aside prior judgements made on the basis of the researcher's personal standards. Some social scientists hold that values and rights are not relevant to empirical research (unless of course they are the topic of the research). While such objectivity remains an ideal, there are two related reasons why values have to enter research: ethical considerations in relation to the subjects of research, and the significance of the research findings.

Partly in response to medical experiments during the Second World War, there has been growing concern about the ethics of research on human subjects. Guidelines have been developed by research institutions and disciplinary associations to make sure that the subjects are not damaged by, and preferably that they benefit from, the research, and that their views and persons are respected in the study. This is a particularly sensitive area with respect to research on children, who, more than adults, have limited experience and competence in dealing with researchers, and whose perspectives are too easily ignored. There can be debate on particular ethical practices, and especially the danger that an emphasis on specific rules for conducting research can obscure or even impede the important principle of respect (for a discussion of difficulties in practice, see Morrow 2012; also Chenhall et al. 2011); but the principle of

---

[2] I acknowledge help from Dr Elisabeth Lickindorf in finalising this chapter. I remain responsible for the substance and for any errors it may contain.

respecting the rights of human subjects of social science studies is now widely accepted.

To ensure that research does no harm requires judgement on what constitutes benefit and harm. Several chapters in this volume (including Spittler, Dougnon, and Mahati) show differences in perspectives on what is beneficial for children and for the communities in which they live, particularly differences between members of the communities and outside officials or activists. An important role of academia is to elucidate such differences and the bases for them. But the human rights movement is not satisfied with an elucidation of differences: it supports a principle that certain treatments of individuals or communities constitute abuse in some objective sense and that such treatment cannot be justified by appeal to particular cultures or legal systems. This way of thinking implies that responsibility is universal; that those with more resources should contribute to those with inadequate resources—the basis of international child protection programmes. There is a long tradition in social anthropology and ethnography of giving voice to people who, for whatever reason, are at the margins of society, a tradition that fits well with concerns for human rights.

Some rights are not disputed, for example, that children should have enough nutrition for their development. But it is not always clear how to resolve tensions between this right and others, such as when earning for food conflicts with the right to leisure or to schooling. Some cultural institutions, such as certain initiation rites or early marriage of girls, may be shown to be medically or physically hazardous to children; but the damage may be of less importance to them than the damage to social relations and social support that can be caused by prohibiting these institutions (see, for example, Boyden et al. forthcoming). To perceive child protection simply in physical terms can be narrow and restrictive: children's place in society, and their opportunities to develop their lives in a variety of ways, also need protection (see Myers and Bourdillon forthcoming). It appears that attention to child rights cannot provide a set of universal moral rules; rather rights provide principles for reflection and their application has to be assessed in terms of their effects on the beneficiaries.

So the question remains as to how to determine what is good or harmful for children when local perceptions conflict with what outsiders perceive to be universal rights. What might academic research contribute to the resolution of such conflict? In the next section, I indicate how such questions affected my research and my personal involvement with working children.

Personal involvement

My involvement with working children started in the late 1980s, when a group of concerned persons established a social welfare organisation, called *Streets Ahead*, to offer support to the growing number of street children in Harare, Zimbabwe. The principal purpose was to provide a drop-in centre for street children and to employ outreach workers to meet them and befriend them where they were living and working. We knew that some of the children were escaping from abuse or extreme poverty at home. Our principle was that the young people were on the streets for a reason, and that we wanted to offer support rather than tell them what they should be doing. One thing that they wanted and needed was livelihoods that were more secure, and we quickly ran into problems with donors who would not support anything that looked like 'child labour'.

After attending an international conference on child labour in Oslo in 1997, I decided that I needed more information about children's work in Zimbabwe, and I started encouraging students to research the topic in a variety of urban and rural situations. My contribution was a study of certain 'earn-and-learn' schools on tea estates in the south-east of Zimbabwe, where as a condition of being admitted to the schools most pupils attended under contract to work on the estates (Bourdillon 2000a). The following points challenged common notions of child labour on the one hand, and laisser-faire attitudes on the other.

- All the pupils I met in the schools were there of their own volition.
- The vast majority had been out of school before they came to the estate school; far from keeping them from school, their work on the tea estates made schooling possible.
- The estate paid the children the same rates for work as they paid to adults, and subsidized their schooling besides: this was not cheap labour.
- Local communities considered the schools an asset and wanted more of them established (unlike some academic colleagues who had depicted them as unacceptably exploitative).
- Nevertheless, the pupils had many complaints about the way the schools were run and especially about their workloads on the estate.

Two brief vignettes illustrate the problem that faced me. A 13-year-old girl was living with her grandmother and three younger siblings after the death of both her parents. The grandmother had no income and a plot of land too small to feed them all. By enrolling in this school (initially below the legal minimum age even for 'light work'), the girl was able to continue her own secondary schooling and to send money home to feed and educate her younger siblings.

A 12-year-old boy had just finished primary school with good grades. He lived with his impoverished single mother who was provided with housing and some employment by a land-owning patron. The boy had helped with his primary school expenses by herding cattle at weekends and undertaking domestic work for the patron. Now he hoped to enter the local earn-and-learn secondary school. Unfortunately for him, under pressure from international buyers, the tea estate had adopted a policy of not employing any more children under the age of 15.

Ideally the state's social services should provide better support for children in such situations, but in Zimbabwe at the time this was an unrealistic dream. What was I to do, as an academic with an interest in the welfare of children? I could get involved in debates about agency and structure, showing how the children, on the streets or in employment, suffered all kinds of constraints, but nevertheless found ways to take some control over their lives and to improve their situation. While such academic debate is relevant to understanding the children's lives, something more urgent was needed to help children whose livelihoods were being threatened by well-intentioned but misguided activists in human rights. I believed it important to try to reach a wider audience to challenge conventional views about stopping child labour. I collected studies by students and colleagues on children's work in a variety of Zimbabwean situations, from formal employment through street work to caring for the sick, which we published under the title *Earning a Life: Working Children in Zimbabwe* (Bourdillon 2000b). The title was carefully chosen: we were not speaking simply of working to survive—a dominant feature in much of the literature; we were looking at children who, through their work, improved the quality of their lives—earned meaningful lives.

Combining academic and practical work

Three things happened to enable me to combine academic and practical work.

1. The book I edited, and my introduction to it, received academic recognition. If our work is to be genuinely useful to practitioners, it must meet sound academic standards.

2. Save the Children Norway considered my work useful, introduced me to people involved with working children in other countries, and engaged me on an occasional basis to help with their work in Zimbabwe and internationally.

3. A problem many academics face is to find enough time for serious practical work; alternatively, they get so involved in the practical side that they have difficulty keeping up with latest theoretical developments and research observations. I was fortunate: for unrelated reasons, I resigned my academic post, which left me more time for practical work; and I was offered several short-term

research fellowships, which enabled me to keep up with academic developments.

So I found myself in a mix of academic and practical. On the one hand, I had my academic background as I tried to develop understanding through careful empirical observations and critical assessment. On the other hand, I was learning how to deal with discourses on children's rights and child protection, often based on values of obscure origin. Sometimes the values and resulting interventions appeared to conflict with empirical observations: indeed I found some of my own assumptions about child labour had to be carefully rethought. Without the motivation of values and concerns about children, the work would have become pointless; without careful empirical observations and critical analysis, the work could become harmful rather than benign. Some kind of difficult balance was needed.

Mitigating the harm from stopping child labour

I involved myself in arguing and publishing, largely at the academic level, to try to mitigate the effects of stopping children from working. Initially, I took the line that several people were taking at the time by pointing to specific reasons why children *have* to work, including the following points.

- There are many child-headed households in my part of the world. If children are supporting younger children without adult help, they clearly need to earn.
- Many street children do not have any adult support on which they can call.
- The high proportion of children to adults in most low-income countries means that resources for children are spread more thinly.
- Children in extremely poor families need to contribute their labour if they and their siblings are to have a tolerable livelihood.
- Undernourishment has been shown to inhibit cognitive development, so it is inadequate it insist on schooling if the children are not first fed.
- Children's work is often needed for the expenses of schooling.

The overall argument is that children should not be prevented from working if they and their lives depend on their work. This argument has helped to mitigate some of the adverse effects of the campaign to stop child labour, and has introduced various cautions about throwing children out of work. However, there remains the problem that this approach encourages nothing more than tolerance of working situations, and does nothing to persuade people to appreciate the value of what children achieve through their work. It encourages a focus on work for survival, rather than attending to the benefits that work often conveys to children.

Benefits of work

The chapters in this volume illustrate many benefits of children's work; here I summarise key points.

Generally, work has economic benefits that extend beyond necessity. Even young people who are not particularly poor can derive economic benefits from part-time work, which gives them a degree of autonomy and the ability to purchase goods and pay for their own entertainment. Moreover, there is some evidence that in certain situations (not in all) work experience can lead to better future employment and earnings, even more than continued schooling.

Working children often speak of the enjoyment they derive from work, especially when it involves the company of peers. This is particularly the case when little such enjoyment is available at home for economic or cultural reasons—in some African societies young adolescents are not expected to waste time in play (for example, see Oloko 1989: 17, 23).

More important are the social benefits that derive from work. Work gives a person not only the means to earn a living, but also a place in society. The same applies to children, who acquire status in their families and their communities through their contributions of work (strongly illustrated by Dougnon in this volume and by chapters on work in the family context).

A further and related benefit is experience of responsibility. In work, young people acquire the experience of doing things that other people depend on. Those who promote a childhood free of responsibility cannot expect young people suddenly to become responsible just because they have reached a certain age.

Through work, children can acquire technical and social skills, and often a sense of achievement. This is evident when children learn the skills of herding and agriculture by participating in the work activities of their communities (Lancy, Spittler, Polak in this volume), or of a craft under the guidance of a master (Köhler). Some work enables young people to learn the value of money and how to handle it. But we pointed out in the introduction to this volume that learning through work is much broader: it is part of the way children develop by imitating and participating in social activities. Through work, children learn not only the technical skills involved, but also how to relate to the people around them: they learn social values and culture.

Children learn to deal with risk and hazards through exposure to them (see Boyden 2009). It is not easy for them to learn how to deal with the high levels of risk that are inevitable in the lives of the poor if all engagement with risk is removed from their childhood. Dougnon in this volume explains how young Dogon people perceive overcoming risk and danger to be a constituent feature of labour migration as a phase in their maturing process. Hashim and Thorsen (2011) also show young migrants learning to cope with a variety of problems through their experiences of labour migration.

So there are many potential benefits that children can derive from work, and these are missed in a discourse that focuses only on harmful effects of work and hazards in workplaces. Because of these benefits, it is not enough to persuade people to tolerate children's work as a matter of necessity, since with such an approach ethnocentric, romantic notions of childhood are left unchallenged. What was—and still is—needed on the topic is a critical appreciation of what children do for themselves through work, based on empirical research and academic analysis.

Rights and Wrongs

In 2007, I joined an international and interdisciplinary team of scholars to look thoroughly at current knowledge on children's work and to produce a state-of-the-art book on the subject, which was published as *The Rights and Wrongs of Children's Work* (2010). The final tone of the book was influenced by a seminar arranged by Plan Canada (and financed by CIDA) that brought together a number of academics and practitioners who had taken time to read rough drafts of our book and who commented on ways to take it forward. One clear effect of this seminar was to drop some of our academic reserve about expressing our opinions on where we should be going. The seminar asked that we state clearly where all our study and thinking had led us. So we did—with conclusions such as, 'ILO Convention 138 [the minimum age convention] should be suspended as a general standard,' and 'Far from using schooling to keep children out of the labor force, educators should make productive work a respectable and widely available component of education...' (p. 213). The result of our enterprise, we believe, was a book that could not only stand up to academic scrutiny, but could also be useful to practitioners.

A book can only be useful if appropriate people read it. Academics are challenging assumptions and developing ideas about children's work in academic publications, conferences, and workshops; practitioners support each other in a different set of conferences and workshops, and may never encounter the challenges posed by academics. Both sides have much to do in their own fields and fail to consult those outside their particular working groups: indeed, even among academics, discussion is often with those of the same discipline or orientation and often fails to incorporate findings from other disciplines. So if academics wish their research findings to improve the lives of children, they have to engage with those involved in policy and intervention, internationally, nationally, and locally.

On the subject of children's work, the 'child labour' perspective is strongly reinforced by sensational, and often ill-informed media attention, which in turn drives much intervention and policy. If this situation is to improve, it is not enough to publish informed academic books that challenge such thinking. We have also to bring these ideas to public attention.

There remains the question of the extent to which empirical research can influence policy and politics. A few years ago, Martin Woodhead (2007) published a chapter entitled, 'Developing policies on child labour: has research made a difference?' His answer was basically that it has not, at least in the case of the International Labour Organisation, which is dominated by adult unions and politics. Other organisations have shown themselves more receptive to research findings, but even when such findings do affect particular practices, lessons learned can be lost when there are staff changes in an organisation (for example, Nelems forthcoming).

Protecting working children

I now return to the conflict in values concerning children's work, with which I started this chapter. The studies in this volume show that the conflict is not simply one of 'advanced' or 'modern' ideas as opposed to ideas that might be conceived of as 'backward' or 'primitive'. There is considerable empirical evidence supporting ideas held by parents in Africa, and throughout the world, that industriousness, including various kinds of work, has important positive functions in the way children grow up.

Nevertheless, things can go wrong at home and in employment, sometimes to the extent that intervention becomes necessary for the welfare of the children. Work can sometimes be physically harmful or hazardous. There is information available on the particular susceptibility of young people to specific work hazards, some of which may only show damaging effects in the long term (Fassa and Wegman 2009). Excessive hours of work can interfere with school, leisure, and even sleep: this interference can come even from domestic chores in the home. Some work can be excessively strenuous and damaging to growing bodies. Work situations can also be damaging psychologically; and such damage can be more serious, and harder to assess, than the effects of physical hazards. Psychosocial damage usually arises from social relations (with employers, fellow workers, controlling adults, and others) rather than the nature of the work. Learning through work sometimes involves learning cultural values and practices that can be damaging to some people in the community—such as certain types of gender discrimination or the marginalization of certain groups in society.

So the question remains: do children have a right to protection from exploitation and damaging work situations? If so, how can appropriate protection be provided? Is it not safest simply to prohibit employment or work by persons under a certain age?

While such an approach may simplify intervention, a prohibition on all work by children deprives them of many benefits, which are illustrated by much of the material in this volume. Simplifying intervention helps the adults involved, but is not necessarily in the interests of children, who often have a more nuanced approach to problems that they encounter in their work. Often children are well aware of the hazards and choose to work on the grounds that benefits outweigh risks; working children may take their own precautions against hazards that worry them (for example, Morrow and Vennam forthcoming). Damaging social relations and excessive demands can affect work in the home as well as in employment outside it: indeed outside employment sometimes offers an alternative to working at home and an escape from intolerable conditions (for example, Grier 2005, 69-109), an alternative that is lost if such employment is prohibited. Although learning through work can transmit damaging prejudices, so can learning in any environment.

To decide how best to protect children, we need to reflect on the purpose of protection. It is frequently perceived in a reactive sense—against particular hazards or forms of abuse; this limited approach can restrict developmental experiences of children in a variety of

ways. I suggest that parents and families are generally more concerned with protecting opportunities for their children, and with enabling them to become constructive and contributing members of their
communities. If protection is understood in this broader sense,
restrictions that merely keep children away from danger are not
always genuinely protective: it may sometimes be more protective to
teach children to deal with risks. In certain situations, practices that
may be considered by outsiders as harmful are perceived by parents
and children as protective (such as the placement of children away
from their parental home). Genuine protection must, therefore, take
account of the local situation and local opportunities: often the best
protective intervention is support for the protection that children and
communities are trying to provide for themselves.

I am not advocating the imposition of universal values on societies, and particularly on those who are restricted by poverty. Nor am
I advocating a kind of cultural triumphalism which assumes that
local tradition is always best. I am asking that academics, and particularly anthropologists, play their part by examining carefully, and
with academic rigour, the place and effects of work by children.
Academic studies need to attend to specific situations of children and
the potential for the children concerned; also to the effects of the
social and economic environment on children and their work,
including the effects of policy and intervention. In this way, we can
hope to engage with others and open up new ways of ensuring that
the work undertaken by children does not impede their development
but rather enhances and enriches it.

References

Bourdillon, Michael (2000a): Children at Work on Tea and Coffee
    Estates. In: M. Bourdillon (ed.): *Earning a Life*. Harare: Weaver
    Press, 147–172.
Bourdillon, Michael (ed.) (2000b): *Earning a Life. Working Children
    in Zimbabwe*. Harare: Weaver Press.

Bourdillon, Michael, Deborah Levison, William Myers and Ben White (2010): *Rights and Wrongs of Children's Work*. New Brunswick, etc.: Rutgers University Press.

Boyden, Jo (2009): Risk and Capability in the Context of Adversity. Children's Contributions to Household Livelihoods in Ethiopia. In: *Children, Youth and Environments* 19(2), 111–137.

Boyden, Jo, Alula Pankhurst and Yisak Tafere (forthcoming): Child Protection and 'Harmful Traditional Practices'. Female Early Marriage and Genital Modification in Ethiopia. In: *Development in Practice* 22(4).

Chenhall, Richard, Kate Senior, and Suzanne Belton (2011): Negotiating Human Research Ethics. Case Notes from Anthropologists in the Field. In: *Anthropology Today* 27(5), 13–17.

Fassa, Anaclaudia F., and David H. Wegman (2009): Special Health Risks of Child Labour. In: H. D. Hindman (ed.): *The World of Child Labor. A Reference Encylopedia*. New York: M.E. Sharpe, 127–130.

Grier, Beverley C. (2005): *Invisible Hands. Child Labour and the State in Colonial Zimbabwe*. Portsmouth, N.H.: Heinemann.

Hashim, Iman M. and Dorte Thorsen (2011): *Child Migration in Africa*. London & Uppsala: Zed Books & Nordiska Afrika-institutet.

ILO (2008). 18th International Conference of Labour Statisticians. Report III. Child Labour Statistics. Geneva: International Labour Organisation.

Morrow, Virginia (2012): The Ethics of Social Research with Children and Families in Young Lives. Practical Experiences. In: J. Boyden and M. Bourdillon (eds.): *Childhood Poverty: Multidisciplinary Approaches*. Basingstoke: Palgrave Macmillan, 24–42.

Morrow, Virginia and Uma Vennam (forthcoming): Children's Responses to Risk in Agricultural Work in Andhra Pradesh, India. In: *Development in Practice* 22(4).

Myers, William and Michael Bourdillon (forthcoming): Introduction. Development, Children, and Protection. In: *Development in Practice* 22(4). Special issue on *Child Protection in Development*

Nelems, Marth (forthcoming): Listening to Iraqi Refugee Children in Jordan, but then what? In: *Development in Practice* 22(4).

Nhenga, Tendai Charity (2008): *Application of the International Prohibition on Child Labour in an African Context. Lesotho, Zimbabwe and South Africa.* Department of Public Law. Cape Town: University of Cape Town. D. Phil.

Oloko, Beatrice Adenike (1989): Children's Work in Urban Nigeria. A Case Study of Young Lagos Street Traders. In: W. E. Myers (ed.): *Protecting Working Children.* London: Zed Books, 11–23.

Woodhead, Martin (2007): Developing Policies on Child Labour. Has Research Made a Difference? In: K. Engwall and I. Soderlind (eds.): *Children's Work in Everyday Life.* Stockholm: Institute for Futures Studies, 15–24.

Notes on Contributors

Erdmute Alber is professor of social anthropology at the University of Bayreuth, Germany. Her research interests in Latin America and Africa include childhood, political anthropology and kinship, and their overlapping thematic fields. Since 1992, she has undertaken field research among the Baatombu in Northern Benin, her themes being the history of power relations, child fosterage, and changing intergenerational relations. She is Vice-Dean of the Bayreuth International Graduate School of African Studies at the University of Bayreuth and the editor of the journal Sociologus.

Michael Bourdillon received his doctorate in Social Anthropology at Oxford University. He is Emeritus Professor in the Department of Sociology, University of Zimbabwe, where he taught for over 25 years. He also taught in Nigeria and has directed training institutes for CODESRIA. Recently he has specialised on children's work, for which he received visiting fellowships at the African Studies Centre, Leiden, the Institute of Social Studies, The Hague, and the Netherlands Institute for Advanced Studies. He is a co-author of *Rights and Wrongs of Children's Work (2010)*. He also has practical experience of supporting working children.

Isaie Dougnon is Maître-assistant at the University of Bamako, Mali. From 1998 to 2003, Dougnon worked on labour migration from Dogon country to the Office du Niger (Mali) and to Ghana, about which he published his book *Travail de Blanc, travail de Noir: La migration des paysans dogons vers l'Office du Niger et au Ghana (1910–1980)* (Paris: Khartala, 2007) and several articles. Recently, he co-edited, with Christophe Daum, *Hommes et Migrations* No. 1279 (May–June 2009), L'Afrique en mouvement: un autre regard.

Cindi Katz, a geographer, is a professor at The Graduate Center of The City University of New York. She is the author of *Grow-*

ing up Global: Economic Restructuring and Children's Every-day Lives (Minnesota 2004), which received the Meridian Award for outstanding scholarly work in geography from the Association of American Geographers. She was a fellow at the Radcliffe Institute for Advanced Study at Harvard University in 2003–4, and the Diane Middlebrook and Carl Djerassi Visiting Professor of Gender Studies at University of Cambridge for 2011–12.

Iris Köhler (Dr. phil.) has done long-term field research in northern Côte d'Ivoire within the DFG-funded research project 'Öffent-lichkeit im Westlichen Sudan' between 1996 and 2000. She did her PhD at the University of Bayreuth about Nyarafolo pottery-making women and learning procedures in northern Côte d'Ivoire in 2005, published as the book *Es sind die Hände, die die Töpfe schön machen* (2008). Her interests especially focus on gender, learning, craft and material culture.

David F. Lancy is Professor of Anthropology Emeritus at Utah State University and author of 8 books including *The Anthropology of Childhood: Cherubs, Chattel, Changelings* and *The Anthropology of Learning in Childhood*. He received the Carnegie award in 2001 as 'Professor of the Year,' and the D.W. Thorne award as outstanding scientist in 2011. He has studied childhood in Liberia, Papua New Guinea and Sweden and is at work on *How Children Learn Their Culture*.

Manfred Liebel is professor of sociology, director of the Institute of International Studies on Childhood and Youth at the International Academy (INA) and of the European Master in Child-hood Studies and Children's Rights (EMCR), both at Free University Berlin. Publications: *A Will of Their Own: Cross-cultural Perspectives on Working Children* (Zed books, 2004), *Working to Be Someone: Child Focused Research and Practice with Working Children* (co-edited by Jessica Kingsley, 2007), *Children's Rights from Below: Cross-cultural Perspectives* (Palgrave Macmillan, 2012).

Stanford T. Mahati is a Zeit-Stiftung Research Fellow in the African Centre for Migration and Society at the University of the Witwatersrand in Johannesburg. His doctoral study focuses on the representations of unaccompanied migrant children in humanitarian work. He has worked as a researcher at the National Institute of Health Research, and also at Biomedical Research and Training Institute in Zimbabwe. His research interests include new social studies of childhood, child migration, postcolonialism, HIV/AIDS and food security.

Jeannett Martin (Dr. phil.) is a post-doc fellow in Social Anthropology at the University of Bayreuth. Presently she leads the DFG-funded research project 'Child Fosterage in the Context of Interethnic Heterogeneity (Borgu/Republic of Benin)'. She has conducted fieldwork in northern Benin and southern Ghana. Her main academic interests include family and kinship, ethnicity, childhood and migration.

Phil Mizen teaches in the Department of Sociology, at the University of Warwick, UK. He has published extensively on young people, children, work and unemployment and his most recent publications (with Yaw Ofosu-Kusi) include an examination of 'Asking, Giving, Receiving: Friendship as Survival Strategy Among Accra's Street Children' (*Childhood*, 14:4, 2012) and 'Engaging With a World Outside of Ourselves: Vistas of Flatness, Children's Work and the Informal Economy' (*Sociological Research Online*, May, 2012).

Yaw Ofosu-Kusi teaches social studies and economics at the Department of Social Studies, University of Education, Winneba, Ghana and is currently the Director of the University's Office of International Relations. He was the Director for CODESRIA's 2011 Child and Youth Studies Institute. His recent publications, together with Phil Mizen, include 'A talent for living: exploring Ghana's "new" urban childhood' (*Children and Society*, DOI: 10.1111/1099–2011.00386.x) and 'Unofficial truths and everyday insights: understanding voice in visual research with the children of Accra's urban poor' (*Visual Studies*, 25 (3)).

Barbara Polak is lecturer at the chair of Anthropology (Bayreuth University). Her research focus is on work, migration and consumption in peasant societies in West Africa. She has accomplished nearly two years of participatory fieldwork among Bamana peasants in Mali. Her forthcoming monograph is entitled *Aus Kindern werden Bauern. Kinder-, Frauen- und Männerarbeit in Mali*.

Gerd Spittler is Professor Emeritus of Social Anthropology at the University of Bayreuth. Since his retirement he has taught at the Universities of Basel, Bayreuth and Niamey (Niger). His publications on work include *Hirtenarbeit* (1998), *Le travail en Afrique noire* (co-editor, 2003), and *Founders of the Anthropology of Work* (2008). He was a fellow at the 'Institute for Advanced Study' (1999/2000), the 'Social Science Research Center' (2005/06) and the IGK 'Work and Human Life Cycle in Global History' (2009/10), all based in Berlin.

Beiträge zur Afrikaforschung

hrsg. vom Institut für Afrika-Studien der Universität Bayreuth

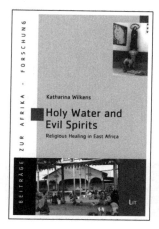

Katharina Wilkens
Holy Water and Evil Spirits
Religious Healing in East Africa
In Tanzania, the Marian Faith Healing Ministry offers Catholic healing rituals under the patronage of the Virgin Mary. Exorcism and a special water service are central to the healing process. People bring physical, spiritual and social afflictions before the group's leader, Felicien Nkwera. Combining the perspectives of the study of religions and medical anthropology, the author analyses Nkwera's pastoral texts and the personal healing narratives of the members. Thus, a complex image of the healing process is created and framed within its Tanzanian interreligious context and its global conservative Catholic context.
Bd. 47, 2011, 304 S., 29,90 €, br.,
ISBN 978-3-643-11179-1

Tebarek Lika Megento
Inter-firm Relationships and Governance Structures
A study of the Ethiopian leather and leather products industry value chain
Interest in the topic of governance and interfirm relationships in the Ethiopian leather and leather products industry was developed after observing a gap in the literature on value chain research at the international level and finding only a few empirical studies on value chains at the local level. Most of the value chain research conducted throughout the world are either too general or are simply functionalistic and, thus, fail to address the socio-cultural context. This study contributes to the literature in several ways: firstly, the present research suggests that a central focus of value chain analysis should be the examination of social networks within local, but also global, value chains, as social relations might play an important and so far neglected role in the struggle to participate in the rapidly changing world economy. Secondly, as a clear departure from mainstream value chain research, this study makes use of a mixture of value chain and network approaches for exploring processes and micro-level interactions used by individuals to construct and maintain networks.
Bd. 48, 2011, 224 S., 29,90 €, br.,
ISBN 978-3-643-11185-2

LIT Verlag Berlin – Münster – Wien – Zürich – London
Auslieferung Deutschland / Österreich / Schweiz: siehe Impressumsseite

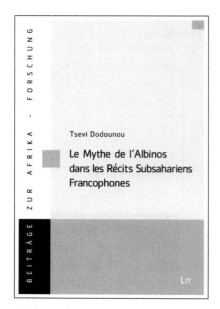

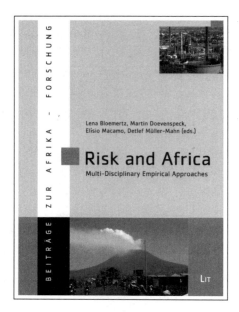

Tsevi Dodounou
Le Mythe de l'Albinos dans les Récits Subsahariens Francophones
Un thème comme celui de l'albinos marque une nouvelle orientation dans le champ littéraire africain. Plus qu'un thème, l'albinos est un mythe survivant dans l'inconscient collectif, voyageant d'ouvre en ouvre, un véritable mythe dont l'origine remonte aux temps anciens. L'apparition d'un albinos semble prédestinée à créer un malaise dans la course ordinaire de la vie. C'est le choc de se voir confronté – selon la formule de Roger Little – à l'autre autre. Mais au-delà du mythique, l'albinos est aussi une figure de la déconstruction, source d'un questionnement, d'un regard critique sur la marginalité et l'altérité. Sa position de « l'entre-deux » est représentative de la position du sujet dans les sociétés postcoloniales, position soustendue par des idées de fluctuation, de mobilité et de labilité de l'identité humaine.
Bd. 49, 2011, 328 S., 34,90 €, br.,
ISBN 978-3-643-11219-4

Lena Bloemertz; Martin Doevenspeck; Elísio Macamo; Detlef Müller-Mahn (Eds.)
Risk and Africa
Multi-Disciplinary Empirical Approaches
Through a range of varied articles this book explores the changing nature of risk in contemporary African societies. It provides a valuable addition to current debate on the concept of risk which has traditionally been skewed in favour of European historical experience. The articles illustrate that technological hazards, pollution and climate change as well as the introduction of new forms of insurance and the restructuring of civil society are just some of the recent developments that invite us to be sceptical of prevailing notions of risk in the African context. The reader is encouraged to move away from focusing on the vulnerability of Africa as a pre-modern society to consider more localised and contemporary perspectives of risk. In exploring new ways of conceptualising risk in Africa the book addresses the challenge of making theoretical and methodological advances in risk research relevant to understanding the processes of social change on the continent.
Bd. 51, 2012, 288 S., 29,90 €, br.,
ISBN 978-3-643-90157-6

LIT Verlag Berlin – Münster – Wien – Zürich – London
Auslieferung Deutschland / Österreich / Schweiz: siehe Impressumsseite